STRANGERS ON THE STREET

Serial homicide in South Africa

Micki Pistorius

PENGUIN BOOKS

PENGUIN BOOKS

Published by the Penguin Group
Penguin Books Ltd, 80 Strand, London WC2R 0RL, England
Penguin Group (USA) Inc, 375 Hudson Street, New York, New York 10014,
USA
Penguin Group (Canada), 90 Eglinton Avenue East, Suite 700, Toronto,
Ontario, Canada M4P 2Y3 (a division of Pearson Penguin Canada Inc)
Penguin Ireland, 25 St Stephen's Grreen, Dublin 2, Ireland (a division of
Penguin Books Ltd)
Penguin Group (Australia), 250 Camberwell Road, Camberwell, Victoria
3124, Australia (a division of Pearson Australia Group Pty Ltd)
Penguin Books India Pvt Ltd, 11 Community Centre, Panchsheel Park,
New Delhi – 110 017, India
Penguin Group (NZ), Cnr Rosedale and Airborne Roads, Albany, Auckland,
1310, New Zealand (a division of Pearson New Zealand Ltd)
Penguin Books (South Africa) (Pty) Ltd, 24 Sturdee Avenue, Rosebank,
Johannesburg 2196, South Africa

Penguin Books (South Africa) (Pty) Ltd, Registered Offices:
24 Sturdee Avenue, Rosebank, Johannesburg 2196, South Africa

www.penguinbooks.co.za

First published by Penguin Books (South Africa) (Pty) Ltd 2002
Reprinted 2003, 2005, 2011

ISBN 9780141003566

Typeset by PJT Design in 10.5/12.5 point Sabon
Cover design: Publicide
Printed and bound by Interpak Books, Pietermaritzburg

This book is dedicated to
General Suiker Britz

CONTENTS

ACKNOWLEDGEMENTS

This book would not have been possible without the assistance of the following people: General Suiker Britz, Dr Mark Welman, Brynne Hodgkiss, Peta Krost, Danie Reyneke, Lawrence Oliver, Tollie Vreugdenburg, Danie Hall, Gert Fourie, Mike van Aardt, Piet Byleveld, S M Naidoo, André Burger, André Fabricius, Derick Norsworthy, Alan Alford, Philip Veldhuizen, Renier Grobler, Tessa Booyens, the staff of the SAPS Museum, my family, friends and my publishers.

INTRODUCTION

The phenomenon of serial homicide holds a certain fascination for people. It seems that we are intrigued by the horrendous deeds that men are capable of, for it makes us feel good that we are not like them. Yet their badness resounds in us and makes us uncomfortable. We manage this uncomfortable feeling by trying to find reasons for their deviant behaviour.

The easiest way to reassure ourselves is to say: 'They must be mad. Only a mad person would commit such terrible acts on another human being.' Unfortunately this is not true. There is more to it than simply labelling bad people as 'mad'.

Serial killers are surely the ultimate 'bad men' for they torture, rape, mutilate and kill completely innocent strangers, with no apparent motive. There are certainly no rational motives – greed, revenge, financial gain – that we might be able to attribute to other murderers.

Why, then, do they do it?

This book is intended primarily for the psychologist, criminologist, student, educator and police officer who may find him- or herself needing background on the behavioural patterns manifest in recorded serial homicide cases in South Africa.

All students researching this field, including myself, have found it difficult to trace research material pertaining to these cases as there is as yet no official database in South Africa. Information is scattered across the country. With the help of dedicated detectives and other friends, I have managed to trace dockets, court cases and newspaper and magazine articles and have combined all we could find in this book, which I believe is the first comprehensive study of South African serial killers. There may be many more cases which I have been unable to trace, and serial killers on trial or awaiting trial at the time of publication are not included in this book as their cases are *sub judice*.

Members of the general public might also find this book interesting but I want to make it clear that, in writing it, it is not my intention to feed serial killers' insatiable hunger for recognition. There is a tendency for these criminals to gain a measure of 'fame' through their deeds and it is unfortunate that in many cases they seem to spark interest and even admiration that they would not have achieved other than through their ghastly behaviour.

This book in no way supports this. It is a serious attempt to understand the mind of the serial killer so that he may be identified and apprehended as soon as possible. The prognoses for serial killers are negative, and I firmly believe that they can never be rehabilitated – they need to be removed from society for the remainder of their lives.

I participated in more than thirty-five serial killer investigations in my capacity as commander of the Investigative Psychology Unit of the South African Police Service for a period of more than six years.

I also completed the thesis for my DPhil in psychology on the subject of serial killers. I wanted to know what makes these men tick. I read several theories on the origin of serial homicide and none satisfied me. I began to develop my own theory, based on Freudian principles, and I applied this theory to more than three hundred case studies of serial killers. It fitted every time. However I do not claim to have all the answers and I would encourage students to continue their research in this area.

In this book, I will present as many cases of South African serial killers as my research has uncovered, and I will also pinpoint some interesting facts about the killers or the cases. I should make it clear that these comments represent my own opinions; not all readers will find them valid.

The different theories on the origins of serial homicide are extremely interesting and it is appropriate to consider all of them first, before discussing my own theory.

Definitions

Before we explore the *origins* of serial homicide, we need to look at different *definitions* of serial killers. It is important to define our subject precisely and to differentiate between *serial killers*, *mass murderers* and *spree killers*, for they differ in their motives.

A review of the literature left me with the feeling that there were shortcomings in different authors' definitions of serial killers – there were questions which remained unanswered for me. I will elaborate on this below.

The definitions are presented in chronological order to indicate how they have evolved from the simplistic to the more comprehensive.

Leyton (1986:18), in his definition, merely highlights the aspect of time as the difference between serial killers and mass murderers by describing serial homicide as murders that are committed over a period of time, and mass murders as murders committed during one explosive event. He attributes the motive for both types of homicide to social failure on the part of the killer (1986:297). A criticism that can be levelled against his theory is that if people become serial killers because their ambitions have failed, why are there comparatively few serial killers? After all, many people's ambitions are unfulfilled.

Cameron and Frazer (1987:17) classify serial killers as a variation of sex murderers. They define serial killers as men (with a few exceptions) who murder their sexual objects, whether they be women, children or other men. The murders are characterised by sexual assault, rape, torture and mutilation. A criticism of this definition is that the motive is defined as solely sexual. As we shall see in the case of Velaphi Ndlangamandla, the Saloon Killer who operated in the Piet Retief area (see page 271), not all serial killers have a sexual motive. Velaphi shot his victims from a distance and there was no sexual interference with the victims. Or was there? We will see on page 278 how Velaphi substituted his rifle for his penis.

Holmes and De Burger (1988:18) differentiate between a mass murderer as a person who kills many people at one time and a spree killer as a person (or persons) who kills several people over a short period, whether it be hours, days or weeks. Although these authors do not define the term 'serial killer', they list the following traits of the perpetrator:

- The central element is repetitive homicide
- They are usually one-on-one murders
- The victim is usually a stranger to the killer
- The motive is murder and not passion, nor is it precipitated by any action of the victim. (For example, when a wife taunts her husband and he kills her, she precipitated the murder. The victims of serial killers do nothing to precipitate their murder.)
- The motivation is intrinsic

In my opinion these traits are accurate in describing a serial killer, but they omit the feature of a 'cooling-off period' and the element of fantasy, both of which are key characteristics of a serial killer's modus operandi and motive.

Leibman (1989) defines a serial killer is a person who kills several people, usually in the same geographic area over a short period of time, which corresponds to some degree with Leyton's definition. My criticism of this definition is that a serial killer does not necessarily confine himself to one area and may kill over a lengthy period. Russian serial killer Andrei Chicatillo was operative for two decades.

Hollin (1989:74) considers a serial killer to be a type of mass murderer who commits murder over a period of time, torturing or sexually assaulting his victims before killing them. Hollin's definition aligns with that of Cameron and Frazer by focusing on the sexual aspect of serial homicide. I do not agree that a serial killer is a type of mass murderer, and not all victims of serial killers are sexually assaulted or tortured before they are killed. David Berkowitz, in New York, simply shot his victims without interacting with them at all.

Levin and Fox (1991:14) regard serial killers and 'simultaneous' killers as two types of mass murderer. Serial killers are defined as mass murderers who murder victims at different times, while 'simultaneous' murderers are mass murderers who kill their victims in one event. This definition again has a lot in common with those of Leyton and Leibman. My criticism of this definition is, again, that serial killers are simply regarded as mass murderers and the authors focus only on the element of time.

Lane and Gregg (1992:3) define mass murder as a deed where several people are killed by the same person at the same geographical site. A spree killing is defined as multiple murder that is committed over a longer period.

Most of the above definitions focus on the element of time in serial homicide, and ignore other criteria. A robber who might kill several people over a period of time in the course of the robberies he commits, will also comply with most of these definitions, but I do not consider him to be a serial killer. The key is the *motive*. The robber's motive is greed.

Robert K Ressler coined the term *serial killer* when he worked for the Federal Bureau of Investigation in the United States of America. He explained the term by using the example of a television serial programme. As each episode ends on a cliffhanger, viewers are kept in anticipation of the next episode, much as the serial killer anticipates his next murder after committing the previous one.

Ressler and Shachtman's (1993) definitions of serial killers, mass murderers and spree killers are the most comprehensive to date.

They define a serial killer as a person or persons who kill more than three victims, during more than three events, at three or more locations, with a cooling-off period in between. Premeditated planning and fantasy are also present.

They define a mass murderer as one person who kills four or more victims during one event at one location. There is no cooling-off period and the victims may be family members.

The spree killer is defined as one or more persons who kill two or more victims during one event which could have a long or short duration, at two or more locations, with no cooling-off period.

After reviewing the different definitions, I propose the following definition of a serial killer:

> *A serial killer is a person (or persons) who murders several victims, usually strangers, at different times and not necessarily at the same location, with a cooling-off period in between. The motive is intrinsic; an irresistible compulsion, fuelled by fantasy which may lead to torture and/or sexual abuse, mutilation and necrophilia.*

I must stress that 'irresistible compulsion' is a psychological explanation and not a judicial term. It does not mean that the serial killer cannot prevent himself from killing. Rather, it means that he does not want to stop killing. It is his choice. The fact that he goes into a cooling-off period confirms that he can control his urge to kill – he just does not want to.

This is a very important concept to understand. Sections 77 and 79 of the South African Criminal Procedures Act (Act 51 of 1977) stipulate that a person should be able to differentiate between right and wrong, and should be able to act according to this differentiation, otherwise he cannot be held culpable for a crime. Therefore the defence counsel of a serial killer might postulate that although his client can differentiate between right and wrong, he cannot act accordingly.

Again, the fact that the serial killer premeditated the murder, selected the victim, committed the murder, took precautions not to be detected and had several cooling-off periods indicates that he did have control and a choice not to commit the crime.

As we shall see in the case of the Station Strangler (page 122), some serial killers actually commit themselves to psychiatric clinics in order to seek help. Unfortunately, they feel it is the psychologist's responsibility to figure out that they are killing people, just as some of them feel it is the police's responsibility to catch them. To think that all serial killers want to be caught is a myth. They don't.

The case of William Heirens provides evidence of this myth. In 1945 Heirens mutilated and killed two women in Chicago. He wrote in lipstick on the bedroom walls of one of his victims: 'For heaven's sake catch me before I kill more. I cannot control myself.'

This is a typical example of a serial killer denying responsibility for his actions. Denying responsibility and projecting it on to the police does not exonerate one from being accountable for one's actions. Heirens clearly realised that what he was doing was wrong, so why did he not give himself up? In effect he was saying: 'It is the police's responsibility to catch me and to protect the community. It is the police's fault that people are being killed by me.' After writing that message on the wall, he abducted six-year-old Suzanne Degnan, chopped up her body and disposed of the parts in the sewers. He displayed no regret or remorse for his deeds.

In my definition of a serial killer I have added the criteria of *intrinsic motive, irresistible compulsion, sexual abuse, mutilation* and *necrophilia* to Ressler's definition in order to cover the motivational aspects. I do not specify that a person is only to be considered a serial killer after he has killed three or more victims, since it is possible for a serial killer to be identified as such if he is apprehended after the second murder.

Classification

Apart from defining serial killers, some authors have attempted to classify them. Although serial killers are unique regarding the type of crime they commit, there is consensus in the literature that they can be classified into several different categories. It is the general opinion amongst some authors (Holmes & De Burger 1988; Nordby 1989; Leibman 1989 and Ressler & Shachtman 1993) that the classification of serial killers should be modelled according to a phenomenological description, rather than based on a quantitative study, because there are so few of them and because each one is unique.

Holmes and De Burger employ a useful descriptive model consisting of four interdependent classification factors and four category typologies. They explain the need for classification as follows:

> Careful study and classification of pertinent data is one of the most fundamental steps in developing adequate knowledge about criminal behaviour patterns such as serial murder . . . The purpose of a 'model' is to list and demonstrate how the major components of a specific phenomenon – serial murder, in this case – are interrelated. The intent of a 'typology' is to provide an inclusive set of categories for describing a particular behaviour or phenomenon – in this case, dominant motives in serial murder (1988:46-47).

Their four categories of classification are:

- Background of behaviour, including psychological, sociogenic[1] and biological etiology[2]
- Victimology, including characteristics, choice and relationship with the offender
- Pattern and method, including process versus deed (some serial killers are more stimulated by the process of planning and fantasising about the murder than about the actual deed); planning versus spontaneity, and organised versus disorganised
- Location of the murders, including concentrated or dispersed

Their four category typologies regarding motive are:

- Visionary type – murder on the orders of someone; for example, the voice of God
- Mission-orientated – murder according to a mission; for example, to kill all prostitutes
- Hedonistic type – including three types namely lust, sensation and comfort
- Power/control type – murder to satisfy a need for control over life and death

Holmes and De Burger's model, depicted in Table 1, is especially useful when a profiler is compiling the profile of an unknown serial killer, since an appraisal of the victims, the method and the location can be correlated with the type of serial killer most likely to have committed the murders. The type of serial killer indicates the motive and the motive, in turn, can assist in deciphering his fantasy. The fantasy is used by detectives as an interrogation tool.

Holmes and De Burger's model is generally accepted as an accurate description of the different types of serial killers. I personally cannot concur with the inclusion of the 'comfort'

---

[1]Sociogenic: factors characterising the social origins of various behaviours, e.g. juvenile delinquency.
[2]Etiology: Study of the causes of a disorder.

type serial killer, since this person would have an extrinsic motive such as financial gain. In my view, paid assassins would fall into this category. An assassin does not comply with my definition of a true serial killer. Once we include assassins we are expanding our subject of study; it gets too broad and invites confusion. I prefer to confine my definition to the true serial killer, that is, one with a deep psychological motivation as the main criterion for his crimes.

Table 1: Holmes and De Burger's model for classification of serial killers

Serial Murder Type	Vision-ary	Mission-orientated	Hedonistic			Power/Control
			Lust	Sensation	Comfort	
FACTORS						
Victims						
Specific/Non-specific	x	x	x	x	x	x
Random/Non-random	x	x	x	x	x	x
Affiliative/Strangers	x	x	x	x	x	x
Methods						
Act focused/Process-focused	x	x	x	x	x	x
Planned/Spontaneous	x	x	x	x	x	x
Organised/Disorganised	x	x	x	x	x	x
Location						
Concentrated/Dispersed	x	x	x	x	x	x

In her classification, Leibman (1989:41) differentiates between the *psychotic*, *ego-syntonic* and *ego-dystonic* killer:

- The psychotic killer murders as a result of a mental disorder and is not in contact with reality
- The ego-syntonic killer commits murder without disruption of his ego function. The murder is rational and acceptable to the murderer
- The ego-dystonic killer disassociates himself on a conscious level from the killings

Leibman considers all serial killers to be ego-dystonic. I disagree. I have found that some serial killers who have even a small degree of an active superego (or conscience) will be ego-dystonic, whilst those with hardly any superego will be ego-syntonic.

Ressler and Shachtman (1993:180) only refer to the two categories of *organised* and *disorganised* and do not use Holmes and De Burger's typologies of visionary, missionary, hedonistic and power-motivated serial killers. Ressler warns that a serial killer could also be a mixture of the organised and disorganised categories.

Ressler and Shachtman (1993:179-196) attribute the following characteristics to the organised serial killer to distinguish him from the disorganised type:

- The murder is planned and effectiveness increases with each murder
- Organised murders signify psychopathy (antisocial personality disorder), while disorganised murders signify psychosis (mental illness relating to break with reality)
- The organised killer's fantasy is the blueprint for the murder
- The organised killer selects his victims according to certain characteristics and they are stalked; while in the disorganised murder the victims are often of a high-risk category
- The organised killer is aware of the victim's humanity and

will interact with the victim
- Some form of confidence trick is used to gain the victim's confidence
- The killer's modus operandi is adaptable and he is mobile
- A weapon is taken to, and then removed from, the scene
- The killer will hide or destroy the body in an effort to avoid detection
- If a vehicle is used, it will be in good working order to minimise the chances of apprehension
- The clothing of the victim may be removed or the victim may be mutilated to prevent identification
- False clues may be left at the scene to confuse the investigators
- The organised crime scene is neat, while the disorganised crime scene is chaotic
- The 'trophy' or 'souvenir' taken by the organised killer may be a piece of clothing or another inanimate object, while the disorganised killer may take body parts
- The organised killer will commit sexual abuse or rape before killing the victim, while the disorganised serial killer is more inclined to necrophilia
- The organised serial killer may have short-term sexual relations with a partner, but not a long-term, emotionally fulfilling commitment
- The organised serial killer is confident, attractive and has a superiority complex
- The organised serial killer may be married, while the disorganised serial killer would more likely be living alone or with parents
- The organised serial killer will probably have a skilled occupation while the disorganised serial killer will have menial employment, if he is employed at all
- A stress factor precipitates the organised serial killer's first murder
- The organised serial killer is more likely to keep newspaper articles about himself and to follow the case in the media

Fox (in Schwartz, 1992:146) does not acknowledge Ressler's differentiation between organised and disorganised serial killers. He is of the opinion that most serial killers torture and rape victims before murdering them and that the bodies are then merely dumped. After reviewing numerous case studies, I have found that not all serial killers torture or rape their victims and some deliberately display the body in order to shock the community or provoke the detectives. Some of them even keep the bodies for different purposes. They are called 'collectors'. Jeffrey Dahmer kept the bodies of his victims in his apartment and John Wayne Gacy kept his victims' bodies under his house.

Jeffers (1993:88-89) illustrates the different characteristics of organised and disorganised serial killers in Tables 2 and 3.

Table 2: Jeffers' differences between organised and disorganised serial killers

DIFFERENCES AT THE CRIME SCENES

Organised	Disorganised
Planned attack	Spontaneous attack
Victim: selected stranger	Victim: random
Personalises victim	Depersonalises victim
Demands submissive victim	Sudden violence towards victim
Methods of restriction (ropes, handcuffs)	Minimal restriction
Scene reflects control	Scene chaotic
Murder precipitated by aggression	Sexual deeds after murder
Body hidden	Body displayed
Weapon absent	Weapon left at scene
Transports body	Leaves body at scene

Table 3: Jeffers' differences between the organised and disorganised serial killers

Organised	Disorganised
Average or high intelligence	Below average intelligence
Socially competent	Socially incompetent
Prefers schooled labour	Unschooled labour
High order of birth	Low order of birth
Father in stable employment	Father in unstable employment
Inconsistent discipline during childhood	Strict discipline during childhood
Controlled mood during the murder	Anxious mood during the murder
Uses alcohol before murder	Minimum use of alcohol
Precipitating stress	Minimal stress
Lives with partner	Lives alone or with a parent
Reads news on case	Minimum interest in news coverage

Besides categorising serial killers, Ressler and Shachtman (1993: 182) also divide serial homicide into four phases, namely:

- Pre-crime phase – the continuous behaviour of the serial killer (i.e. the killer's normal daily behaviour, including fantasising about the murder)
- The murder – including the selection of the victim
- Disposal of the body – the body may be destroyed, dumped or displayed

- Post-crime phase – getting involved in the investigation or contacting the families of the victim

Theories on the origins of serial homicide

While studying these theories I tried to find the answer to the question: *Why will one person with a certain type of background, and who is exposed to certain environmental factors, become a serial killer, whilst another, with a similar background and circumstances, will not?*

Socio-cultural theories

Regarding the socio-cultural origin of serial homicide, Holmes and De Burger state:

> Sociogenic forces, especially in the form of violence-associated learning, are undoubtedly present in the cultural and behavioral background of the serial killer. However, sociogenic theories are also unable to account *directly* for the appearance of serial homicide. (1988:48)

Holmes and De Burger (1988:64) name two socio-cultural sources that are important in the origin of serial homicide. The first is a continuous culture of violence coupled with a continuous change in the relationship between the individual and his environment. The second source is the pattern of early development and interaction within the serial killer's family.

These authors identify the following characteristics of the American culture that are associated with an increase in violence (Holmes and De Burger, 1988:65):

- Normalising of interpersonal violence
- Emphasis on personal comfort
- Emphasis on thrills
- Extensive violence

- Magical thinking[3]
- Unmotivated hostility and blaming of others
- Normalising of impulsiveness
- Excessively violent role models
- Anonymity and depersonalising in overcrowded areas
- Extensive and accelerating spacious geographic mobility
- Emphasis on immediate and fast gratification of needs

These characteristics align with the first mentioned socio-cultural source that Holmes and De Burger regard as a possible origin of serial homicide, that is, the continuous culture of violence coupled with a continuous change in the relationship between the individual and his environment.

In my opinion, the above characteristics also exist within our South African culture, especially within the so-called townships and in the rural communities. The political unrest in the province of KwaZulu-Natal serves as an excellent example of the normalisation of personal violence, hostility and blaming of others, and violent role models, anonymity and depersonalising in overcrowded areas.

Leibman (1989) also supports the socio-cultural theory of the origin of serial homicide. She addresses two elements in a serial killer's early development, namely a cruel and violent childhood and rejection by parents, which correlate with Holmes and De Burger's identification of early developmental patterns as a possible source of serial homicide.

She (1989:42) identified the following five common social factors in an analysis of case studies of four serial killers and theorises that they are key factors which may result in a person becoming a serial killer:

---

[3]Magical thinking: The belief that thinking is equating with doing. It is seen in children as a normal stage of development during which the child believes that his thoughts and hopes are the cause of events happening around him. It is also observed in adults in a variety of psychiatric disorders.

- Childhood marked by cruel and violent patterns
- Rejection by parents
- Rejection by a member of the opposite sex during adulthood
- Confrontation with the law during youth or adulthood
- Admittance to psychiatric hospitals

Leibman (1989) identified these five characteristics in the following four case studies in the USA: Ted Bundy (nineteen female victims) was rejected by his biological father and was not supported emotionally by his mother; Albert de Salvo, the 'Boston Strangler' (thirteen female victims), was physically abused by his father; Edmund Kemper (eight female victims, including his mother and grandmother) was abused and humiliated by his mother; and Jerry Brudos (four female victims) was physically abused by his father and rejected by his mother. According to Leibman, all four of these men were unable to act out their aggression directly towards those who abused them. All four were loners and had no one with whom they could discuss their emotions.

I concur with Leibman's theory in as much as these elements may contribute to a person's becoming a serial killer, but would point out that many individuals are exposed to Leibman's five social factors and not all of them become serial killers. Her theory, therefore, does not answer my persistent question as to why a particular individual will resort to serial homicide, while others who have been subjected to the same circumstances will not.

Albert Bandura's theory of social learning states that a child models the behaviour of his parents and the example set by his environment and it can therefore also be regarded as a socio-cultural theory which may be applied to serial killers. However, I have not found any record of a serial killer whose father was also one. The intrinsic elements of serial homicide – namely multiple murder of strangers, torture and in some cases necrophilia and mutilation – are not learned behaviours. In my opinion, these elements are idiosyncratic to the serial killer.

Leyton is an anthropologist who also proposed a socio-cultural theory on the origin of serial homicide. He describes all serial homicide as a type of subcultural political and conservative protest which implies a social gain of revenge, star status, identity and sexual gratification for the serial killer. He acknowledges that these people kill for pleasure. He regards all serial killers as the 'missionary' type – the mission being a primitive rebellion against the social order to which they would have liked to belong, but were rejected (Leyton 1986:26).

Leyton is of the opinion that the victims of serial killers are all of the same social class and this class is usually a step higher than the class to which the serial killer belongs. He regards the sexual motive as a basis for the motive of social revenge. He comments that Ted Bundy, a law student, achieved the social status which he craved, but felt uncomfortable in that position. To take revenge on the higher social classes, he robbed them of their most precious possessions – their talented and beautiful young women (1986:110).

Leyton differentiates between serial killers and mass murderers by maintaining that while both are rebelling against society, the mass murderer usually ends his own life. He considers the murder of many people in one event to be the 'suicide note' of the mass murderer, since the mass murderer will almost invariably also commit suicide during this event. The serial killer, on the other hand, wants to live and attempts to ensure 'fame' by planning and committing a series of crimes (1986:298).

My criticism of Leyton's view is that he describes the murder sprees of mass murderers as 'planned careers'. The mass murderer may well plan the murder as a last, despairing cry for help, or out of desperation or revenge arising from a feeling of being duped by the community. However, these murders are not compulsions and may be prevented by counselling. Another aspect of Leyton's theory with which I disagree is his postulate that the victims of serial killers are people of a social class to which the killers themselves would have liked to belong. Many serial killers actually prefer high-risk victims, such as prostitutes, hitch-hikers and street children, who often belong to a lower social class. The social rejection to which Leyton refers has merit, but I would rather interpret it as a repetition of the rejection the serial killer first experienced from his parents. Leyton does not refer to any intrinsic psychological motivation in his theory.

Ressler's motivational model

Robert Ressler and his colleagues at the Federal Bureau of Investigation in the United States of America interviewed thirty-six serial killers in prison. The material obtained from these interviews was then used as a basis for qualitative and quantitative research on serial killers and sexual homicide. Based on the knowledge he gained from both the interviews and the qualitative research, Ressler (in Ressler, Burgess and Douglas, 1988:69-97) designed a model to explain the origin of serial killing. The model has five dimensions, which will be discussed individually. They are:

- Ineffective social environment
- Formative years
- Patterned responses
- Action towards others
- Feedback

Ineffective social environment
In his description of the serial killer's social environment as a child, Ressler addresses the dysfunctional family.

According to Ressler, the serial killer's social bonding as a child fails or becomes narrow and selective because his caretakers either ignore, rationalise or normalise unacceptable behaviour. The parents of the serial killer ignore pathological behaviour. Ressler cites the example of Jeffrey Dahmer's[4] father who did

---

[4]Jeffrey Dahmer was the Milwaukee serial killer who committed necrophilia and ate the flesh of his victims.

not mind that his child was dissecting animals.

Ressler and his colleagues found that in about 70 per cent of cases drugs and alcohol were problems in the family homes of serial killers.

There were psychiatric problems, usually linked to aggression, in more than half of the families – in most of these cases the mother had been institutionalised for a period of time. In 50 per cent of cases serial killers' family members were involved in criminal activity, usually of a sexual nature.

Ressler found too that the family members of serial killers have inconsistent contact with each other as well as dysfunctional interpersonal relationships. This, Ressler maintains, indicates that the serial killer did not have any close relationships with his siblings as a child. He was a so-called loner.

Many of the families of serial killers were nomadic. Only one third of the cases on whom the research was conducted lived in one place for any length of time. About 40 per cent of serial killers grew up away from the nuclear family before the age of eighteen years. They were denied the opportunity to form close relationships with people outside the family because they were uprooted so often. The families also had minimal contact with any community, resulting in extreme loneliness for the killers as children.

The research showed that in almost half the cases the father had left home before the serial killer reached the age of twelve years. But Ressler and his colleagues concluded that physical absence of the father did not have as much of a negative effect as his emotional absence. Therefore, even if the father was present, if he had a negative relationship with the boy, it had a greater negative effect on the potential serial killer.

Ressler cites the example of the father of one serial killer who threw a glass bottle at his son before the boy was one year old. He tried to strangle him when he was four years old and shot at him while he was playing in the backyard as a child.

Ressler proposes that serial killers also have ambivalent relationships with their mothers. They subconsciously both love and hate the mother. The mother gives the son *double bind*[5] messages which he cannot decipher as a child.

In their quantitative research Ressler and his colleagues found that serial killers were usually the oldest sons, which means that not only were their parents poor role models, but there were no older brothers or sisters who could substitute as good role models. The parents of serial killers were often divorced and if the mother remarried the son's birth order might have changed due to the arrival on the scene of additional stepbrothers and stepsisters. This would be confusing for the child, especially if the situation at home was unstable.

According to Ressler, the lack of closeness in family ties is transferred to childhood friendships. The serial killer as a child is a loner who seldom, if ever, has close friendships with other children. Generally their schoolmates cannot even remember them.

Formative years

In this dimension Ressler focuses on the traumas a serial killer was exposed to during his formative years. As a child the serial killer is likely to have been exposed to direct trauma, such as emotional, physical and/or sexual abuse. The direct trauma results in a developmental failure because the child's distress is ignored. Ressler describes the developmental defect as the forming of negative social relationships (wrong friends) and a decrease in the child's ability to experience positive affect[6] and emotions. As a result he becomes very desensitised. His interpersonal relations are weak and lack depth. His role models are defective or lacking altogether.

Witnessing events such as rape, suicide or murder could be considered examples of indirect trauma. The child remembers

---

[5]A term used to characterise the situation faced by a person who is receiving contradictory messages from another, powerful person.
[6]Affect: A general term for feelings and emotions.

these images and this destabilises his impulse control. He becomes confused regarding human responsibility – who is responsible for the trauma? – and so he begins to fantasise about revenge at an early age.

Ressler maintains that the neglect of serial killers during their childhood is more subtle than one would have expected. They were mainly psychologically abused through humiliation and the discipline at home was usually unfair, alien, inconsistent and abusive.

Sexual and violent experiences during childhood also have a negative effect on the formation of the personality of serial killers. Within the family, sexual abuse was committed by parents, step-parents, siblings and step-siblings, and outside the family by friends, extended family members or by prison mates when they were incarcerated either as juveniles or, later, as adults.

Ressler found that the adult sexual behaviour of serial killers is visually orientated and that they prefer autoerotic activities (masturbation). The following results of the quantitative study conducted by Ressler and his colleagues support this statement:

- About half of the group of thirty-six serial killers had a total aversion to sex
- Three-quarters reported having sexual problems
- 70 per cent reported feelings of sexual inadequacy

The traumas to which these children are exposed lead to the development of fantasies. Ressler quotes the example of one serial killer who had a sexual fantasy between the ages of four and five years and who was aroused by the image of sticking needles and knives into his stomach.

Ressler and his colleagues propose that most abused children fantasise as a way of escaping reality. The serial killer's early fantasies are not about escaping from a negative physical situation to a better one, as are those of other abused children. The serial killer fantasises about aggression, dominance over others and a repetition of what happened to him, but in his fantasies he is the aggressor and not the victim. The serial killer therefore develops his aggressive fantasies during childhood and discusses them with no one. He is committed to his violent and sexual fantasies. The fantasies before the first murder focus on the murder itself and the fantasies after the first murder focus on improving the four phases of the murder (see page 14). The motivation for committing the sexual murder is therefore that it provides the means of acting out a fantasy.

Patterned responses
In this dimension Ressler postulates that the child's memories of frightening and distressing life experiences shape his developing thought patterns. The type of thinking that emerges develops structured, patterned behaviours that in turn help generate daydreams and fantasies. Ressler's term for the structure and development of thought patterns is *cognitive mapping.*

In the serial killer, cognitive mapping is fixed, negative and repetitive and manifests in daydreams, nightmares, fantasies and thoughts with strong visual components. Ressler defines a *fantasy* as an extended thought filled with preoccupation, which is anchored in an emotion and exists in daydreams. Although the fantasy is usually expressed in thought, there are also images, emotions and internal dialogue present. When the fantasy reaches a point where it causes unbearable inner stress, the killer is ready to act it out.

According to Ressler the serial killer's thought patterns as a child have the following characteristics:

- Daydreams and nightmares with strong visual components
- Internal dialogue where he rationalises his aggression
- Kinaesthetic arousal levels (ie arousal levels of the body) which accompany the thought patterns
- The themes of the daydreams are dominance, rape, violence, revenge, molestation, power, control, mutilation, inflicting pain on others, and death

In their interviews with thirty-six incarcerated serial killers, Ressler and his colleagues found that none of them remembered positive childhood fantasies. Although other children may have occasional aggressive fantasies, serial killers have *only* aggressive fantasies and they are totally committed to them and to the secret reality which the fantasy represents to them.

The basis of the aggressive fantasy will already have been acted out during latency[7] in the child's handling of animals, in rehearsals for the murder (eg practising killing, strangling or skinning an animal), or in play. The serial killer will not easily speak about his youthful fantasies because he realises that he still had control over them then, but has since crossed the line of reality. Ressler (1988) refers to one serial killer who sodomised fellow hostel boys in the showers at the age of fifteen, in the same way as he was sodomised at the age of ten. He did not, however, see any connection between being sodomised himself and the sodomising of others.

The serial killer is egocentric in his fantasies or play. He regards other children or adults merely as extensions of his own inner world and has no insight into their needs or the impact his behaviour has on them.

In this dimension, Ressler lists the personality characteristics of serial killers as children as follows:

- Social isolation
- Autoerotic activities – masturbation
- Fetishism
- Rebelliousness
- Aggression
- Lies
- Self-entitlement (self-righteousness)

---

[7]Latency: The fourth of Freud's psychosexual developmental phases, covering the ages of 6-12 years. This is a socialisation phase and not a sexual one – therefore sexuality is latent.

He believes that these personality traits interact with the cognitive mapping to generate fantasies.

Action towards others
Ressler gives examples of how the fantasies are acted out during the childhood years in the serial killer's behaviour towards other people. The repetitive patterns, as described in the previous dimension, manifest at an early age. Ressler cites the example of Ed Kemper who, as a child, asked his sisters to tie him to a chair. He would then play that he was being shocked to death. When John Joubert was eight years old he fantasised that he was going to kill his babysitter and eat her. As a little boy he would stand behind her chair and play with her hair with one hand and with the other hand he would stroke a knife in his pocket. Ressler also refers to Harvey Glatman who, as a child, tied a piece of string around his penis, tied the string to a door knob and swung himself on the door.

Feedback filter
As an adult, the serial killer begins to act out the fantasies that have developed during his childhood years and he measures his performance according to the fantasy – this is the 'feedback filter'.

By committing his first murder the serial killer departs from his fantasy world and enters the real world. He justifies the murder and evaluates the mistakes he made. He reaches a point where he becomes very good at what he does and this is usually when he starts making mistakes, because he gets overconfident.

Summary
Ressler's motivational model emphasises that, as a child, the serial killer grows up in a negative environment where the home atmosphere is characterised by negligence, alcohol and drug abuse and a lack of positive role models. Interpersonal relationships are dysfunctional and the child is emotionally isolated. He is exposed to direct and indirect emotional, physical and sexual traumas. He starts to develop aggressive and revengeful fantasies,

which he acts out in play and towards other children and animals. According to Ressler, these fantasies are conscious thought patterns and they condition the child to be able to act them out as an adult by murdering other people. After the first murder the serial killer has departed from his fantasy world and has crossed the boundaries into reality. Each murder provides him with feedback on how to improve with the next murder so that it will resemble the perfect fantasy.

I agree in principle that the elements of childhood abuse and the early development of sadistic and revenge fantasies play a part in the origin of serial homicide. I disagree, however, that the motive for serial homicide can be explained on a cognitive level as conscious thought processes. The case studies of most serial killers indicate that they themselves cannot explain why they murdered their victims. Many of them can only ascribe it to an 'impulse' or 'urge' over which they allege they have no control. In my opinion the motivation lies not on a cognitive level, but on a deep unconscious psychological level. Ressler's model has acceptable and logical points, but once again it does not explain why one man becomes a serial killer while his brother, who has been exposed to the same environment, does not.

Systemic theories

The systemic theories on the origin of serial killers focus on how the whole social system, including family environment, the educational system, social structures like the churches and welfare organisations, law enforcement, the judicial system and correctional facilities, can contribute to the development of a serial killer. This is in accordance with the general systems theory which focuses on the interaction between the individual and different societal subsystems. Some of the authors who support systemic theories also pay attention to how the system may act to prevent the development of a serial killer.

Holmes and De Burger (1988:155) identify the following

elements of a system that may make a contribution to the prevention of serial homicide:

- Components of the criminal justice system, namely police services, courts and correctional services
- The media
- The public

According to Holmes and De Burger these elements of the system should focus on the early identification of violent personalities in an attempt to prevent serial homicide. This statement implies a relationship between that which can prevent serial homicide and that which causes it.

Lane and Gregg (1992:15) question how much freedom the state, social workers and the police services should have in interference in the domestic activities of families and individuals where abuse is suspected. These authors also consider the defects of the system as a contributory factor to serial homicide – for example, lack of involvement in child abuse/neglect cases, heavy case loads, lack of manpower, loopholes in the system.

The case of Jeffrey Dahmer is a good example of how the system failed to prevent the murder of innocent victims. In 1989 Dahmer was charged with possession of child pornography. During the court case a psychologist described him as schizoid and manipulative and it was recommended that he be institutionalised. Dahmer's defence made the following statement during his plea: 'We don't have a multiple offender here. I believe he was caught before the point where it would have gotten worse, which means that that's a blessing in disguise . . .' (Schwartz, 1992:67)

At this time Dahmer had already killed five people, but this fact was unknown. Dahmer was sentenced to a year's imprisonment, but he was allowed to go out to work every day. Two years and twelve murders later he was finally apprehended again. In the five years he was on probation, his probation officer suspected that something wrong, but did not investigate further because the suburb in which Dahmer lived was too dangerous.

Schwartz (1992:94) refers to two police officers who ignored the plea of a member of the public on 26 May 1991 concerning the boy Konerak Sinthasomphone, who was found naked and drugged on the street. Dahmer arrived on the scene and convinced the officers it was a lovers' tiff. They escorted him back to Dahmer's apartment and Konerak was murdered a few hours later. The police officers, who are a part of the system, were negligent in their duty in this instance.

I am in agreement with the principle that the early identification of certain patterns in the behaviour of children could prevent them from becoming serial killers. I am also of the opinion that society and the system, comprising the family and the authorities, are negligent in failing to identify potential serial killers. The system is geared to react to a serial killer, but not to prevent his development in the first instance.

As a component of the system, the media play a major role in the dynamics of the organised serial killer. Ressler and Shachtman (1993:106) state that most organised serial killers keep newspaper clippings of their crimes and fantasise about them later. Ressler reported that David Berkowitz only took on the name 'Son of Sam' after a newspaper reporter referred to him by that name. Ressler blames the reporter for irresponsibly enticing Berkowitz to murder. He published the names of the counties in which Berkowitz had already murdered and speculated whether he was going to attempt to commit a murder in each of the remaining counties. In an interview with Ressler, Berkowitz admitted that the idea to commit a murder in each county only occurred to him after he had read the speculation in the newspaper.

Ressler (in Jeffers, 1993:94) identifies social, environmental, psychological, cultural and economic factors, as well as stress, as elements in the American culture that contribute to the increase in serial homicide. He singles out the media as an exacerbatory factor. Monty Rissell, who murdered five women in 1978, admitted that he was inspired by the news coverage on David Berkowitz. Ressler regards the media as a catalyst in the sense that the organised serial killer craves acknowledgement and likes to see his name in print.

I am in complete agreement with other authors regarding the often irresponsible attitude of the media. Their coverage of serial killings can interfere with and hamper police investigations. In the case of Cedric Maake, the Wemmer Pan/Hammer Killer (page 291), I discuss the adverse results of media reporting. But, in all fairness, it must be acknowledged that there are journalists who act very responsibly when covering these cases.

Schwartz (1992:134) points out that district attorney Michael McCann condemned the *New York Times* for the premature publication of Dahmer's confession, since it could have influenced the jury.

Jeffers (1993:231) refers to Robert Graysmith's book *Zodiac*, which relates the exploits of the serial killer called Zodiac who operated in San Francisco in 1986. He was never apprehended. After the publication of the book in 1986 a second serial killer, also calling himself Zodiac, applied a similar modus operandi in New York.

American television programmes such as 'Unsolved Mysteries' and 'America's Most Wanted' often screen material about serial homicide. Although these programmes render an important service by generating public awareness, they also serve as a source of inspiration to potential serial killers.

In my opinion films such as 'Silence of the Lambs', 'Seven', 'Copycat' and 'Natural Born Killers' glorify serial killers and spree killers as supernatural beings, adding to the myth that they are either raving lunatics or super-intelligent human beings. These films provide negative role models. Several films have been made about the lives of Ted Bundy, David Berkowitz, John Wayne Gacy, Wayne Williams and John Reginald Christie. These films may serve a documentary purpose and in my view are not as harmful as fictional material.

While I agree that there are several systemic factors that contribute to serial homicide, to me they do not explain its *origin*.

Demonic possession

There is a common misconception that serial killers are possessed by demons. A possible reason for this is that 'normal' people cannot conceptualise that other seemingly normal people are capable of the atrocities that serial killers commit. When asked what the worst act of a serial killer could be most people are inclined to say necrophilia or cannibalism. They cannot stretch their imagination to visualise a serial killer masturbating into the decapitated heads of his victims. The uninformed usually do not grasp the symbolism of these acts. The serial killer himself may not be aware of it. People are therefore inclined to attribute such behaviour to demonism.

In the article 'Psychodynamic aspects of demon possession and Satanic worship' (1993), Ivey described the symptoms of demonic possession as follows:

- Radical personality change
- Loss of self-control
- Blasphemy
- Dissociative states
- Voice changes
- Auditory or visionary hallucinations of demons

None of these symptoms was evident in the recorded case studies of serial killers available to me.

Ivey explains demonic possession with regard to object relations as the internalisation of the bad object that derives from a disturbed relationship between the parents and the child. 'Object relations' is a psychological concept describing a situation where a child forms a relationship with the parent in his/her mind and ascribes certain good or bad traits to the parent which may not necessarily concur with the traits of the parent in reality. By internalising the 'bad object' the child is identifying with the ascribed bad traits of the parent in his/her mind. The case of David Berkowitz (Son of Sam) illustrates how 'demonism' can actually be explained as being caused by incorporation of a bad object.

Berkowitz attributed his behaviour to demonic possession. He made the following entry in his diary: 'There is no doubt in my mind that a demon has been living in me since birth. All my life I've been wild, violent, temporal [sic], mean, sadistic, acting with irrational anger and destructiveness' (Jeffers, 1993:3).

Berkowitz was born in 1953 as the illegitimate child of a mother who abandoned him (Lane and Gregg, 1992:36). According to Ressler and Shachtman (1993:106), he had problems with his adoptive parents. His adoptive mother died when he was fourteen years old and Berkowitz attempted to locate his biological mother. He succeeded in tracing her but she rejected him. His first sexual experience was with a prostitute and he contracted a venereal disease.

Although Berkowitz referred to a demon in his diary there is sufficient evidence that he had the opportunity to internalise the bad object. There is no evidence that he ever manifested any of the symptoms put forward by Ivey.

After his arrest Berkowitz said that he committed the murders in the name of a demon, a six-thousand-year-old man who lived in the dog of his neighbour, Sam. He shot this dog before he began to murder. Berkowitz later reported that any dog had the ability to point out his next victim. He was traced as a result of the evidence of an elderly woman who was walking her dog late one night and spotted him with a firearm.

During an interview with Berkowitz, Ressler (1993:108) confronted him with the fact that the stories about dogs and demons were nonsense. Although Berkowitz had managed to mislead psychiatrists with this story to the extent that they diagnosed him as a paranoid schizophrenic, Ressler did not believe it. Berkowitz indeed admitted to Ressler that the story was a ploy to secure a plea of insanity. He admitted that he had committed the murders because he resented his own mother and could not establish a relationship with any woman.

Berkowitz referred to himself as the 'Wicked King Maker',

the 'Chubby Monster', the 'Duke of Death' and 'Sam's Creation' before he took on the name 'Son of Sam'.

Jeffrey Dahmer's case also provides an example of how a serial killer justifies his acts by believing it to be the work of a demonic entity. Schwartz (1992:195) reported that Dahmer was fascinated by the devil and enjoyed films such as 'The Exorcist III' and 'Return of the Jedi'. Ressler (1995, personal communication) reported that Dahmer wanted to build a shrine in his apartment with real skulls and a skeleton from which he could draw power. He also bought yellow contact lenses which he often wore. Although Dahmer was interested in the occult, there is no evidence that he manifested symptoms of demonic possession. Dahmer admitted to an evil influence in his life: 'I have no question whether or not there is an evil force in the world and whether or not I have been influenced by it.' (Schwartz, 1992: 200)

Based on an extensive review of the available literature, I have drawn the following conclusions about demonic possession as a factor in the origin of serial homicide:

• Serial killers do not manifest the symptoms associated with demonic possession
• People who abduct children and rape or murder them in Satanistic rituals do not have the same intrinsic motives as serial killers
• Satanists belong to covens, while serial killers prefer to work alone. There have been cases of two or three working together, but these instances are rare

And again, we can ask the question: 'Why are not all Satanists or people possessed by the devil serial killers, and why are all serial killers not Satanists?' Several South African serial killers were religious. Bongani Mfeka and Nicolas Ncama (pages 235 and 244 both studied to become Methodist ministers and Mhlengwa Zikode, the Donnybrook serial killer (page 219), was a Catholic.

Neurological theories

Authors who support the neurological theories propose that serial killers suffer from brain injury or a neurological defect which causes them to murder strangers.

Money (1990) refers to paraphiliac serial rape (biastophilia) and lust murder (erotophonophilia) and attributes these two forms of sadism to neurological damage. According to him, the section of the brain that is damaged is the limbic system,[8] which is responsible for attack as a means of defence of the self or the species. Persons suffering damage to the limbic system tend to confuse this response by combining the aggressive mode with the sexual mode.

According to Money, in the case of sexual sadism, the brain is pathologically activated to transmit the signal for attack coupled with the signal for sexual arousal. He attributes this defect in functioning to a brain tumour or brain injury. The defect is not a continuous phenomenon, but occurs intermittently in the same way that epileptic fits manifest.

He states that contributory factors to sexual sadism are inherited vulnerability, hormonal functioning, pathological relationships and syndrome overlapping. Syndromes which overlap may include epilepsy, bipolar disorder, schizoidal preoccupation, antisocial tendencies and dissociative disorders. When the person experiences a paraphiliac attack his level of consciousness undergoes change. In this state of changed consciousness he may revert to another personality.

Jeffers (1993:100) discusses the case of Bobby Joe Long, who murdered ten women and raped several others. Long had suffered several head injuries, the first being at the age of five when he fell from a horse. He was also injured in a motorbike accident. He complained of headaches and had outbursts of temper. Long

---

[8]Limbic system: A complex system of nerves and networks in the brain that control basic emotions and drive, including sexual and defensive responses.

had an insatiable sexual drive. He had intercourse with his wife twice daily and masturbated five times a day. He also suffered from a genetic dysfunction and developed breasts, which were surgically removed.

Although these biological factors support Money's theory, there were other circumstances that influenced Long. He was allowed to share his mother's bed until the age of thirteen. His mother was twice divorced. He married as a teenager and had intercourse with his mother as well as his wife. Both these women dominated him. In my opinion, these circumstances may indicate a psychodynamic related pathology.

The records and case studies which I have researched indicate that not all serial killers have brain damage and not all of them dissociate during the act of murder. Also, not all people with brain damage become serial killers.

Psychopathological theories

Holmes and De Burger (1988) believe that biogenic[9] factors, with rare exceptions, can never be regarded as the cause of serial homicide. They do not elaborate on what a 'rare exception' to a biogenic factor might be. They consider the origin of serial homicide to be psychogenic.[10]

In considering psychogenic factors it is necessary to enquire whether a serial killer can be classified according to the DSM-IV[11] diagnostic categories. We will consider here the most probable psychiatric disorders that serial killers may suffer from.

---

[9]Biogenic: Pertaining to aspects of behaviour which are biological or organic in origin.

[10]Psychogenic: Psychological in origin. The term is used as a qualifier for disorders that are assumed to be functional in origin, ie those in which there is no known organic dysfunction.

[11]Diagnostic and Statistical Manual. It is the guidebook of the American Psychiatric Association which is regularly updated. DSM-IV was published in 1994.

> *Schizophrenia is a general label for a number of psychotic disorders with various cognitive, emotional and behavioural manifestations. Although there are various distinguishable schizophrenias which display differing etiologies, certain features are taken as hallmarks of all: deterioration from previous levels of social, cognitive and vocational functioning; onset before midlife; duration of at least six months; and, most tellingly, a pattern of psychotic features including thought disturbances, bizarre delusions, hallucinations (usually auditory), disturbed sense of self, and a loss of reality testing.*

A diagnosis of schizophrenia brings to mind Ressler and Shachtman's (1993:180) definition of the disorganised serial killer, which relates more to psychosis[12] than to psychopathy.[13] Kaplan and Sadock (1991:332) state that schizophrenia commences during the teenage years. Ressler is of the opinion that a period of ten years is necessary for schizophrenia to take on the characteristics that are found in disorganised serial killers. This period of ten years will place the operative serial killer in his early to mid-twenties. According to Ressler, an older person's schizophrenia will already have taken on such proportions that he is no longer able to function in society, and will probably be a chronic patient in an institution.

Trenton Chase is an example of a disorganised serial killer who was diagnosed with schizophrenia. Ressler's knowledge of schizophrenia led to the correct profile and subsequent arrest of Chase in 1978. His schizophrenia began during his high school years and in 1976 he was committed to a psychiatric institution after injecting himself with rabbit blood.

---

[12]Psychosis: Term used to describe the condition of a person who loses contact with reality.

[13]Psychopathy: Traits of antisocial personality disorder. This is not a mental illness.

While he was in the institution, Chase bit off the heads of birds and was often found with blood on his clothing. He believed that he was being poisoned and that his blood would turn to powder, and he needed other blood to replace his own. Chase was discharged in 1977 but remained an outpatient. He often killed animals, including his mother's cat. He also set fire to the houses of people he disliked. On the day he murdered his second victim Chase broke into a house, defecated on a child's bed and urinated on the clothing.

Ressler and Shachtman (1993:203) also refer to the case of Herbert William Mullin, who was diagnosed with paranoid schizophrenia. His schizophrenia commenced during his high school years and he manifested several personality changes. Although most schizophrenics are not dangerous, Mullin was extremely violent. He believed that he should commit murder on the orders of his father. His mission was to murder people as a sacrifice to prevent an earthquake in California.

Lane and Gregg (1992:166) discuss the case of Joseph Kallinger, who was diagnosed with schizophrenia and who believed he committed murder in the name of God. He blamed his alter ego, whom he called 'Charlie'. Kallinger spoke in several languages during his trial and foamed at the mouth. He was found to be able to differentiate between right and wrong and was convicted. After he set fire to his prison cell he was transferred to a psychiatric hospital. When he tried to suffocate himself with the plastic cover on his bed he was transferred to the Pennsylvania State Hospital for the Criminally Insane.

Cameron and Frazer (1987:105) provide further insight into Kallinger's background. In 1975 he killed a woman with a knife after she refused to bite off the penis of a captured male victim. Kallinger believed it was his mission to relieve people of their genitals. He also fantasised about the mutilation of female victims.

During his youth, Kallinger was operated on for a hernia. When he returned home from hospital his adoptive parents told him that the doctor had removed a devil from his penis and that it would always remain soft and small. Shortly afterwards he had a daydream in which his penis rested on the blade of the knife his adoptive father, who was a shoemaker, used for carving the soles of shoes. According to Cameron and Frazer, the combination of the symbolic castration by the parental figures, the vision of the knife, and the real pain of the operation formed the basis of his delusion.

Kallinger could only obtain an erection when he held a knife in his hand. 'These events fitted in with what Kallinger later did, and with the notion that he was defending himself against castration anxiety, as well as revenging himself on his parents who castrated him.' (Cameron and Frazer, 1987:105)

Cameron and Frazer also quote Dr Terrence Kay, who made the following statement when defending Peter Sutcliffe, the 'Yorkshire Ripper':

A sadist killer can very rarely relate to adult women and therefore is very rarely married; secondly he has a rich fantasy life, dreams about sex and is usually very anxious to discuss his fantasies; thirdly such people would stimulate their fantasy with pornography and would be interested in torture, whips and female underwear. (1987:130)

Kay was of the opinion that since Sutcliffe was married, he did not conform to these requirements. Sutcliffe tried to present himself as a schizophrenic who committed the murders on the orders of God in order to enter a plea of diminished responsibility before the court. Sutcliffe had raped Helena Rytka while she was dying and inserted a wooden plank into the vagina of Emily Jackson. He repeatedly stabbed Josephine Whitaker with a screwdriver. He was therefore sadistic and acted out his sadistic fantasies. According to Cameron and Frazer, Kay's defence that Sutcliffe was schizophrenic and not sadistic held no water. Later Sutcliffe admitted to his brother that he committed the murders because he wanted to rid the world of prostitutes.

Although there is no doubt that some schizophrenics are capable of serial homicide, not all schizophrenics are serial killers, and many serial killers only claim to be schizophrenic in order to enter a plea of mental disorder.

Schizoid personality disorder

> *A personality disorder characterised by an emotional coldness, secretiveness, solitude, withdrawal and a general inability to form intimate attachment to others. It is not regarded as a form of schizophrenia and is diagnostically differentiated from a schizotypal personality disorder.*

Case studies indicate that schizoid tendencies are more common among disorganised than organised serial killers. Reference has already been made to Jeffrey Dahmer's schizoid tendencies. He had no close ties to family members, with the exception of his grandmother; he preferred solitary activities and did not have friends. Schwartz (1992:191) mentions that acquaintances, neighbours and teachers described him as a loner.

As far as sexual behaviour is concerned, the criterion for schizoid personality disorder is a person who avoids sexual contact. Jeffrey Dahmer avoided sexual contact with living human beings. He tried to turn his victims into zombies by drilling holes in their heads and pouring acid into the holes. He said he wanted to create a sex slave who would comply with all his wishes, without having a personality of his own (Ressler, 1995, personal communication). Dahmer was unsuccessful in his attempt to create 'zombies' and settled on committing necrophilia with the bodies of his victims. This indicates that he preferred sexual intercourse where no interpersonal relations were possible.

Another criterion for schizoid personality disorder is restricted affect. Dahmer exhibited this criterion. During the court case he seldom showed any facial expression. Schwartz (1992:191) states that Dahmer stared in front of him and laughed only once about the false news report that he had eaten his prison cell mate. An early acquaintance describes Dahmer as follows: 'I felt un-comfortable around him because he was so weird and emotionless.' (Schwartz, 1992:41)

It should be emphasised, however, that schizoid tendencies are not found in all serial killers, and nor do all people with schizoid tendencies become serial killers.

Schizotypal personality disorder

> *A personality disorder characterised by markedly eccentric and erratic thought, speech and behaviour and a tendency to withdraw from other people. The disorder is characterised as similar to but less severe than schizophrenia, although it is occasionally called borderline schizophrenia. It is distinguished from a schizoid personality disorder where eccentricities of thought, speech and behaviour are not present.*

Jeffrey Dahmer also provides us with an example of someone with schizotypal tendencies. He said that the reason he committed cannibalism was because he believed the spirits of his victims would live inside him. This is an example of magical thinking. Eccentric behaviour is another criterion of schizotypal personality disorder which Dahmer exhibited. He wore yellow contact lenses, planned to build an altar of human skulls and bones from which to draw power, and he did not wash often. He had no confidants, which is another criterion of this personality disorder (Schwartz, 1992).

Again, it is necessary to point out that schizotypal tendencies are not found in all serial killers, and not all people diagnosed with this disorder become serial killers.

Antisocial personality disorder

> *A personality disorder marked by a history of irresponsible and antisocial behaviour beginning in childhood or early adolescence and continuing into adulthood. Early manifestations include lying, stealing, fighting, vandalism, running away from home and cruelty. In adulthood the general pattern continues, charac-*

terised by such factors as significant unemployment, failure to conform to social norms, property destruction, stealing, failure to honour financial obligations, reckless disregard for one's own or others' safety, incapacity to maintain enduring relationships, poor parenting, and a consistent disregard for the truth. Also noted as an important feature is a glibness accompanied by a lack of remorse and a lack of or lessened ability to feel guilty for one's actions. Other labels that have been used over the years to capture this syndrome include psychopathic personality and sociopathic personality.

Holmes and De Burger describe the psychopathic inner structure of the serial killer as follows: 'The single most important one of the basic behavioral sources in repetitive homicide is the existence of a sociopathic character structure or personality in the perpetrator', and 'he has sociopathic tendencies and a capacity for aggression and raw violence'. (1988:66)

These authors emphasise that the typical serial killer is not mentally ill, but that his lack of remorse can be attributed to a psyche that is socially defective. 'This sociopathic pattern, originating in early childhood, separates them from the rest of humanity and results in a lack of empathy for it. Yet they are otherwise rational, logical, appropriate, competent, even charming and persuasive.' (Holmes and De Burger, 1988:66)

All authors seem to agree that several of the criteria for antisocial personality disorder may manifest in serial killers. The criteria manifesting before the age of fifteen, namely physical cruelty towards animals and other people as well as forced sexual relations, are found in many serial killers. For instance, Jeffrey Dahmer slaughtered and dissected animals as a child. (Ressler, 1995, personal communication)

Some serial killers also commit arson. Notes on 1400 incidents of arson were found in David Berkowitz's diary. It is estimated that he committed about 2000 cases of arson (Jeffers, 1993:143) but it is not known whether this commenced before the age of fifteen.

Theft before the age of fifteen is also one of the criteria for antisocial personality disorder. The Boston Strangler, Albert de Salvo, already had a criminal record at the age of seventeen for housebreaking. (Jeffers, 1993:2) Monty Rissell had raped twelve women and murdered five by the age of nineteen. At the age of nine he shot his cousin; he was caught driving without a licence at thirteen; and at fourteen he was charged with housebreaking, car theft and two rapes. (Ressler and Shachtman, 1993:122)

An unstable employment record is another criterion for antisocial personality disorder and is commonly found in the case histories of serial killers. According to Ressler, serial killers often work in occupations beneath their intellectual or social standards. Dahmer worked in a chocolate factory and Peter Sutcliffe was a truck driver. Dahmer was often truant from work, especially after a murder. In 1991 he was dismissed for being late and for being absent without leave. (Schwartz, 1992:109)

Aggression and violence are other manifestations of the antisocial personality disorder and are common characteristics among serial killers. Apart from torturing their victims, they are often involved in fights and woman battering. Albert de Salvo beat his first wife when she refused to comply with his sexual desires. (Jeffers, 1993:2) Dahmer's father Lionel reported that his son was often involved in bar fights. (Schwartz, 1992:49)

Another characteristic of the antisocial personality disorder is the inability to commit to a long-term emotional relationship with a partner. Although some may be married, serial killers as a rule do not have the ability to commit to a long-term, fulfilling relationship. Ted Bundy, charged with nineteen murders, was married but admitted that he was unable to sustain a relationship with a partner. He claimed the fact that he was illegitimate contributed to this inability.

David Berkowitz was offended by a newspaper article that referred to him as a misogynist (Jeffers, 1993:59), but he later admitted to Ressler that he murdered women because he could not have a fulfilling relationship with them and that he blamed his mother for this. (Ressler and Shachtman, 1993:108)

The criterion of antisocial personality disorder which is most applicable to serial killers is the lack of the ability to feel remorse or guilt. Ted Bundy made the following statement: 'What's one less person on the face of the earth anyway; I don't feel guilty for anything; I feel sorry for people who feel guilt; I'm the most cold-hearted son of a bitch you'll ever meet.' (Jeffers, 1993:78)

Levin and Fox refer to Clifford Olson who murdered eleven children and at the time of his arrest made an offer to the police that he be paid ten thousand pounds for every body he pointed out. He argued that if the police agreed to this they would be able to clear up unsolved cases and the families could bury the victims. The police agreed to pay the money to Olson's wife. She was paid nine thousand pounds. When he was asked to point out the rest of the bodies without payment, Olson remarked: 'If I gave a shit about the parents, I wouldn't have killed the kid.' (1991:167)

Again, not all serial killers are diagnosed with antisocial personality disorders, and not all people diagnosed with antisocial personality disorder become serial killers. Antisocial tendencies are found most often in organised serial killers. My own explanation for the absence of guilt feelings in serial killers is based on Freud's theory of the superego, which will be discussed later.

Paraphilias

> *Paraphilia is an umbrella term for any mode of sexual expression in which arousal is dependent upon what are generally considered to be socially unacceptable stimulating conditions. Typically, a paraphiliac is rather obsessively concerned with and responsive to the particular erotic stimuli of his or her sexual mode. A large number of paraphilias have been identified.*

Kaplan and Sadock (1991:443) describe paraphilias as being characterised by sexual fantasies and intense sexual urges and practices that are repetitive and upsetting to the afflicted person.

Paraphilias are considered to be divergent behaviour, which is hidden by the person affected and directed at the exclusion of damage to others. They disturb the person's potential for binding with others and become a substitute for an intimate sexual relationship with another. Paedophilia, sexual sadism, fetishism, oralism, sadism, voyeurism and necrophilia are paraphilias that may manifest in serial killers.

The question arises whether serial homicide can be classified as a paraphilia. Elements of paraphilia are certainly present in serial killers, but need not necessarily dominate their lives. Another problem encountered when considering whether serial killers can be diagnosed as paraphiliacs is that one of the criteria for paraphilias is that it is upsetting to the person who manifests it. Ego-syntonic serial killers do not perceive the perversion as offensive and they do not hide it. In my own experience, I have found that they sometimes even provoke the police with their perversions and generally they do not experience any feelings of guilt.

Jerry Brudos is an example of a serial killer who had a fetish. According to Lane and Gregg (1992:55) Brudos already had a shoe fetish at the age of five years. At seventeen he was arrested for ordering a woman to undress and threatening her with a knife. He was detained for nine months in a mental institution and was diagnosed as suffering from an early personality disorder. He often paraded in his wife's underwear and took photographs of himself. In 1968 he murdered a woman, chopped off her left foot and threw the body into a river. He kept the foot in a deep freeze and dressed it in different shoes. Apart from committing necrophilia, he also mutilated victims' breasts and kept the breasts.

If the serial killer is offended by his own sexual deviation, as Kaplan and Sadock's description of paraphilia requires, I would postulate that his ego would defend itself against the offensive impulses by dissociation. He would then be an ego-dystonic serial killer.

Dissociative disorders

*This is a general term for those psychological disorders charac-
terised by a breakdown in the usual integrated functions of
consciousness, perception of self and sensory/motor behaviour.
Multiple personality disorder is generally included here.*

Carlisle (in Holmes and De Burger) is of the opinion that serial
killers have a multiple personality structure. Holmes and De
Burger state:

> Carlisle holds to the position that the serial killer has an
> overwhelming urge to kill, and that this urge to kill, which
> some serial killers call their 'beast' or their 'shadow' can take
> over the complete task of murder. The beasts are only visible
> to the serial killers, who outwardly appear to be 'nice people'.
> With some of the serial killers, the person is no longer in
> charge, only the impulses of the beast. (1988:98)

Cameron and Frazer analyse the case of Dennis Nilsen who
murdered sixteen young men between 1978 and 1983. Nilsen
experienced the murders as ego-dystonic. 'I seem not to have
participated in the killings, merely stood by and watched them
happen – enacted by two other players . . . I always covered up
for that "inner me" that I loved . . . He just acted and I had to
solve all his problems in the cool light of day.' (1987:151)

Ted Bundy also tried to pretend that his murders had been
committed by another entity inside him. (Cameron and Frazer,
1987:179) Lane and Gregg (1992:59) refer to Bundy's statement that an unknown 'urge' hides within the murderer. Bundy
confessed to the murders in the third person singular.

Lane and Gregg (1992:173) also discuss Kenneth Bianchi,
one of the 'Hillside Strangler' duo of Los Angeles, who pretended
to suffer from multiple personality disorder. One of his alleged
personalities was named 'Steve', a violent individual who committed the sex crimes.

Another case referred to by Lane and Gregg (1992:156) is that of William Heirens, who alleged that his murders were committed by his alter ego called 'George Murman'.

Norman Simons, the Station Strangler (page 122), told detectives that the voice of his older brother Boyzie ordered him to kill the children and that it was Boyzie's hands who murdered them.

In my opinion, multiple personality disorder/dissociative personality disorder develops during early childhood as an escape and defence mechanism against excessive abuse. The child fantasises about escaping an unbearable situation and creates different personalities to manage the abuse. According to Ressler's motivational model, the serial killer, on the other hand, fantasises about revenge and manages the abuse by acting out the fantasies. The origins of serial homicide and multiple personality disorder therefore differ fundamentally as different defence mechanisms come into play in each case. The child's ego can choose either of these defence mechanisms – either by splitting into personalities or by developing and acting out revenge fantasies – but it cannot choose both.

Normality

Normality is not a DSM-IV category, but the question is often asked whether a serial killer can be a 'normal' person and I would therefore like to discuss the issue.

Cameron and Frazer quote the following statement made by a psychologist about serial killers:

> Most of them are very normal and very friendly, that you maybe went into a pub to have a drink, and you'd sit there and talk to him and he'd all of a sudden become one of your good friends, you can't look at him and tell that there is something strange about him, they're very normal. (1987:157)

Leyton writes:

. . . madness is not like cancer or any other physical ailment. Rather it is a culturally programmed dialogue. It should not therefore be surprising that no matter how hard our psychiatrists search, they are unable to discover much mental disease among our captured murderers (except in the nature of their acts). Therein lies the special horror, for the killers are as 'normal' as you and me, yet they kill without mercy, and they kill to make a statement. (1986:22)

Ressler and Shachtman indicate that organised serial killers often exhibit acting out and violent behaviour during their childhood, but this is not necessarily the childhood behaviour pattern of the disorganised serial killer. When he is arrested and his identity is publicised his neighbours, school friends and teachers hardly remember him: 'And when his neighbours are interviewed, they characterise him as a nice boy, never any trouble, who kept to himself and was docile and polite.' (1993:194)

The question of whether a serial killer is 'normal' or whether he is mentally ill often arises during their trials. Levin and Fox (1991:175) discuss the dilemma when a plea of insanity is entered and results in an accused being found not accountable for his actions. Many serial killers have avoided the death penalty by successfully entering such a plea and have been institutionalised for the rest of their lives. A psychotic person can, however, still be held legally accountable in the United States of America and sentenced to a prison term. Twenty-seven American states accepted the criteria of the American Legal Society which state: 'A defendant is not criminally responsible if "as a result of mental disease or defect he lacks substantial capacity either to appreciate the criminality of his conduct or to conform his conduct to the requirement of the law".'

Some American states accept the verdict 'guilty but mentally insane' and such a person will receive therapy in prison.

Jeffrey Dahmer attempted to enter a plea of insanity before the court. Schwartz (1992:213) reports that Dahmer, who showed the characteristics of both an organised and a disorganised serial killer, was found guilty and mentally accountable for the murders he committed. His plea of insanity did not succeed. The question remains whether the following description of his behaviour, presented by his defence attorney during the trial, is that of a normal person:

Skulls in locker, cannibalism, sexual urges, drilling, making zombies, necrophilia, disorders, paraphilia, watching videos, getting excited about fish eggs, drinking alcohol all of the time, into a dysfunctional family, trying to create a shrine, showering with corpses, going into the occult, having delusions, chanting and rocking, picking up a road kill, having obsessions, murders, lobotomies, defleshing, masturbating two, three times a day as a youngster, going and trying to get a mannequin home so he could play sex with a mannequin, masturbating into the open parts of a human being's body, calling taxidermists, going to graveyards, going to funeral homes, wearing yellow contacts, posing people who are dead that he killed for pleasure, masturbating all over the place. (Schwartz, 1992:212)

Ressler related that when he asked Dahmer whether he ate the human flesh raw, Dahmer answered: 'Mr Ressler, I'm not that sick.' (Ressler, 1995, personal communication)

In South Africa an accused may be referred for thirty days or longer for observation in a state-appointed psychiatric hospital. According to Sections 77 and 79 of the Criminal Procedures Act, 1977 (Act no 51 of 1977) the accused may be found mentally ill or not mentally ill, fit to stand trial or not fit to stand trial and to have the capability to appreciate the wrongfulness of the act in question and to act accordingly, or not, and to be found mentally ill or not mentally ill at the time of the alleged offence.

In my review of the case histories of South African serial killers I found that only two men were found unfit to stand trial, one was Cornelius Burger and the other was Raymond Govindsamy. Although their actions can be explained using the tool of psychoanalysis, I am of the opinion that the majority of organised serial killers are not mentally ill. To me, psychoanalysis provides an explanation for the origin of serial homicide but does not provide an excuse for the actions of the perpetrators.

Fantasy

> *Fantasy is a term generally used to refer to the mental process of imagining objects, symbols or events that are not immediately present. In general, fantasy is assumed to be normal, the pathological aspects often cited being restricted to those cases in which fantasy becomes delusionary or when it dominates a person's mental life and serves as a retreat from reality rather than an adjunct to it.*

MacCulloch, Snowden, Wood and Mills (1983) studied a group of sixteen sexual sadists. In thirteen of the sixteen cases, sadistic masturbatory fantasies were found to have inspired the sadistic acts. MacCulloch *et al.* found that thirteen of the sadists had behavioural 'try outs' where their fantasies corresponded with their sadistic behaviour. In nine cases they found a progression in the contents of their sadistic fantasies.

Prentky, Wolbert-Burgess, Rokous, Lee, Hartman, Ressler and Douglas (1989) examined the role of fantasy by comparing twenty-five serial killers with seventeen murderers who committed only a single murder. The authors hypothesised that the drive mechanism for serial killers is an intrusive fantasy life manifesting in higher prevalences of paraphilias, documented or self-reported violent fantasies and organised crime scenes in the serial homicides. All three of their hypotheses were supported.

Prentky *et al.* (1989) report that Burgess, in a study she conducted in 1986, had found evidence of daydreaming and compulsive masturbation in over 80 per cent of a sample of thirty-six serial murderers in childhood as well as adulthood.

Prentky *et al.* summarise the MacCulloch *et al.* research as follows:

While the precise function of consummated fantasy is speculative, we concur with MacCulloch *et al.* that once the restraints inhibiting the acting out of the fantasy are no longer present, the individual is likely to engage in a series of progressively more accurate 'trial runs' in an attempt to enact the fantasy as it is imagined. Since the trial runs can never precisely match the fantasy, the need to restage the fantasy with a new victim is established. MacCulloch *et al.* suggested the shaping of the fantasy and the motivation for consummation may be understood in terms of classical conditioning . . . While it is unlikely that the translation of fantasy into reality conforms precisely to a classical conditioning model, it does appear that the more fantasy is rehearsed, the more power it acquires and the stronger the association between the fantasy content and sexual arousal. (1989:890)

I agree that fantasy is the blueprint for serial homicide. Whereas Prentky *et al.* were unable to explain the lack of inhibition that causes the fantasies to be acted out in reality, I will later attempt to explain this phenomenon according to Freud's theory of the id, ego and superego. Prentky *et al.* do not support MacCulloch *et al.*'s suggestion that the repetitive fantasy can be attributed to classical conditioning, but they themselves do not provide an adequate explanation for repetitive fantasy or why a serial killer commits a series of murders. I will also attempt to explain this phenomenon in terms of Freud's theory on the compulsion to repeat.

Literature on serial killers is mainly of American and British origin. Several authors have attempted to explain the elusive motive of serial killers by proposing socio-cultural, demonic, neurological and systemic theories. I have also attempted to explore the psychogenic categories to determine whether serial killers could be classified according to the DSM-IV. Although several criteria of the DSM-IV categories are evident in some serial killers, they do not all conform to a specific diagnostic category.

It is evident that socio-cultural factors and a violent and alienating system are contributory factors to serial homicide, but none of these theories adequately explains the *origin* of serial homicide.

After I had studied all the above theories on the origin of serial homicide, I still had what I regarded as one valid question: If two boys in the same family are both exposed to family abuse – be it emotional, physical or sexual – and both are equally exposed to violent and criminal external factors such as faction fighting, armed robbery and murder, as well as to poverty and illness, why is it that one may develop into a serial killer and the other not?

To my mind, the answer lies within the individual's internal reaction to all these adverse external circumstances and not in the circumstances themselves. The debate about the normality or abnormality of serial killers also does not provide an explanation for this phenomenon.

I had to find a tool, a medium, by which I could try to decipher what went on in the mind of the serial killer, and this tool had to be of such a nature that it could be applied to all serial killers. I discovered the tool in some of Freud's psychoanalytical theories. I found that I could generalise these theories to the more than three hundred serial killer case studies I have examined and all the cases I have personally worked on.

Pistorius' theory

In a nutshell, my theory proposes that a serial killer fixates in one of what Freud called the psychosexual developmental phases. This fixation[14] is the seed from which his particular fantasy germinates within the subconscious. The serial killer does not socialise like other children and does not develop a conscience.

---

[14]A layman's term for a fixation is a mental short circuit. It is an individualistic reaction to being exposed to too much or too little of something.

Due to the lack of conscience, the fantasy is allowed to emerge from the subconscious to the conscious.

When the serial killer's self-esteem is challenged or threatened (which he perceives as loss of power), he has to act out his fantasy (he is omnipotent in his fantasies and regains the power which he felt he was losing) in order to restore mental homeostasis[15] regarding power and control. There is no conscience to inhibit the acting-out of his fantasy. There is a correlation between the serial killer's early fixations and the fantasy he acts out on his crime scene. My theory answers the questions I posed regarding Prentky and his colleagues' research. I believe that it takes us a step closer to understanding the enigma.

Freud's theory on the psychosexual developmental phases provides an answer to my first question as to *where* the serial killer's fantasy originates. According to this theory every human being passes through five psychosexual developmental phases. They are the oral phase, anal phase, Oedipal or phallic phase, latency phase and the genital phase. A person can fixate in any of these phases and failure to resolve the fixation would be cause for pathology.

The first phase is the *oral* or breast-feeding phase, existing from birth to about two years. All the infant's basic needs – such as survival, hunger, love and security – are satisfied orally by the mother's milk. The oral phase is divided into two stages, namely oral erotic, which is the sucking stage, and oral sadistic, which is the period when the infant bites the mother's nipple.

An infant can fixate in this phase by either not getting enough milk or by getting too much. If the infant feels that he is not getting sufficient milk, he perceives that his needs are not satisfied. He will develop into an adult who is forever searching to have his needs gratified and who is oversensitised to rejection. He is, after all, totally dependent on the milk for all his needs. If

---

[15]Homeostasis – maintaining equilibrium – implies an in-built tendency to keep psychological tension at a constant optimal level.

he perceives that he is getting too much milk, he will develop into an adult who expects the whole world to attend to his needs immediately. Preverbal sexual and aggressive fantasies already exist in the infant's subconscious, since sex and aggression are the two most basic instincts we are born with.

The *anal phase* is the so-called 'potty-training phase', existing from approximately two to four years. This is also called the *control phase* since the toddler is learning to control his own bodily functions, he is exercising control over his environment by becoming more mobile and less dependent on his parents, and he is learning to control his parents. The toddler is engaged in a battle of power with his primary caretaker, usually the mother, who tries to teach him to use the potty. He can sit on the potty for hours and either 'give' or 'retain' faeces which he perceives to be a product of his own body and of which he is very proud. The mother patiently waits, usually sitting on her haunches in front of the mighty toddler, for him to give or retain. He is controlling the most powerful person in his life – she is the most powerful because he is dependent on her for his survival.

Fixations can occur in this phase if children are forced to use the potty before they are physically ready to, or a toddler can fixate on the immense feeling of power. The passive infant is developing into an active toddler. The sexual and aggressive fantasies in the subconscious become more defined since the toddler is learning how to speak and to interpret symbolism. He is becoming consciously aware of his fantasies and verbalises them. One should listen to the noises children at this age make when they play. They also seem to be preoccupied with bodily functions and verbally express these fascinations.

The *Oedipal* or *phallic phase*, existing from approximately four to six years, is a most interesting phase when the little boy subconsciously falls in love with his mother and hates his father. A father can be replaced by any father figure and need not necessarily be the biological father. He vies for his mother's attention and has subconscious sexual fantasies about her and subconscious aggressive fantasies towards his father. This is also the period during which children show a natural curiosity in the difference between the genders' genitals – 'Show me yours and I'll show you mine.'

It is natural for children to masturbate up to this phase, for they are experiencing their bodies and its sensations. The little boy discovers that the little girl has no penis and cannot imagine that she was actually born like that. He subconsciously perceives her to be castrated and consequently fears castration himself.

A fixation may occur in this phase when a boy beats his father in the battle for his mother's affection, or where he perceives himself mentally castrated either by the father or by the mother. The father may castrate him for coveting his wife and the mother may castrate him by rejecting his adoration.

At the end of this period the boy decides it is safer to identify with his father in order to one day marry a woman like his mother. As a result of this identification with the father and the fact that the boy is ready to go to school and socialise, a conscience, or superego as Freud called it, develops. Up to this age, a child will avoid doing something he knows is wrong for fear of punishment. After this phase he incorporates right versus wrong internally in the superego.

The *latency phase* exists from the ages of approximately six to twelve years, beginning at the time when the boy is sent off to school. All sexual thoughts and subconscious fantasies from the previous phases are repressed as the boy concentrates on social-ising, developing empathy for others, sharing, incorporating moral and ethical values and thereby developing his internal conscience or superego.

Fixation in this phase results in the boy's failure to socialise and empathise, and the primitive sexual and aggressive fantasies are not repressed. He also fails to develop a conscience. A fixation could also occur when the conscience develops too strongly, in which case the boy will develop into an adult who is tortured by guilt feelings. Another fixation here is that the boy will continue to masturbate.

During the *genital phase*, existing mainly during the teenage years, the boy becomes sexually orientated again, but this time he enters into a heterosexual relationship with an appropriate partner and he has a last chance to resolve issues resulting from fixations which developed during the previous phases.

Children are very sexually orientated during the first three phases and masturbation is a natural occurrence and a manner in which they explore their bodies. Most of us do not remember the explicit sexual and aggressive fantasies we had then, since most of them have been repressed to the subconscious and our incorporation of moral and ethical values has banished these fantasies as taboo. Masturbation and accompanying sexual and aggressive fantasies are repressed during the latency phase, but re-emerge as censored and more subliminal versions during the genital phase. In the case of neurosis, these fantasies may re-emerge as neurotic symptoms.

Freud's theory on the topological structure of the psyche, namely the *id*, *ego* and *superego*, provides an answer to my second question, namely the lack of an inhibiting censor, such as a conscience, to prevent the serial killer from acting out his fantasy.

This theory postulates that every human being is born with an id. The id is situated within the subconscious and contains the instincts and all the energy needed to have the instincts satisfied. The first basic instincts are sex and aggression. Sex comprises all the instincts for the reproduction of the species, and aggression the instincts for survival, attack and defence of the self. Both have to do with self-preservation. The id is like the witches' cauldron in Shakespeare's *Macbeth*. It bubbles, toils and is full of trouble. It knows no time, no morality and cannot discriminate between good and bad. There is no logic in the id. It operates on the pleasure principle and it wants all its needs satisfied immediately. It is like a very demanding baby. Since the id is situated in the subconscious it communicates with the ego by means of dreams, symbols and symptoms.

From the id develops the ego, the second structure. The ego is the executive manager of the psyche. It adheres to the reality principle and understands logic. It can communicate in language.

The ego exists within the conscious. Its main task is to act as negotiator between the id, the superego and external reality. Since this is such a difficult task, the ego has an army of mental defence mechanisms to assist it. One of the main defence mechanisms is its ability to repress anything it finds threatening to its self-preservation to the subconscious. Unfortunately the subconscious demands that the ego deals with whatever it has repressed and this can cause pathology.

At about the age of six, during the commencement of the latency period, the *superego*, or conscience, develops as a result of an identification with the father figure and the incorporation of society's norms and values. The superego sets up an ideal self, by which it measures the ego. Should the ego fail to meet the standards of this ideal self, or fail to comply with the superego's moral and ethical values, the superego punishes the ego with guilt feelings. The superego is situated partly within the subconscious and partly in the conscious. Sometimes we know why we feel guilty, but sometimes we cannot pinpoint the exact source of our guilt feelings because the reason has been repressed to the subconscious by the ego. Where the id says 'yes' to everything, the superego says 'no' to everything and can be just as unrealistic in its demands on the ego as the id.

The id's sexual and aggressive fantasies, which all children experience during the first three developmental phases, cause anxiety to the ego because of the development of the child's superego during the latency phase. In an adult the superego has grown much stronger and will force the ego to repress any upsetting need or urge originating from the id. These fantasies are then repressed to the subconscious.

The serial killer has a particularly strong and dominating id and consequently very strong sexual and aggressive urges. Owing to a lack of bonding with his mother or primary caretaker, or due to a symbiotic situation in which he fails to differentiate his own personality from his mother's, he has a weak ego. Furthermore, the serial killer has no positive father figure with whom to identify during the latency period and he does not manage the socialisation process. He does not, therefore, develop a superego, or develops only faint traces of a superego. The fixation he experienced during any of the developmental phases germinates into a fantasy which becomes more defined and more conscious as the child becomes older. As a result of his weak ego and virtually non-existent superego, these penetrating fantasies cause no anxiety to the ego and are therefore neither repressed nor are they sublimated into more acceptable versions.

The serial killer is in absolute command and is omnipotent in his own fantasies. When the adult serial killer's fragile ego and self-esteem are threatened by any form of rejection or pain, the original childhood agony is triggered and he feels the irresistible urge to act out this powerful fantasy, which is the only way he perceives he will be able to resolve the psychological imbalance.

All serial killers fixate in the latency phase, although they will also fixate in one or more of the other psychosexual phases. They always feel like outsiders. The case history of any serial killer will indicate that the father figure was perhaps physically, but definitely emotionally, absent when the boy was in his latency phase. As a boy, therefore, he had no positive father figure with whom to identify.

Case histories also indicate that serial killers report themselves as very lonely children who felt alienated and isolated from their peers. During the latency phases they did not learn to socialise, they did not learn to empathise with others and they did not incorporate moral and ethical values. Because of the fact that they failed in their socialisation process, serial killers treat their victims as mere objects that exist for the gratification of their own needs. They show no empathy for their victims.

Serial killers can be either ego-dystonic or ego-syntonic. The ego-dystonic serial killer has a very slight sense of conscience and cannot identify himself with the fact that he kills other humans to relieve his own suffering. He may indicate slight guilt feelings, especially after his arrest, but the guilt is not strong enough to motivate him to stop. The ego-syntonic serial killer has no conscience whatsoever and does not feel the slightest sense of guilt.

The last question I asked after studying the work of Prentky and his colleagues was why serial killers feel compelled to repeat the acting-out of their fantasies and to commit repetitive murders. Freud's theory on the compulsion to repeat provides an answer to this tendency.

The theory states that the ego experiences any trauma passively, but in order to master the trauma, it repeats it actively in a weakened position.

Anyone who observes children will notice that they tend to repeat any new experience. When they learn a new word they will repeat it frequently, or when they learn to tie their shoelaces they will tie and untie them a hundred times until they get it right.

The passive-active role reversal can be explained by the everyday example of a husband returning home in a foul mood because his boss has berated him. He criticises his wife as he walks in the door. The wife yells at their son for not doing his homework and the boy kicks the dog for being in his way. The dog chases the cat (and the cat, of course, is smart enough to understand the whole situation and merely shrugs the dog off). The point, of course, is that all the role-players converted their passive victim status into active aggressor status in order to master their anxiety.

The serial killer does the same. He repeats what was done to him either directly or symbolically in order to master it and he will keep on repeating it until he gets it right. Unfortunately he never will get it right for he is using the wrong method to master it. Prentky and his colleagues, especially Ann Burgess, correctly assessed this process when they pointed out that reality is never as perfect as fantasy.

The passive-active role reversal process and compulsion to repeat the trauma also influences the serial killer's idiosyncratic selection of victims. As I have said, he can either indirectly repeat what was done to him, like Norman Simons (page 122), and will then most likely choose victims who represent himself; or he may symbolically avenge his suffering, and would then be more likely to select victims who represent the original tormentor.

I believe my theory may explain the intrinsic development of the urge to kill in serial killers. A fixation occurs when an individual has too little or too much of something. Why some individuals are more prone to certain fixations I do not know, but I trust some bright student will be able to expand on this theory to bring us closer to understanding the enigma of serial homicide. I also trust that another bright student may explore the objects-relations theory with regard to serial killers.

I hope that this chapter has provided some insights as to why 'normal' men do bad things.

Lastly, I am often asked why serial killers are mostly men and I would like to quote Roy Hazelwood – a retired FBI agent who specialised in research on serial rape and was one of my mentors – who explained the difference between men's sexuality and women's sexuality to me as follows:

- Men and women differ in their primary sexual sense. A man's sexual sense is visual – many sexual crimes have this element attached to them. Think of voyeurism, fetishism, sadism, etc. Men are stimulated by what they see. A woman's primary sexual sense, on the other hand, is touch. Women are aroused when they are touched and stroked.
- Men and women differ regarding their sexual dysfunctions. Men's dysfunctions centre around their performance – think about impotence, etc. Women's dysfunctions centre around pain.
- Men reach their sexual peak at the age of eighteen to twenty-four years and women in their mid-thirties. By this age women are often settled in marriage, child-rearing, etc and are unlikely to go off on a killing spree.
- Men and women react differently to sexual abuse. Men tend to take out abuse on others and women tend to take it out on themselves.

- When a man wants to dominate a woman, he will demand sex – think of rape. When a woman wants to dominate a man, she will refuse him sex.
- A woman equates sex with emotions but a man does not necessarily do so.

Hazelwood's explanation makes sense. It is against a woman's nature to commit a sexual crime. This is not to say that women serial killers do not exist. I have never met or investigated a female serial killer, but I tend to believe that if a woman turns against her nurturing nature, she will commit worse atrocities than a man.

Female serial killers often work with male partners. Myra Hindley and her partner Ian Brady – dubbed the Moors Murderers in Britain – killed three children in the mid-1960s. Fred West and his wife Rosemary were a notorious serial killer pair in Britain in the 1990s. Prostitute Aileen Wuornos killed several of her clients in the States. South Africa's Daisy de Melcker was not, however, a serial killer. She poisoned her husbands and son for material benefit. She had an external motive – financial gain – and she did not target strangers who had symbolic value.

In the pages that follow I will be discussing a selection of South African serial killers. There has never been any official record keeping of South African serial killers, but I have endeavoured to research as many as I could. In some cases the information is sparse. The MTN Centre for the Study of Crime Prevention at Rhodes University, under the directorship Dr Mark Welman, is currently developing a data bank on South African serial killers.

It is only by understanding the motives and behaviour of serial killers that the police will be in any position to secure early arrests. Detectives need to receive specific training for this kind of investigation and the South African Police Service has benefited greatly in the past from such specialised training.

It is, however, important to extend training to other officials as well. State prosecutors, judges, parole officers and pathologists need also to take note of the psychodynamics of serial killers in order to carry out their duties effectively.

The Police, Justice and Correctional Services Departments are, however, only involved in a reactive way. It is crucial that a proactive approach be followed by educating the general public, particularly teachers and others who work with the young, to be able to identify possible traits and psychological problems in children. Not all serial killers were abused as children, but all of them were neglected. I was always astounded when I asked serial killers about their most disturbing childhood experiences. None of them described physical or sexual abuse as the worst; all of them said that verbal criticism by their parents and teachers was their most awful experience.

Preventing serial homicide is only possible once every member of society takes an active interest in preserving the mental health and well-being of our children. Serial homicide is a double tragedy. It is a manifestation of how a neglected child grows into an adult who murders innocent victims. Every one of us has to take up the responsibility to break this cycle.

MILNERTON

1934-37

One of the very first identifiable cases of serial homicide in South Africa was in Milnerton in the Cape. The murders took place between 1934 and 1937 and remain unsolved to this day.

On the morning of 4 March 1937 Detective Chief Constable W J Herbst was called out to investigate the murder of 28-year-old Connie Adams of Woodstock, whose body had been found on the way to the Rugby station along the old coast road. To Herbst, it was obvious that Connie had been murdered elsewhere and that her body had been dumped next to the road. She had several wounds on the right side of her neck and face. There were no indications that she had been raped or that she had had sex the previous evening.

Connie's murder recalled the case of 24-year-old Madeleine Sharkey of Mowbray, whose body had been discovered on 17 June 1934 in Forestry Lane, Pinelands, some 6 kilometres from the place where Connie's body had been found. Madeleine had similar wounds to Connie, but she had been murdered on the spot where she was found.

On the evening of 9 March 1937, five days after Connie's body was found, detectives were called out to yet another crime scene. Two motorists had discovered a body on the Malmesbury road which ran parallel to the old coast road where Connie's body was found. The body was identified as that of 25-year-old Getrude Willemberg, a prostitute of Chapel Road. She was lying on her back and was partially clothed – her stockings were around her ankles and her panties were missing. Getrude had only one wound – a deep gash on her throat – and this was the cause of her death.

Pathologist Dr R Turner was convinced that all three murders had been committed by the same person, and that this person had a knowledge of anatomy.

The only lead Detective Herbst had was that both Connie Adams and Getrude Willemberg had been seen getting into a black Austin motor car. The police offered two rewards of £100 each for information about the murders, but they were never claimed as the cases were never solved.

Notes

This was one of the earliest cases of serial homicide in South Africa that I uncovered in my research, but there is little information about it.

It often happens that a pathologist, or even a state mortuary attendant, notices that incoming bodies display similarities in the manner in which they were killed. This sort of informal 'network' is invaluable to the police, especially when bodies are discovered in different jurisdictions and the investigating detectives do not have the opportunity to discuss cases with one another.

CORNELIUS BURGER

Johannesburg, 1936-37

During 1936 and 1937 Cornelius Burger, who was then in his mid-thirties, murdered five prostitutes and dumped their bodies on the road between Johannesburg and Potchefstroom. He took their handbags as 'souvenirs' and kept them in a cupboard at his home. Burger was married, but he and his wife lived separate lives. They did not share a bedroom and hardly spoke to each other.

Burger had contracted a venereal disease, but by the time he found out it was too late for treatment. He had sworn revenge on prostitutes whom he held responsible for his affliction.

The case was referred to Lieutenant Ulf Boberg of Marshalls Plain, Johannesburg. After the fourth body was found Boberg decided it was time for concerted action. He assembled a team of detectives and devised a plan for them to look after Johannesburg prostitutes while they worked. Since prostitution was illegal, this required permission from a very high authority.

One or two detectives were assigned to each prostitute. They watched her all night and recorded the registration numbers of the vehicles which picked her up. The prostitutes agreed that before they got into the vehicle they would elicit an undertaking from their clients to drop them off at the same place where they had picked them up. Only when all the prostitutes had checked in for the night and all of them were safely home, were the detectives allowed to go off duty. This routine was followed for a number of months.

Just after midnight one night, Boberg was waiting for his detectives to check in. All but one were present. As Boberg was about to send out a search party the missing detective arrived with the news that 'his' prostitute, Mavis Davids, had not returned. He gave Boberg the registration details of the vehicle which had picked her up and the address of the owner was traced.

Boberg decided it was more important to find Mavis before they confronted the suspect. Detectives were sent out to search the Potchefstroom and Heidelberg roads. Mavis was found on the Potchefstroom road, bleeding but alive. She told the detectives that a man in a large black car had picked her up. She became nervous when he drove out on the Potchefstroom road. When he stopped the vehicle, Mavis tried to escape, but he grabbed her and tried to strangle her. That was all she could remember. Mavis was fortunate to have survived.

Detectives went to the home of the suspect. They arrived before he did and lay in wait for him. When Cornelius Burger returned home in the early hours of the morning he was accosted by armed detectives. He did not resist arrest and led them to his room where they found the handbags of his earlier victims in a cupboard. Mavis' handbag was still in his vehicle. Three of the handbags were positively linked to three murdered prostitutes.

Medical examination established that Burger's venereal disease had already affected his mind and he was found not capable of standing trial on the grounds of mental illness. Burger's illness progressed rapidly and he died in an institution.

Notes

Not much is known about Burger's personal circumstances, or about the police investigation for that matter, but it is interesting that, like so many other serial killers, Burger kept 'souvenirs' of his victims. Serial killers often masturbate with these souvenirs, thereby reliving the murders.

Years later, in the 1990s, a serial killer preyed on prostitutes in Cape Town and police were again compelled to protect the prostitutes rather than arresting them. Catching a serial killer is clearly far more important than apprehending prostitutes for soliciting. Whether it is right to bend the law in this manner is a matter that is open to debate.

SALIE LINGEVELT

Cape Town, 1940

On 14 September 1940, Mrs Evelyn Chalmers was in her kitchen in Wellington Road in Wynberg in the Cape when a young man burst into the room and attacked her. She screamed, whereupon her assailant fled on a bicycle. Mrs Chalmers would never forget the man's face, and she became an important witness in the trial of one of South Africa's first known serial killers.

Nineteen days after the failed attack on Mrs Chalmers, on 3 October 1940, Mrs Ethel Marais was on her way home after seeing her husband off at the railway station. She lived in Brockhurst Road, Lansdowne – a suburb separated from Wynberg only by the Kenilworth race course – but before she reached her home, she was brutally attacked. Her head and face were battered with a blunt object, her hands were tied together with her stockings and a scarf was wrapped around her mouth. Her underwear was missing. Mrs Marais was rushed to hospital but she never regained consciousness and died of her injuries. There were more than twenty wounds on her mutilated body; her ring and the clasp on her turban were missing.

Exactly nineteen days after the attack on Mrs Marais, Mrs Dorothy Marie Tarling, the owner of boarding kennels in Prince George Drive in Wynberg, was found hacked to death in her dining room. She was half naked and pillows were scattered on her head and buttocks. Her skull had been bashed and there were also about twenty wounds on her body. The assailant had entered her home during the night by way of the bedroom window. He ransacked the house and a foreign fingerprint was discovered inside a drawer.

On 11 November 1940, nineteen days after Mrs Tarling was murdered, Miss Evangeline Bird, a lodger at the home of Mr and Mrs Oswald Spolander in Myrtledene Wetton Road, Wynberg, went outside at 10 am to give an order to a delivery man named Achmat Rawoot. Five minutes later, Mrs Spolander went to the kitchen to get a glass of water. She noticed that there was blood on the outside stairs and that a shoe was lying there. She investigated, and found Miss Bird lying under a bush. She had been badly beaten. Her dress had been pulled up and her underwear pulled down to her knees. She died as a result of her head injuries, but she had not been raped. Achmat Rawoot had noticed a young man with a bicycle with a red tyre in the vicinity. When he later returned to the Spolanders' home he saw the same man chopping wood nearby. A Mrs Pieterse, who worked for the Spolanders, also noticed the man with the bicycle and reported that his hands appeared to be covered in blood.

At this stage Major P H Golby, the chief of police, took charge of the case.

Fourteen days after the attack on Miss Bird, at 9 am on 25 November 1940, Mrs Mary Overton Hoets of Thornhill Road, Rondebosch – approximately 6 kilometres north of Wynberg – went to visit a friend, returning home some two hours later. At seven o'clock that evening Mrs Hoets' lodger, a Mr Jones, returned home to find the upper part of the front door open. When he went into the house and investigated, he found water boiling on the stove. The window in his room had been broken. He then discovered Mrs Hoets' body lying spreadeagled on her bed. There was a gash on her neck, her head had been smashed in, and there were about twenty wounds on her body. The room had been ransacked. The police found fingerprints in both Mrs Hoets' and Mr Jones' rooms, as well as a footprint outside Mrs Hoets' bedroom and bicycle tyre tracks outside.

The head of the detective unit in Pretoria, Colonel J Coetzee, went to Cape Town to take over the investigation. The only description the police had of the suspect was that he was a man about five feet ten inches tall with a copper complexion, and that he rode a bicycle with a red tyre. The police contacted owners of bicycle shops to try and trace the bicycle. The fingerprints found on the crime scenes did not match any in the police records.

The police announced to the media that they had the left thumb print of the suspect. This was intentionally misleading: the police actually had the right thumb print but they did not want to advertise this information. A private citizen offered a one thousand rand reward for information leading to the arrest of the suspect.

Nineteen days passed, and the police waited in anticipation of the next murder, but none was forthcoming. Instead, there were three complaints about a young man committing indecent behaviour in public.

The first complaint concerned a young man who exposed himself to a woman in Ainsley Road, Plumstead – about 2 kilometres south of Wynberg – before he cycled away. In the second instance a woman was accosted in Bayview Road, Wynberg. A young man tried to lift up her dress and remove her underwear. She struggled with him and managed to break free. The third incident took place in Timour Hall Road, Wynberg, when a young man cycling past a woman grabbed her around the neck and then followed her home.

The next day the woman saw the same man loitering with his bicycle opposite her house. She called the police, but when they arrived he was gone. Three days later she spotted him again and asked a delivery man to follow him to see where he lived. The police contacted the delivery man, who worked at the local butchery, and he told them that he knew the young man by sight and that he frequented the Gaiety Cinema in Wynberg. The police organised a stake-out at the cinema and it was there that Sergeant Ernest Engelke arrested the suspect on the charge of indecent assault. He did not charge him with the murders.

At the Wynberg police station the man identified himself as 20-year-old Salie Lingevelt, who lived with his father in Douglas

Road, Wynberg. He was wearing the ring which had been taken from Mrs Marais' body. A house search turned up the clasp of Mrs Marais' turban and the red bicycle tyre was found under Lingevelt's bed. What was most extraordinary, however, was that Lingevelt had chopped off the tip of his left thumb. The ingenuity of the police had paid off: his right thumb print matched the print they had found in Mrs Hoets' house.

Lingevelt was pointed out at an identity parade by Mrs Chalmers, who was fortunate enough to escape being his first victim. Neither Rawoot nor Mrs Pieterse was able to identify him.

Lingevelt refused counsel, saying that he preferred life in prison to the one he had outside. His mother had died many years before and he felt sorry for his father, who was good to him. He said he had committed the murders because his 'boss' ordered him to do so, but he did not want to divulge who his boss was. Lingevelt was interviewed by psychiatrists but he refused to co-operate with them. He said that he wished to be hanged. The psychiatrists found no indication of mental illness and declared him fit to stand trial. Lingevelt did not know the names of his victims and he showed no remorse for killing them. In fact, he revelled in the attention he attracted during his trial.

A plea of not guilty had to be entered, although Lingevelt had made a full confession and even pointed out where he had hidden the murder weapon – it was an iron bar. But the onus was on the State to prove his guilt, which it eventually did. Mr Justice R P B Davis found Lingevelt guilty of the murders and sentenced him to death. Judge Davis did not, however, agree with the psychiatrists that Lingevelt was not mentally disturbed, and concluded that he must have acted out of some sexual perversion. But Lingevelt refused to acknowledge that there was any sexual element in his crimes. During the trial it was pointed out that he had had no need to tie Mrs Marais' hands with her stockings as she was already unconscious from the blows he had inflicted on her head. Lingevelt refused to say anything in his defence.

When the date of his execution finally dawned in Pretoria, Lingevelt walked cheerfully to the scaffold.

Notes

Lingevelt never explained who the 'boss' was, but most probably it was the internal urge to kill that most serial killers experience and he would not be the first, or the last, serial killer to give this urge a name.

Lingevelt had a need to control his victims, evidenced by the fact that he tied up Mrs Marais when she was already unconscious. This need to control is termed *bondage*. He was probably very perfectionistic in asserting this bondage, which indicates sexual perversion and a fixation in the anal (control) stage. The judge was right in his estimation that Lingevelt was sexually perverted, but this does not indicate mental illness, nor does it exempt him from responsibility. Perversion is a paraphilia.

The police used the press to their advantage in this case by deliberately giving them false information. The issue of transparency versus the interests of the police investigation is a matter that could be endlessly debated. In my opinion, the well-being of the community at large should be the ultimate yardstick by which police action is measured. Sensationalism might sell newspapers, but it does not save lives.

ELIFASI MSOMI

KwaZulu-Natal, 1953-55

On 28 September 1955, Elifasi Msomi, the notorious axe murderer who caused a reign of terror from August 1953 to January 1955 in the KwaZulu-Natal midlands, was sentenced to death in the Pietermaritzburg Supreme Court by the Honourable Mr Justice J Kennedy for committing fifteen murders.

Elifasi Msomi was born in 1910 at the Indaleni Mission near Richmond. His father was a herbal doctor (*inyanga*) and Msomi had learned this trade from him. In 1945 or 1946 Msomi's father died and he took over family duties, including his father's practice. For seven years he ran a successful practice and then the number of his patients began to diminish and Msomi realised he would have to devise another plan to make a living.

Some time during late 1952, Elifasi Msomi arrived at the homestead of the late Ngongolwana Zaca on the Greenhill farm in the Richmond district. There he met Nomhlambi Zaca, recent widow of Ngongolwana, who had one child and was two months pregnant. Msomi said that he was an *inyanga* and obtained permission from Nomhlambi's bother Elijah to stay at his home and to treat patients. Nomhlambi assisted Msomi in his practice and eventually they fell in love. Msomi invited her to go with him to his home at Mamtalane and she agreed. They left her first child behind at Elijah's homestead.

After travelling and living outdoors for a few months, Nomhlambi asked Msomi why it was taking so long for them to reach his home. He replied that he was afraid of going home, but did not say why.

Eventually, during the winter of 1953, the couple and Nomhlambi's newborn baby arrived at the homestead of Zibeville Khambula at Kwa Gubuza in the Ixopo district. Msomi told Nomhlambi that they were to take on the name of Ndlovu of the Mgwane clan. He told Zibeville that he was looking for a doctor for his wife, who was ill, and Zibeville agreed that Nomhlambi could remain at the homestead while Msomi went to look for a doctor. In the mean time Zibeville treated Nomhlambi himself. Msomi returned without having found a doctor. The couple stayed for a week and then left. Two months later they returned to the homestead, and Msomi again reported to Zibeville that he had been unable to find a doctor. He asked Zibeville to continue treating Nomhlambi. Zibeville refused to do so, but allowed them to stay for a further two weeks.

During these two weeks Msomi met Zibeville's daughter, 20-year-old Olivia Khambula. One Sunday night Olivia went to sleep at the neighbouring homestead of her aunt, and early the following morning Msomi and Nomhlambi arrived to collect her. Msomi told Olivia's aunt that he was going to marry Olivia, but the story he told Olivia was that she should go with them to marry Nomhlambi's brother Elijah. The three set off, carrying only a suitcase containing the women's clothing and blankets. Hidden in this suitcase was a knife.

The first night of their journey was spent out in the open, about 7 kilometres from Zibeville's home, with Msomi sleeping between the two women. Nomhlambi awoke to Olivia's complaints that Msomi had forced her to have sex with him. Msomi was angry that Olivia had woken Nomhlambi and proceeded to rape her again in Nomhlambi's presence. Nomhlambi then witnessed Msomi stabbing Olivia in the chest and back with a knife. He dragged the dead girl away and attempted to hide the body in an anthill. This was not successful and so he dumped her body a short distance away. He returned to Nomhlambi and her baby and told her to pack up. He threw the knife away in the veld. The pair continued travelling for another two weeks until they reached the homestead of Mzobe, about 27 kilometres from Zibeville's home.

Nomhlambi reported the murder of Olivia to Mzobe who called his neighbour, Essau Maphanga. Nomhlambi repeated her story in Msomi's presence and he did not deny that he had murdered Olivia. Mzobe and Essau decided to take the couple to the local chief, but since it was already growing dark they decided to stay overnight at the nearby Dhlamini homestead. Although the men shared a hut, Msomi managed to escape during the night.

The next day Nomhlambi was taken to the police station at Ixopo where she made a statement to Detective Sergeant Paul Moore. She also led the detectives to the murder scene where Olivia's decomposed body was found. Sergeant Moore ascertained that Msomi had tried to hide Olivia's body in the anthill for her head cloth and earring were found inside. Olivia was identified at the mortuary by her father and her body was released for burial.

Nomhlambi and her baby returned to her brother's homestead on Greenhill farm in the Richmond district. She would later testify that Msomi had arrived there a few times after his escape but that he fled every time she confronted him and threatened to call the police.

Msomi's uncle and aunt, Magapa and Ma Mkize Ngongo, were an elderly couple living on the farm Clonmel in the Richmond district. Some time during November 1953 Msomi arrived at his uncle's homestead. He was introduced to the neighbours, including Gcinokwanke Dhlamini who lived about 200 paces from Magapa's home.

On Sunday 30 November 1953, Dhlamini set off to visit his in-laws. He passed Magapa's homestead at about nine o'clock that morning and saw both Magapa and his wife sitting outside their hut. On the Monday evening, Dhlamini returned from his in-laws and decided to pay Magapa a visit as he had not been well. When Dhlamini entered Magapa's hut he found Msomi there. Msomi told him that Magapa was sleeping – Magapa was indeed covered with a blanket. The aunt, Ma Mkize, was not there. Msomi told Dhlamini that she was in another hut, but Dhlamini did not check this.

On Tuesday 1 December 1953, Nkulumo Ngongo, a relative living on the same farm but a short distance away, decided to pay Magapa a visit as he knew that he had been ill. Nkulumo found the door of Magapa's hut closed. He none the less entered and found Magapa lying under a blanket. When he pulled the blanket off him he made the gruesome discovery that Magapa had been brutally attacked. Nkulumo called the farmer and then reported the incident to the Roman Catholic Mission.

Sergeant Botha from the Richmond police went to the scene. He called on Dhlamini who accompanied him to Magapa's hut, which they found in disarray. There was no sign of Ma Mkize. Magapa's hands were folded neatly over his chest, but he had multiple axe wounds.

Two days later Totolena Ngcamu, who lived on a nearby farm, left for Magapa's home to attend the vigil before his funeral. On the way she discovered Ma Mkize's mutilated body on a hill not far from her hut. She, too, had been attacked with an axe. Totolena reported her discovery to the farmer and Sergeant Botha was again called to the scene. Msomi was nowhere to be found.

Banana Ndlovu lived at Elandshoek in the Impendhle district, about 18,5 kilometres from Magapa's home. He had two children: Cisho, a 13-year-old boy, and Dombolozi, a 20-year-old woman. Dombolozi had a young daughter, Balekile. Banana's sister Gertrude also had two young children: a daughter Catherine, and a son Hinloti. Banana's second sister Losette had a 14-year-old daughter, Ntingilisi.

During December 1953, Msomi arrived at Banana's homestead claiming to be an *induna* who was looking for labourers. He introduced himself as John Ngcobo and he told Banana that the labourers would be paid five pounds per month for work on the nearby farm of a Mr Durose. Msomi then left, but returned a week later.

In the mean time Banana had recruited labourers, including the children in his family. The children Cisho, Hinloti, Balekile and an adult woman, Catherina, accompanied by Balekile and her mother Dombolozi, left for the farm with Msomi. Msomi promised Banana that they would return before Christmas.

But two days later, Dombolozi, Balekile and Msomi returned to Banana's homestead. Msomi told him that Dombolozi was suffering from a headache and he took 14-year-old Ntingilisi to work in her place. Two days after this Msomi visited Banana and told him that the children were working well. He stayed the night, but disappeared the following day, taking Dombolozi and Balekile with him. Banana went to look for Msomi at Durose's farm but found no trace of him or any of the children. He reported the matter to the police at Boston.

In late April 1954 a relative of Banana, Siboya Madlala, who lived at Brentwood, also in the Impendhle district, was surprised when a woman named Dombolozi accompanied by her daughter Balekile and a man calling himself Ndhlovu arrived at his homestead claiming to be relatives of his. Dombolozi said that Ndhlovu had married into the Madlala clan. They left after staying only one day. Three days later they returned, again spending only one night at the homestead. After a week Ndhlovu/ Msomi returned alone. He presented Siboya with the skirt that Dombolozi had been wearing, explaining that she had sent it in gratitude for the hospitality they had received during their previous visit.

Msomi stayed on for a few days and then, on 9 May 1954, he asked Siboya if his teenage daughter Dano could go with him to fetch potatoes for the family. When they had not returned after three days Siboya reported the matter to the police.

Dana's body was discovered soon afterwards by Reuben Ngcobo and pointed out to a Sergeant Kruger. On 15 May 1954 local pathologist Dr Albert Nethercott performed a post mortem on her body and found that the cause of death was a fractured skull and that she had multiple other injuries.

On 5 June 1954, Detective Sergeant Daniel Myburgh of the Boston police station was called to the New Fornset farm. A woman named Elinah Ntuli showed him part of a human leg that her dog had brought home. He asked her not to feed the dog for a day, and the next day he followed the dog to a place called Lundi Hill. There he discovered the body of an adult woman, who was later identified as Dombolozi, and the skull of a child – Balekile. Although her body was severely decomposed, Dr Nethercott later testified that Dombolozi had probably died as a result of about thirteen injuries to her head inflicted with an axe.

On 28 July 1954 Sergeant Myburgh was called out to the farm Elandshoek, which was the home of Banana Ndlovu, where three skulls were pointed out to him by Nsiwana Dlomo. These were identified as the remains of Hinloti, Cisho and Catherina. They had been bludgeoned to death with an axe.

In May 1955 when the skull of 14-year-old Ntingilisi was examined by Dr Nethercott, he found the cause of death to be multiple wounds caused by an axe.

Meanwhile, in June 1954, Msomi arrived on horseback at the Mapumulo homestead at Llangallen in the Camperdown disctrict. He again introduced himself as Ndhlovu and told 70-year-old Mahleza Msomi that he could get him a horse at a good price. As was his usual practice, Msomi stayed only one night, returning a day later. He promised Mahleza he would get him a horse if he could borrow a saddle and a bridle. Msomi left again and returned with a spare horse. He left the horse at the homestead and departed, again for one night. The following morning Msomi and Mahleza left to go and buy another horse. Mahleza never returned home.

Between August and September 1954 Msomi arrived at Zayo Ngcobo's homestead at Expectation in the Umzimkulu district.

He had two horses with him. On the day of his arrival, a Monday, the matriarch, Mtomubi Ngcobo, was not at home. He introduced himself as Isaac Mmthembu and began to pay court to the eldest daughter, Ntombeni, who had one child. When Mtomubi returned home on the Tuesday she met Msomi, but Ntombeni and the younger daughter Teselina were out cutting grass. Mtomubi was thus unaware that Msomi had already met her daughters. Msomi enquired about a *sangoma* in the area and then departed.

When the girls returned home that evening their mother told them of Msomi's visit. The next day, Wednesday, both girls went to cut grass again. They returned in the afternoon, left again and then later only Teselina came home. She told her mother that Ntombeni had gone with Msomi to get married to him, but that he would return on the Saturday to pay *lobola* for his bride. But he never returned, and nor did Ntombeni.

Ntombeni travelled with Msomi for some weeks and during this time the horses ran away. Ngungunyana Mbanjwa, who lived in the Ixopo district, met Msomi during the harvest season when he arrived on foot, calling himself by his true name, Msomi. Ntombeni was with him. Msomi asked Ngungunyana if he could leave two saddles at his homestead and Ngungunyana agreed. Msomi never returned to collect the saddles.

Willem Rooi was a Griqua who lived on the Bantam farm in the Umzimkulu district. He had adopted Zulu customs and lived at his homestead with his wife Grace. Msomi arrived at his home during September 1954, giving his name as Shabalala and introducing Ntombeni as his wife.

Msomi used the same ruse he had employed when Nomhlambi was his partner. He told Willem that his wife Ntombeni was ill and that he was looking for a doctor. They stayed for one night, departing the following morning. After a week and five days, Msomi returned to Willem's home without Ntombeni. He said that he had left her with the doctor. Msomi asked Willem if his wife could accompany him to fetch potatoes in payment for his lodging – the same tactic he had used to lure Dano away from her home. But Willem said that his wife could only accompany Msomi if Msomi's wife was also present. Msomi stayed on for a few days before asking one of the other men if he could borrow two horses so that he could go and fetch his wife.

During the periods that Msomi was absent from Willem's home, he stayed at the nearby Shabalala homestead. He repaid Shabalala for his hospitality by stealing his boots and an axe on his last night there, after which he returned to Willem's home to fetch the horses.

A week after Msomi left Willem's home, Ntombeni's body was discovered about 5,5 kilometres away. On 11 September 1954 Detective Sergeant Noel Crossman of the Umzimkulu police station was called out to the farm Expectation (also the home of Zayo Ngcobo). He was shown Ntombeni's body, which had been hidden in a hole. She was identified by Willem, Grace and several other people as the wife of the man who had visited them and she was known to them as Ma Ngcobo. Her body was eventually claimed by her mother Mtomubi Ngcobo.

Msomi arrived at the homestead of Muntuwani Wanda, probably in early October 1954, and met the female *sangoma* Ma Nkehli Wanda. He introduced himself as Zuma. As was his usual practice, he stayed one night, left, returned, left again and returned again. He requested Ma Nkehli and her assistant Ma Dlomo Mkhize to accompany him home to treat his sick wife, and they agreed. On 12 October 1954, while walking along a footpath, he attacked Nkehli, striking her on the head with an axe, and then pursued Dlomo who had fled. She managed to evade him. He returned to find that Nkehli too had escaped. She was later taken to hospital where she recovered from her injuries.

Msomi met Thembeni Shusha when he arrived at Dinga's homestead in the Bizana district. He introduced himself also as a Shusha, claiming to be a relative of Thembeni's deceased husband. He stayed with Thembeni for a week and then convinced her that she should accompany him to Ma Pulangweni's home for a prayer meeting. She left with Msomi and eventually they arrived at Molo's homestead near Redoubt some time during October 1954.

Thembeni had a baby with her. Msomi slept in the hut of Mancucwini Molo, a widowed woman. A teenage boy, Punu Molo, also shared the hut. Msomi, Thembeni and the baby left after one night. They travelled for a week, staying at several different homesteads along the way. Thembeni later testified that Msomi would slaughter a sheep and deliver meat to some of these homesteads. He was known to the local people as 'the person of the meat' and it was obvious to her that he was well known and well liked.

One night Msomi forced Thembeni at knifepoint to have sex with him, and thereafter she consented because she feared he would kill her. Some nights they had sex three times. Eventually they reached the Ibisi river in the Umzimkulu district. After visiting a homestead where Msomi had drunk beer, he sat down next to the road to sleep. Thembeni managed to get away from him. She hid in one of the nearby homesteads and borrowed money to catch a bus back to Bizana. Msomi returned to her hut in Bizana one night, took back a handkerchief he had given her and threatened her with a revolver. Fearing for her safety, she moved back to her parents' home

On his fourth return to the Molo homestead, Msomi was alone. He left on 31 December 1954, taking Punu with him as he had promised the boy that he would find him a job with a white man. He had used the same ruse to abduct Dano Madhlala. Two days later, Msomi returned without Punu. He stayed for two days and then left once again, taking with him an adult woman, Makaki, who was ill. He returned after two days without Makaki, saying he had left her with the doctor. He told Mancucwini, also an adult woman, that she would have to accompany him to the white man to receive Punu's money. They left two days later at dawn. Msomi returned alone later that same day. He stayed the night and left the next morning, never to return.

The families became concerned and started searching for their missing relatives. On 20 January 1955, the same Sergeant Crossman was called out to the Mzizi location where two bodies had been discovered. They were the bodies of Mancucwini Molo and Makaki Molo.

On 9 February 1955 Sergeant Crossman was out called to the farm Rooiwal in the Harding district where the body of Punu Molo had been found about 8,5 kilometres from Willem Rooi's home.

Msomi continued to travel, finally finding work at Mpandlana's farm near Port Edward. He used the name Zuma and had accommodation in a compound on the farm. Shortly after his arrival the police held a meeting at the neighbouring Reid farm to warn the community that a killer was active in the area.

Hulumeni Dimane, who worked at the nearby Larkan farm, noticed one day that some sweet potatoes had been stolen from the land. He followed a trail of footsteps which led him to the Mpandlana compound. He spoke to the *induna* who told him that Msomi was the culprit. Msomi tried to raise an alibi by saying that he had bought the vegetables from a store, but when the owner of the store was questioned he was unable to verify this. Msomi then offered to pay for the sweet potatoes.

Dimane told Msomi that the farmer would decide whether or not to take the matter further. Msomi disappeared, but was apprehended in his hut later that night by four men, one of them being Dimane. They tied him up and took him to the Larkan compound. He escaped during the night but a week later Dimane found him hiding at a nearby homestead and took him to the police.

So it happened that Elifasi Msomi, who had murdered fifteen people, was eventually arrested for stealing sweet potatoes.

Elifasi Msomi was about forty-five years old when he went on trial. During the trial he claimed that because his *inyanga* practice was losing patients he had gone to consult another herbal doctor, Madondo, and to obtain *muti* (medicine) that would benefit his practice. This doctor had introduced him to a *tokoloshe* – a supernatural being who, according to Msomi, was invisible to others. He said that Madondo had put an evil spell on him, telling him that the *tokoloshe* would not leave him until he brought back the blood of sixteen people.

Msomi denied that he had committed the murders and the rapes, claiming that it was the *tokoloshe* who identified prospective victims to him and instructed him to lure them from their homes. It was the *tokoloshe* who raped the women and killed the victims with an axe. Throughout this time, he was the only one who could see or speak to the *tokoloshe*. However, all witnesses described Msomi as a normal person who had never mentioned witchcraft. According to Msomi, shortly after Mancucwini was killed, the *tokoloshe* had collected enough blood and he left Msomi, thus breaking the spell.

Msomi decided to get an honest job and to give up any ideas of practising as a herbal doctor. He acknowledged that he had been aware that the police were searching for him. They had in fact been on his trail soon after the murders of his uncle and aunt, Magapa and Ma Mkize Ngcongo, with whom he had stayed under his real name in November 1953.

On 1 February 1954 Sergeant Willem Sterrenberg Naude of Pietermaritzburg took over the investigation into the deaths of Msomi's uncle and aunt. The investigation into the death of Olivia Khambula was being conducted by Detective Sergeant Moore from Ixopo. On 6 July 1954, after receiving information from Sergeant Myburgh, Sergeant Naude went to Boston police station, taking Dombolozi's head with him. It was identified by her father, Banana Ndlovu. Later in July Sergeant Myburgh took Sergeant Naude to the spot where the missing children's clothing had been found. There was still no trace of Ntingilisi.

On 16 August 1954, Sergeant Naude went to Richmond where

Sergeant Botha pointed out the belongings of the missing Mahleza Msomi. Sergeant Naude took over the investigation of this case. On 16 September 1954 Sergeant Naude found the clothing of the missing Ntombeni Ngcobo. On 12 October 1954 he was called to Umbumbulu police station where he met the bleeding and seriously injured *sangoma*, Nkehli Wanda. He had her admitted to the King Edward hospital in Durban, where she recovered.

At this time Sergeant Naude had 120 men helping him search for Msomi. By 7 January 1955 he had come to the conclusion that the same modus operandi had been used in several murders in the area, and he had also visited the crime scene where Dombolozi and Balekile were found. The next day he took over the investigation into Dano Madlala's death.

On 21 January 1954 Sergeant Naude went with Sergeant Crossman to the spot where the bodies of Makaki and Mancucwini had been discovered. On 10 February 1954 the place where Punu's skull was found was pointed out to Sergeant Naude.

On 3 May 1955 Sergeant Naude met Msomi while he was being held in custody in Port Shepstone for the theft of the sweet potatoes. Sergeant Naude had already been alerted by the Port Shepstone police that they might have detained the man he had been looking for for so many months. An identity parade was arranged and Msomi was identified by several witnesses, although under different aliases. He was wearing Punu's blazer. Sergeant Naude arrested Msomi and he was charged with the murders.

On 4 May Sergeant Naude took Msomi to the Bizana area. They went to Shusha's homestead and the community searched for, and found, the axe he had used as a weapon. On 5 May, they went to Bostonview in the Impendhle district where Ntingilisi's skull had finally been found. On 12 June 1955 Zibeville Khambula pointed out to Sergeant Naude the spot where his daughter Olivia's remains had been found.

Two doctors – Dr Cheze-Brown, a psychiatrist of twenty-seven years' standing, and Dr Hemming, a general practitioner with ten years' experience in mental diseases – both testified that

Msomi had syphilis, but they agreed that he was not mentally ill. He had a gift for confabulation and a higher than average intelligence. Both medical experts found him to be a sadist.

On 28 September 1955 Mr Justice J Kennedy said that he was not convinced by Msomi's story about the *tokoloshe* having committed the crimes and sentenced him to death on each of the fifteen counts of murder. In his judgment he referred to the fact that Msomi had denied stealing money, and that he had claimed that the crimes were committed by the *tokoloshe*. Mr Justice J Kennedy said:

> The accused's reasons for denying these various factors, if the Crown evidence is accepted, is apparent, because they would reveal the accused not as a person acting under the influence of his *tokoloshe*, but as a rapist, a robber and a murderer, and they would reveal that his requests to the various women (who did not accompany him for one reason or another) were not made for any professed motive that they were required by the *tokoloshe*, but for reasons personal to the accused.

Mr Justice J Kennedy pointed out that eight months had elapsed between Msomi's first visit to the *inyanga* Madondo and the time he committed the first murder, and that Msomi had apparently been prepared to live under the alleged curse for two years. The judge found this hard to believe.

Msomi told the judge that he accepted the verdict, but that he knew that 'Europeans' did not believe in the *tokoloshe*. He would have preferred his case to be heard by Zulus who, he said, did believe in the *tokoloshe*. Elifasi Msomi was hanged on 10 February 1956.

Notes

Many serial killers perceive their internal urge to kill as an external force and some of them even give a name to this perceived separate entity. Msomi never indicated that he committed the murders under an irresistible compulsion or in a state of compulsion. Most serial killers do not understand where the urge to kill comes from and the more intelligent ones attempt to provide a rational explanation for it. They know they are not mentally ill and they need to find a reason for their behaviour. The urge is, however, buried deep in their psyches and germinated during their developmental phases.

Msomi acknowledged that he knew it was wrong to commit murder. He was therefore able to distinguish between right and wrong, and the fact that he travelled with some of his victims for months before killing them proves that he could prevent himself from killing and was capable of acting according to his knowledge of right and wrong. Finding an explanation for one's deeds does not necessarily excuse them.

Msomi's defence advocate, Mr Feetham, argued that while agreeing that Msomi committed the murders, he was in fact a sadist, and as such he was suffering from a mental disease; he attempted to rationalise the impulse to which he was subject by bringing into being the *tokoloshe*, at whose door he laid the blame for the killings.

Mr Feetham was correct in his opinion of Msomi's rationalisation, but he was wrong in describing sadism as a mental illness for it is at most a personality disorder. Secondly, the fact that Msomi carefully planned the murders proved that he was not reacting to an irresistible compulsion. Msomi's planning included scouting out each homestead before staying there and, as has already been pointed out, he travelled with many women for months before killing them.

The judge in Salie Lingevelt's case was correct in concluding that Lingevelt had a perversion but he, too, was wrong in thinking that this would influence his mental capabilities. Sometimes even mentally ill people can differentiate between right and wrong, and act accordingly.

Many serial killers have roamed the green hills of KwaZulu-Natal. The Donnybrook area was to be plagued by Mhlengwa Zikode in 1995 (see page 219). Msomi's behaviour was also later repeated in the selection of victims by Bongani Mfeka (see page 235), the Kranskop serial killer who also spent months in the company of his girlfriends before killing them.

Time frame and summary

Late 1952
Msomi arrives at homestead of Ngongolwana Zaca – Greenhill farm, Richmond district
He meets Nomhlambi Zaca and her brother Elijah

Winter of 1953
Msomi arrives at homestead of Zibeville Khambula – Kwa Gubuza, Ixopo district
Uses name of *Ndlovu*
He meets *Olivia Khambula (20 yrs)

November 1953
Msomi arrives at home of uncle and aunt *Magapa & *Ma Mkize Ngongo – Clonmel, Richmond district

December 1953
Msomi arrives at homestead of Banana Ndlovu – Elandshoek, Impendhle district
Uses name of *John Ngcobo*
He meets Banana and children:
    *Cisho (13 yrs)
    *Dombolozi (20 yrs)
            *Balekile
He also meets sister Gertrude and her children:
    Catherine
    *Hinloti
and sister Losette and her daughter:
    *Ntingilisi (14 yrs)
as well as adult woman *Catherina

Late April 1954
Msomi arrives at homestead of Siboya Madlala – Brentwood, Impendhle district
Uses name of *Ndhlovu*
He meets *Dano Madlala

June 1954
Msomi arrives at Mapumulo homestead – Llangallen, Camperdown district
Uses name of *Ndhlovu*
He meets *Mahleza Msomi

August-September 1954
Msomi arrives at homestead of Zayo Ngcobo – Expectation, Umzimkulu district
Uses name of *Isaac Mmthembu*
He meets Mtomubi Ngcobo and her daughters:
   *Ntombeni
   Teselina

September 1954
Msomi arrives at home of Willem Rooi and his wife Grace – Bantam farm, Umzimkuku district
Uses name of *Shabalala*

October 1954
Msomi arrives at homestead of Muntuwani Wanda
Uses name of *Zuma*
He meets Ma Nkehli Wanda (*sangoma*)
and
Ma Dlomo Mkhize

October 1954
Msomi arrives at Dinga homestead – Bizana district
Uses name of *Shusha*
He meets Thembeni Shusha

October 1954
Msomi arrives at Molo homestead near Redoubt
He meets
   *Mancucwini Molo
   *Punu Molo
   *Makaki Molo

Early 1955 (exact date unknown)
Msomi finds work at Mpandlana's farm – Port Edward
Uses name of *Zuma*

*Indicates Msomi's victims

NIEU-DOORNFONTEIN & CROWN MINES

1970 & 1972

Captain Ben Kruger of the Brixton Murder and Robbery Unit in Johannesburg was a legendary figure in the early 1970s, but there were two murders which baffled him and which remained unsolved when the time came for him to retire.

On the night of Saturday 11 April 1970, Kruger and his partner Koos van Aswegen were called out to a murder scene on the corner of Third and Miller streets in Nieu-Doornfontein, downtown Johannesburg. The body of a young woman was lying against a factory wall. Kruger carefully noted the woman's injuries. She had been hit on the head with a blunt object and there was a knife wound under one breast. She had also been cut from her navel down to her pubic area.

From her clothing it was obvious to Kruger that she was a prostitute. She was also covered in tattoos. On her left arm the name 'Barend' was engraved and the letter 'P' marked her left thigh. A tattoo of The Saint was on her left wrist and there was one of cartoon character Andy Capp inside her elbow. It was therefore not very difficult to identify her as Anna Christina Swarts, a local prostitute.

Anna's pimp and live-in boyfriend told the detectives that she was working on the night of her murder. At ten o'clock that night she handed him nine rand, which she had just earned. An hour later he saw her get into a Volkswagen combi on the corner of Bok and Banket Streets. She did not return and the pimp went home to the flat he shared with Anna in Omega Building in Nieu-Doornfontein.

Anna had not had an easy life. As a three-year-old girl, she was passed on to step-parents, but they soon sent her to foster care. Although she was a pretty child, no one really wanted her and the young Anna was passed from one family to another like an unwanted puppy. She attended school up to grade nine in Benoni on the East Rand, but bad behaviour resulted in her being transferred to an institution in Standerton. She ran away from the institution and ended up on the East Rand where she got into bad company.

Anna met and married a man and had a baby with him. The marriage did not last very long, because she had many other boyfriends. Then she married a man with the surname of Swarts, but this did not last either. Eventually she found her way to Johannesburg where she became a prostitute. She was also involved in crime and, ironically, a few days after she was buried, her name came up in court as a co-accused in an armed robbery case.

Kruger followed up all the leads he could find and the case occupied him for quite a while. However, Johannesburg in the 1970s was rather like the Al Capone era in Chicago and Kruger had to set Anna's case aside on his desk, although not in his mind.

Two years later, on 8 July 1972, Kruger was called to a murder scene at number 17 shaft, Crown Mines. The body of a naked adult woman had been found lying in a road. She was wearing only her shoes and she had a ring on her finger. Kruger's pulse began to race when he noticed the wounds. She had been hit on the head with a blunt object, there was a knife wound below her breast and a 30-centimetre wound ran downwards from her navel to her pubic area. To Kruger this signalled that the killer was the same person who had murdered Anna Swarts two years before.

The body was identified as Dorothy Hattingh. Apart from the nature of their deaths, the women had much in common. Both were prostitutes and both lived in Nieu-Doornfontein.

Dorothy also lived with a man and she was the mother of two children. Both were killed on a moonless Friday night. Dorothy was last seen alive a mere two blocks from the spot where Anna had disappeared.

Pathologists confirmed Kruger's suspicion that both women were murdered by the same man, but, much to his frustration, he was never able to solve these two murders.

Notes

Anna's and Dorothy's murders brought to Captain Ben Kruger's mind the notorious case of Jack the Ripper, arguably the world's most infamous serial killer, who murdered five prostitutes in Whitechapel, London, between August and November 1888.

The Ripper's first victim was Mary Ann Nicholls, a prostitute of Bucks Row. Her badly mutilated body was found on 31 August 1888. Barely a week later, on 8 September, Annie Chapman, also a prostitute, was viciously slaughtered in Hanbury Street. On 30 September the bodies of Lizzy Stride and Catherine Eddowes, both prostitutes, were discovered in Berner Street and Mitre Square respectively. Both women had been mutilated. The worst scene of all was that of Mary Jane Kelly, a pretty prostitute whose horribly mutilated body was found in her room at Miller's Court on 9 November.

An full-scale investigation was launched to catch Jack the Ripper and even His Royal Highness Prince Albert Victor, the Duke of Clarence and grandson of Queen Victoria, was a suspect.

As in the Nieu-Doornfontein case, the perpetrator of the Whitechapel murders was never apprehended. Author Shirley Harrison in her book *The Diary of Jack the Ripper* presents evidence that Liverpool cotton merchant James Maybrick was the most likely suspect. Maybrick had been in London on business during the times that the women were murdered. He lodged not far from the murder scenes.

The diary was brought to light in Liverpool in 1992 by scrap metal dealer Michael Barret, who said he had received it from a friend named Tony Devereux. Barret took it to Shirley Harrison to have it authenticated. In fact, Barret's wife Anne had inherited the diary from her father, who received it from his grandmother, who was a friend of one of Maybrick's servants. Michael was suffering from depression at the time and Anne wanted to give him the diary to keep him occupied, but she knew he would not be interested if she gave it to him herself. So she asked Devereux to give it to him.

The diary contained exact descriptions of the crime scenes, which had never been made public at the time of the murders. Shirley Harrison spent a great deal of money having the diary authenticated. Even the ink was tested. In a twist of irony, Maybrick was killed by his wife, a year after the last Whitechapel murder. She was imprisoned for fifteen years and thereafter led a quiet life.

JOHN PHUKO KGABI

Atteridgeville & Limpopo Province, 1974-78

As a member of the South African Police Force, John Phuko Kgabi was assigned to a mortuary. His duties involved cutting up and preparing bodies for the pathologist to complete the autopsies. One day Kgabi had to cut up the body of a pretty girl in early puberty. When he made an incision in her throat, he got an unexpected erection. He was surprised, as he had been impotent for quite some time. After the post mortem was completed, Kgabi masturbated to the image of cutting the young girl's throat. This caused a sexual fixation. A certain stimulus (cutting the girl's throat) caused a pleasant reaction (the erection) – and people are inclined to search for similar stimuli to experience the pleasant reaction. The more the process is repeated, the more entrenched the fixation becomes until eventually it excludes all other stimuli.

Kgabi was dishonourably discharged from the police force in 1972, and his fixation boded ill for many young girls.

On 16 October 1974, five-year-old Helen Tiny Ramskin of Sompane Street, Atteridgeville, Pretoria, was waiting for her sister in a street in Atteridgeville when a man approached her and led her away. Her body was discovered in Church Street West. Her throat had been cut.

Five months later, on 9 March 1978, young Mavis Masekwaneng was walking past a playground in Bandolierskop in the Louis Trichardt district, about 400 kilometres north of Atteridgeville. The children in the playground saw Mavis and also noticed a man following her, but they did not pay much attention. A little while later Mavis came running down the road, clutching her throat. She could not utter a sound, but tears were streaming down her face. Bystanders bundled Mavis into a blanket, noticing that blood was gushing from a wound in her throat. Mavis died at the police station.

The next month, on 20 April 1975, eight-year-old Ouma Magdaline Seopela of Sithole Street, Atteridgeville, and a friend climbed over a fence to play on the local sports grounds. A man followed them over the fence. He asked Ouma if she would buy him cigarettes and gave her money. According to the friend, the man followed Ouma when she climbed back over the fence. It was the last time she saw Ouma alive. Her body was found in a dam in Church Street West.

A year later, on 4 April 1976, the same fate befell eight-year-old Josephine Mabena. She was lured by a man who slashed her throat twice with such force that her vocal cords were exposed. Amazingly, Josephine survived the attack, but in June that same year she died in Kalafong Hospital in Atteridgeville. Because of the nature of her injuries, she was unable to give the police details of what had happened to her.

A year and seven days after the attack on Josephine, the perpetrator was in the Louis Trichardt district again, probably because he had heard that Josephine had survived. On 11 April 1977, young Rosina Manetja was walking along a road in Bandolierskop when a man stopped and asked her for directions. He then grabbed her, dragged her into the veld and sat on her while he cut her throat with a piece of corrugated iron. He left her for dead. Rosina was hospitalised for a month, but she survived. Later she was unable to point out her assailant at an identity parade, but she did recognise him in court.

Five attacks had taken place, but they were years and miles apart and no one connected them. The killer gained confidence and his urge to kill increased during the following two years.

On 28 May 1977, Mr Kleinbooi Phora was walking his dog near the Kalafong Hospital when he made a gruesome discovery.

It was the body of seven-year-old Gemma Shabangu, who had gone missing ten days before. Her throat had been cut and flesh had been cut out of her leg.

The Atteridgeville community remembered the three previous cases and were up in arms. Since body parts were missing, the most logical conclusion was that the killer was a witchdoctor who used body parts for *muti*. During the ensuing investigation the community raided the houses of local *sangomas* and *inyangas*. But these traditional doctors do not use body parts.

In July 1977 nine-year-old Lekgowa Magdaline Zondi left her home in Atteridgeville. She was living with her aunt, Mrs Letta Makhoba, and told her she wanted to visit her mother. It was not until a few days later, when her mother arrived at the aunt's house on 31 July, that they realised that Lekgowa had never reached her destination.

On 6 August Mr Gilbert Jbewe and his friends were herding sheep near the Kalafong Hospital. When the sheep started to behave strangely, Gilbert went to investigate and found the mutilated body of Lekgowa. Like Gemma, her throat had been cut and flesh was missing from her leg.

The day after the discovery of Lekgowa's body, on Sunday 7 August, ten-year-old Eva Mavis Phalamohlaka of Ramapuputhla Street, Atteridgeville, was walking to her uncle's house. A man grabbed her from behind and pulled off her jacket. She turned around and demanded he give back her jacket, whereupon he dragged her into the veld. She remembered that he sat on her and began to cut her throat with a piece of corrugated iron before she lost consciousness. When she came to, the man had gone and she realised that a piece of flesh had been cut from her leg. She stumbled to the nearest house, which happened to belong to one of her teachers, and was taken to hospital. Eva remained in hospital for three months, but she recovered. She was later able to identify her attacker at an identity parade.

Since the victim had survived, the killer's confidence was shaken, but this time he did not move to another province. He merely moved to Mamelodi, which is situated to the east of

Pretoria, while Atteridgeville is situated to the west of the city.

On 2 October 1977, seven-year-old Gloria Kathazile Khoza was last seen alive playing with her friends in Mamelodi. Her body was discovered the following day at the Bantule Station near the market in Pretoria West. Her throat had been cut and her tongue, larynx and oesophagus were missing.

Members of the Pretoria Murder and Robbery Unit took over the investigation and formed a task team. Divisional Commissioner J A N Grobelaar promised that no stone would be left unturned in their efforts to find the killer. A powerful *sangoma* named Mpapane from the (then) Eastern Transvaal, was brought in to assist the detectives, but no one was arrested. Kgabi's mother was also a *sangoma* and he may have heard from her that Mpapane was involved in the investigation. This may have scared him off, because there were no further murders for a while.

Then, on 14 May 1978, ten-year-old Evelyn Mothoa of Voortrekker Heights went to buy a bus ticket to visit relatives in Atteridgeville. Kgabi spotted her and offered her a lift in his car. He told her he was the elder brother of a friend of hers and she believed him. At Erasmia Street, Kgabi pulled over and dragged her out of the car and into the veld. She lost consciousness, waking later to find herself covered in blood. A man riding past on a bicycle found her and took her to hospital. She survived and was able to describe the car.

On 25 June 1978, eight-year-old Jennifer Ramalekane of Khudu Street Atteridgeville, went missing. Her mutilated body was found on 2 July. Flesh had been cut from her thigh and forehead and her tongue was missing. Her nose and toes had been removed. Unbeknown to anyone at that stage, John Phuko Kgabi was also living in Khudu Street.

On 27 August 1978 nine-year-old Elaine Tsitsana Mokwena's body was discovered at the Mangwema Mokone Higher Primary School, between the ablution block and a dustbin. She was found about 200 metres from the police station and two blocks from her home in Masemola Street. Fingerprints were found at this crime scene.

On 10 September 1978 the body of nine-year-old Loretta Edwards was found. Her head had been almost completely severed. Loretta lived in Swartberg Street, Eersterust, a suburb bordering Mamelodi, but her body was discovered in the veld between the suburbs of Hercules and Ga-Rankuwa in the west. Her tongue had been removed. She had been missing since 15 August.

By now the community was so enraged that Mrs Sarah Mashele, a prominent *sangoma* from Soweto in Johannesburg, called a meeting of the *sangomas* and *inyangas* in the area to pledge their support for the investigation. They wanted to clear their name as good traditional doctors who served the community and who did not use body parts to make evil medicine.

On 11 October 1978 ten-year-old Cynthia Mathabe of Ga-Rankuwa, north west of Pretoria, disappeared. Her mother Linky had asked her daughter to take the rubbish to the dustbin outside the house, and she never returned.

On 20 November 1978 young Nomonde Florence Sebolai from Alexandra, on the northern borders of Johannesburg, and her friend Jessie were on their way to church when a man offered Florence fifty cents to help him offload beer. Florence got into his car. Her body was discovered the same day near Saulsville in Pretoria West. Some body parts were missing.

The killer became nervous once more and moved to Seshego near Pietersburg (now Polokwane) in the far Northern Province (now Limpopo), not far from Louis Trichardt. On Sunday 26 November 1978 he spotted young Martha Hluni Mothiba at a shop. He offered her a lift in his silver-grey car. When Martha did not arrive home her father Simon became concerned and initiated a search.

Twelve-year-old Simon Molesa told him he had seen Martha climb into the car. Simon and a few other men went looking for the car, which they eventually found. John Kgabi was sitting inside it. Simon asked Kgabi where his daughter's body was for he knew intuitively that she was dead. Although Kgabi denied killing her, the men attacked him and assaulted him severely. He was taken to the police station and later agreed to take the police and the girl's father to the place where they would find Martha. He had still not confessed to killing her. As they made their way across the veld, Kgabi told the men he wanted to urinate and he walked away from them. One of the policemen noticed that Kgabi had dropped something and was trying to grind it into the ground. It was a piece of human windpipe. Kgabi was immediately confronted with the murder and he then led them to Martha's mutilated body. Her father covered her with a shirt and knelt down to pray.

Kgabi was arrested for Martha's murder. Since the area was under the jurisdiction of the Pretoria Murder and Robbery Unit, detectives were sent to fetch Kgabi and take him to Pretoria. He made a confession to Captain Steve Oelofse, and Captain Dirk Engelbrecht officiated at the pointing out of the crime scenes.

Kgabi was sent to Weskoppies Psychiatric Hospital for observation, but stayed there for only seven days as the doctors feared he would be harmed or killed by other inmates. He was found to be sane and competent to stand trial.

In June 1979 John Kgabi appeared before Mr Justice Schriber. Advocate D Bester acted as *pro deo* defence counsel and Advocate S A Engelbrect prosecuted. Kgabi was not charged with all the murders because of lack of evidence, but he was found guilty of the murders of Gemma Shabangu, Gloria Kathazile Khoza, Jennifer Ramalekane, Loretta Edwards and Elaine Tsitsana Mokwena, as well as that of Martha Hluni Mothiba, and was sentenced to death on each of these six counts. He was also found guilty of the attempted murder of Evelyn Mothoa and sentenced to five years' imprisonment.

Kgabi said he did not sell the body parts as *muti*, but used them to masturbate after he had cut the girls' throats. He was the father of a young girl about the same age as his victims.

John Phuko Kgabi was hanged at Pretoria Central Prison on 6 February 1980.

It could be asked why, if Kgabi was discharged from the police in 1972, two years elapsed before he started murdering? The

Atteridgeville police had murder dockets of eight-year-old Magrietha Goliat and ten-year-old Patricia Goliat who died under similar circumstances in 1973, and of young Olga Mokwane who died in November 1976. Kgabi denied involvement these cases and there was no evidence to prove otherwise.

Notes

Atteridgeville seems to be doomed to be a playground for serial killers.

In 1956 an unknown man murdered and mutilated six boys over a period of five months, but was never apprehended. In the 1970s a man dubbed 'The Ironman' clubbed seven people to death with an iron bar and robbed them as they were on their way home from shebeens. The killings eventually stopped, but he was never arrested.

In 1988 and 1989, ten years after John Kgabi's reign of terror in Atteridgeville, Johannes Oupa Mashiane, dubbed 'The Beast of Atteridgeville', sodomised and stoned to death young boys in the same area. They were Surprize Desmond Kola (11), Tebego Thomas Khoza (8), Khayalakhe Mlangeni (11), Joseph Sibande (14), and Bakae Mathabe (9). Bakae's cousin Tebego, who was the same age, was seriously injured. The skeletons of two young boys were discovered in June 1989, a few metres from the place where Bakae and Tebego were attacked. A 13-year-old unidentified boy was also found naked and injured, but alive, on the outskirts of Atteridgeville in June 1989.

Mashiane had a droopy eye and a tattoo of a cross and a dagger on his left forearm. Warrant Officer Johan Koegelenberg investigated this case and the South African Defence Force, as well as the municipal police, joined in the search for the suspect. Mashiane was also involved in several assault and robbery cases. Late on a Saturday night in July 1989, Mashiane ran in front of an oncoming car on the Apies River Freeway in Marabastad and was killed instantly. The police identified his body at the mortuary the following day.

Mashiane started his killing spree after his release from a five-year prison sentence for killing his girlfriend.

After John Kgabi's arrest it was once again safe for the young girls of Atteridgeville to play in the streets. None of them knew that twenty years later, as adults, they would run the risk of becoming the prey of Moses Sithole, the Atteridgeville serial killer of the 1990s.

RONALD FRANK COOPER

Johannesburg, 1976

Ronald Frank Cooper succeeded in killing only one boy, but he is included in this collection as his diary revealed the typical fantasies of a serial killer. Cooper planned to kill thirty boys and thereafter to commence killing girls and women. He botched four attempts to kill young boys.

As an 11-year-old child in 1963, Cooper attempted to kill another child, but did not succeed. In April 1976, the 24-year-old Cooper was living in an apartment in Berea, Johannesburg, when he forced ten-year-old Tresslin Pohl into a park at gunpoint. His nerve failed him and he released the boy, who promptly told the police what had happened to him. Despite the fact that the police had a good description, they were unable to find Cooper.

Cooper kept a diary of his fantasies – many serial killers do – and on 17 March 1976 he made the following entry:

I have decided that I think I should become a homosexual murderer, and shall get hold of young boys and bring them here where I am staying and I shall rape them and kill them. I shall not kill all the boys in the same way; some I shall strangle with my hands, others I shall cut their throats. I can also suffocate or smother others . . . (Lane & Gregg, 1992)

A week after this entry Cooper attempted to stab a ten-year-old boy in the chest, but the boy screamed so much that he only managed to inflict a few minor cuts. Shortly after that he tried to strangle another young boy, but also abandoned this effort when the boy started to scream.

On 16 May 1976, Cooper resolved that he would follow through and complete the deed. He abducted 12-year-old Mark Garnet and strangled him. Then he tied a rope around his victim's neck and unsuccessfully attempted to sodomise him. Realising that he had finally become a murderer, Cooper was overcome with remorse and wrote in his diary:

> It's a really dreadful thing that I did; I only wish I could undo it. I never want to do such a thing again. (Lane & Gregg, 1992)

Young Tresslin Pohl had spotted Cooper in the street some time before Mark's murder. He followed Cooper and found out where he lived, but he kept this information to himself. Coincidently, Mark and Tresslin were friends and it was only after Mark's disappearance that Tresslin led the police to Cooper's apartment, where he was arrested.

Cooper was tried and convicted and sentenced to death. He was hanged on 16 January 1978.

Notes

Cooper's diaries provided valuable evidence during his trial. Many serial killers keep some kind of record of their crimes.

Robert Berdella of Kansas City (USA) had fixated in the hippie-era. He owned a shop specialising in hippie memorabilia, but his greatest passion was to abduct young men, keep them hostage in his house and torture them for weeks. Between July 1984 and August 1987 Berdella tortured and killed six men. He killed them because eventually he became bored with them. He dismembered the bodies, threw some body parts into the trash can and buried others in his yard. Berdella's last victim was Christopher Bryson. After weeks of torture, Bryson managed to escape on 1 April

1988. The police found him wandering naked in the streets in a disoriented state, with a dog collar around his neck. He led them to Berdella's house.

In the house the police found stacks of photographs Berdella had taken of his victims. They also discovered the diaries in which he meticulously recorded every minute detail of the tortures he inflicted on his victims. Berdella would, for example, write at precisely what time he would insert drain cleaner in his victim's eyes and what the effect would be. The diaries not only helped in identifying the skulls the police discovered buried in Berdella's yard, but they also proved strong incriminating evidence at his trial. Berdella was sentenced to five life terms on 20 December 1988.

JOSEPH MAHLANGU

Soweto, 1979

On 9 January 1979, Sheila Mamodidi Kgaladi was at work with her colleague, Catherine Mothuku. Catherine stopped work at about 4.30 pm when Sheila's boyfriend, Happy Joe Mangali, arrived in his red Peugeot to pick Sheila up. The last time Catherine saw Sheila alive was at 5 pm when she was sitting in Happy's car.

On the evening of 15 June 1979, 31-year-old Joseph Mahlangu, who became known as the Lover's Lane Killer of Soweto, told Lieutenant Swart of the Meadowlands police station that he had found Happy and Sheila in the Peugeot which was parked under a tree. He approached them and asked what they were doing. Happy told him it was none of his business, whereupon he shot Happy in the face. Sheila tried to escape from the car, so he shot her in the head as well. Later, during Mahlangu's trial, it became evident that the firearm he had used was a .38 Smith and Wesson that had gone missing from the Orlando Police Station on 2 July 1977.

On 9 February 1979, exactly a month after the murders of Happy and Sheila, Mahlangu accosted Sergeant Andries Mongwe and his girlfriend Dinah Shao in their parked car in Soweto. He shot Andries three times in the head and when Dinah told him that he had killed a policeman, he shot her too, killing her instantly. He robbed Andries of his 7.65 service pistol, and took the car and set it on fire.

A week later, on 17 February 1979, Mahlangu found Ishmael

Binky Mamakwe and his girlfriend Anna Mogoje in similar circumstances. He shot them both and dumped their bodies.

On the evening of Saturday 10 March 1979, Valerie Tsolo worked until 8 pm at her job in a bottle store. Her boyfriend, Samuel Socaza, arrived in his Chev Constantia when she finished work and they drove to Roper's Lounge in Kliptown where he bought four bottles of milk stout. They then drove to the police station in Kliptown and made love in the car in the station yard. Later, they drove to a piece of open ground between the golf course and the rugby grounds in Kliptown where they drank the milk stout. Some policemen arrived in a van and they chatted to them.

Between midnight and 1 am Samuel drove to Valerie's home in Soweto, parking the car about five houses away from her door. Samuel and Valerie were sitting in the front seat of the car when a man walked past, on the driver's side. It was Mahlangu. He was wearing blue overalls, a black leather jacket and a woollen hat. Neither Samuel nor Valerie paid much attention to him. The next thing Valerie saw was a torch shining through the driver's window. Samuel did not see this as he was reaching down, feeling for something under his seat. Suddenly a shot rang out and Samuel slumped down on top of her. She grabbed her handkerchief and pressed it on the right side of his face, which was covered in blood. Mahlangu opened the passenger door on the driver's side. Valerie told him to leave them alone, but he placed his firearm against Samuel's right temple and pulled the trigger. He then got into the driver's seat and, with Samuel lying between them, he started the car. He drove to the Zulu section of Kliptown and parked the car. He opened the door and dragged Samuel's body out.

After searching Samuel's pockets for money Mahlangu got back into the car and drove in the direction of a stream between Klipspruit and Orlando. He stopped the car and told Valerie to get out. Her clothing was soaked in blood which she tried to wring out. The police found the blood the following day. Telling Valerie to follow him, Mahlangu walked towards the stream. The banks of the stream had been cemented into an embankment and as Valerie climbed down her bloodstained hands left prints on the cement, which the police also found the next day. Mahlangu then raped Valerie. Afterwards, they walked back to the car and Mahlangu told Valerie to remove her belongings. She managed to get a good look at his face in the interior lights of the car before he drove off. Valerie ran to the nearest house. The owner, Emily Mantsha, took Valerie inside and at first light they went to the Kliptown police station. Valerie took the police to the place where Mahlangu had dumped Samuel's body.

Valerie was later able to point Mahlangu out at an identity parade as the man who had raped her and killed Samuel. One of the things she had noticed was that the man's right eye continually streamed with tears. Mahlangu had been shot in the right eye some years before and it watered perpetually.

Thandi Nxumalo, a single woman, lived at 663 H Meadowlands. On 6 April 1979 she saw Mahlangu for the first time when he brought his car, a Valiant, for repairs to the house opposite hers. Thandi's friend Gerald Engelbrecht picked her up that evening and they drove to the veld near the Kliptown power station. Thandi and Gerald were making love in the car when she saw two men approaching the vehicle. They were carrying beer bottles. One of the men smashed a bottle against the driver's window and Gerald was struck on the head. He cried out and Thandi, lying underneath him, saw blood flowing from his head. The front passenger door of the car was opened and a man told her to get out. It was Mahlangu. He asked her how old she was and where she lived. She said that she did not know her age. Mahlangu then led her into the veld, a firearm in his hand. He asked her whether she knew 'what a girl was supposed to do'. Thandi refused to take off her clothes. Mahlangu berated her for wasting his time, forced her to lie down and ripped her panties off. He then raped her and when he was finished he called his friend. At that point Thandi managed to run away, leaving her panties and shoes on the scene. As she fled, she heard two shots being fired in the direction of the car.

When Thandi reached the tarred road, she saw the car speeding off. A taxi stopped and took her home, where she told her grandmother what had happened to her. She went to the Meadowlands police station to report her rape and Gerald's murder. Later, Thandi was able to identify Mahlangu at an identity parade, as she had been able to see him clearly in the spotlights of the power station.

On the evening of 25 April 1979, Pinky Mantile, who lived at 4229 Mafu Street, Dobsonville, went out her with boyfriend, Nelson Roberton Mutswaletswale. They went to Meadowlands, returning at about 11 pm. Pinky and Nelson were fondling in the car outside her house when a torch light was shone into her eyes. The man holding the torch asked if they always parked the car there at night and whether they knew that people died in Dobsonville. The man was Mahlangu. He asked Nelson where he lived and Nelson replied that he lived in Dobsonville. Pinky heard a gunshot and the window on Nelson's side shattered. He fell on to her lap, splattering her with blood.

Mahlangu got into the car and pushed Nelson's body over to Pinky's side. Pinky jumped out of the car and managed to get into her house unharmed. She hurriedly told her brother what had happened and they both rushed outside, but the car was gone. They then went to the Dobsonville police station, where Pinky made a statement. The police, accompanied by Pinky, set out to search for Nelson's body which they eventually found. His wristwatch was missing. Mahlangu was wearing the watch when he was arrested. They also found the car which had been set on fire.

Mafa Cain Ngojo was Pinky's neighbour. On the night that she and Nelson were attacked he was sitting in his kitchen when he heard a knock on the door. Before he could open it a man burst in and asked him if he knew him. Mafa said that he did not. The man switched off the lights, shone the torch on Mafa and shot him in the head. Mafa needed major surgery, but he did not die. Mahlangu later confessed that after he had dumped Nelson's body and set the car on fire he returned to Pinky's house. But he made a mistake and entered the neighbour's house instead.

Mahlangu was a police informer who had worked for Lieutenant Viljoen of the Brakpan police station on the East Rand since 1977. Viljoen was aware that Mahlangu was wanted on several murder charges and, acting on information, he arrested Mahlangu in Benrose at about two o'clock on the afternoon of 15 June 1979. He took Mahlangu to the Meadowlands police station, where they waited for an hour and a half for Major Engelbrecht to arrive. Viljoen handed Mahlangu over to Engelbrecht and returned to Brakpan.

Engelbrecht interrogated Mahlangu, who later took him to the house of James Morapedi in Orlando East. Morapedi said that he had known Mahlangu for eight years and that Mahlangu had at one time stayed with him, but had moved out before 1979. He occasionally spent the night with him during 1979. Engelbrecht called for back-up. When the detectives arrived Mahlangu pointed out a disused stove and the detectives removed the lid with a screwdriver, uncovering several boxes of ammunition. Mahlangu insisted that Morapedi should hand over a firearm to the detectives, but Morapedi maintained that he had given the gun back to Mahlangu on an earlier occasion. When Mahlangu became belligerent, Morapedi hit him on the chin in front of the detectives. Morapedi also pointed out some of Joseph's clothing to the detectives, as well as two torches that Mahlangu had used.

No firearm was found at Morapedi's house and Mahlangu then took the detectives to No. 5682 Kliptown, but no firearm was found there either. They returned to the Meadowlands police station, where Engelbrecht received a radio message from his colleagues which led him, accompanied by other detectives and by Mahlangu, to No. 1211 Orlando East, the home of shebeen owner Isaac Shaumang. Shaumang was known to Mahlangu, who had visited him before. Mahlangu never drank strong liquor but he had upon occasion fired several shots in the backyard of the shebeen in a show of bravado.

Isaac Shaumang testified during Mahlangu's trial that at about eight o'clock on the morning of 15 June 1979 Mahlangu came to his house and pointed a revolver at Shaumang's two-year-old son. The child grabbed the firearm and dropped it. Mahlangu told Shaumang that he was going to change his clothing and that he would return within half an hour, which he did. Mahlangu had both the revolver and the pistol with him. He gave them to Shaumang and told him to look after the firearms while he went to town. Shaumang took them to the backyard and hid them in a drum. That same evening Engelbrecht and other detectives arrived at his house with Mahlangu. Mahlangu told Shaumang to give the firearms to the police and they were handed over to Engelbrecht with several rounds of ammunition.

Eventually, at about ten o'clock that night, they returned to the Meadowlands police station, where Engelbrecht handed Mahlangu over to Captain Swart. Although Mahlangu spoke fluent Afrikaans, Sergeant Shemba was also present to act as interpreter if need be. Swart warned Mahlangu of his rights, but he declined legal representation.

Swart then began to take Mahlangu's statement, during which Mahlangu confessed to the murders. Swart warned him that he was incriminating himself and asked him if he wanted to make a confession to a magistrate. But Mahlangu declined, saying that he wanted to 'open his heart' to Swart, so the policeman continued taking the confession. By one o'clock the following morning both men were exhausted and Mahlangu was booked into the cells. At ten o'clock that morning Swart had Mahlangu booked out of the cells, warned him again, and then completed taking the confession. It was fifty-eight pages long.

Mahlangu agreed to point out the crime scenes.

Mahlangu's trial began on 5 February 1980. He was charged with nine counts of murder, two of which were coupled with robbery, one charge of attempted murder, two charges of rape and two charges of unlawful possession of firearms and ammunition. The trial ended on 25 February 1980.

Before sentencing, Mahlangu's criminal record was laid before the court. In 1960 he had been convicted of robbery and received five cuts with a cane; in 1961 he was sentenced to eighteen months for the theft of a car; in 1963 he was sentenced to two years for rape and to eighteen months for robbery. He was also convicted for theft, illegal possession of firearms and escaping from custody, which resulted in his being declared a habitual criminal in 1964. In 1964 he was again convicted of robbery. He was released on parole on 6 August 1974.

Mr Justice Human sentenced Mahlangu to seven years for each of the rapes, ten years for the attempted murder of Mafa, two years each on the illegal possession of firearms and he gave him the death sentence for each of the nine murders. Mahlangu's appeal failed and he was executed.

James Morapedi and Isaac Shaumang were charged as accomplices in the illegal possession of ammunition and firearms, but were acquitted due to their truthful evidence.

Notes

It is undesirable that an officer should take the confession of a suspect if he is involved in the case. Captain Swart was the investigating officer in two of the murder charges against Mahlangu. Mahlangu alleged during the trial that he had not made the confession, that Swart had written it himself and that he had been forced to sign it. Judge Human rejected this allegation and accepted the confession on the basis that the fifty-eight-page document contained so much detail that Swart would never have been able to fabricate it. In addition, Mahlangu had pointed out crime scenes that no one else would have known about.

It is preferable that a magistrate should take a suspect's confession, but even a member of the public can do so. The only legal requirements are that it should be given free and voluntarily. Detectives often take suspects to a district surgeon before and after confessions to prove that the suspect was not coerced into making the confession. A policeman who is not an officer may not take a confession, nor officiate at the pointing out of a crime scene.

PHILLIP KHEHLA MAGOSO

Pietermaritzburg, 1983

At about two o'clock on the afternoon of 21 July 1983, 22-year-old Winile Ntombizonke Sydness Gabuza of Plessislaer near Pietermaritzburg was walking in Church Street in Pietermaritzburg when she was approached by two men. They threatened her with a knife and forced her to go with them. They walked to the Epic Oil Mills where one of the men told her that he had stolen three boxes of cooking oil and that she was to help them sell it.

The man forced Winile on to a bus which was bound for Woodlands. The other man did not go with them. When they arrived at Woodlands, the assailant took Winile to a plantation. She was reluctant to follow him and so he dragged her along a slope. He demanded money from her and she gave him eight rand and a few cents. He dragged her deeper into the plantation to a place where a bedsheet had been spread on the ground.

The man raped Winile repeatedly and kept her captive during the night. The next morning he told her that he was going to tie her to a tree. When he reached for a bag, she noticed the body of another woman not far from her. Winile bolted, jumping into a deep ditch behind her. She did not know that there was yet another body in this ditch, as she was running for her life.

The following day she went to the Mountain Rise police station where she recounted her ordeal and made a statement. The case was referred to Warrant Officer D Holby.

A colleague of Holby's, Warrant Officer Mthembu, and a police photographer went to the plantation. To their horror they discovered the decomposed bodies of five women in close proximity to one another. They had all been strangled with their pantyhose.

The detectives put word of the murders out to their informers and soon received the information that the suspect might be 31-year-old Phillip Magoso who had been found guilty of rape in 1979 and sent to prison in 1980 for three years. Holby contacted the prison authorities who confirmed that Magoso had been released and he obtained an address for the suspect in Plessislaer. Holby went to the address, but Magoso was not there. However, he managed to obtain a photograph album belonging to the suspect. When he showed the album to Winile she immediately pointed out her assailant. It was Phillip Magoso.

Holby asked that news of the murders be broadcast on the radio, requesting that relatives of missing women come forward. Angelina Zanele Mkhize, Hazel Dladla and Sibongile Agrineth Mbatha were the first victims to be identified.

Twenty-seven-year-old Ernest Masokana Ndlovu said that his girlfriend, 22-year-old Angelina Zanele Mkhize, had visited him at the bakery where he was employed in Pietermaritzburg on 12 July 1983. Later that day he dropped her off in Church Street where she planned to catch a bus to Claridge where she worked. That was the last time he saw Angelina alive. He had heard that the bodies of several women had been found in the Woodlands plantation and went to the mortuary on 26 July 1983, where he identified Angelina's body. Angelina's mother, Gemaima Mkhize, also identified the body at the mortuary.

Fifty-five-year-old Philda Khulelaphi Mbatha last saw her daughter, 23-year-old Sibongile Agrineth Mbatha, alive on 5 July 1983 at her home where she had asked her mother for five rands which she was supposedly to pay to a furniture store. When she did not return home that night Philda was not unduly concerned as Agrineth often found piece-work which prevented her from returning home. But when the family had heard nothing from her for a week, Philda became concerned and sent Agrineth's twin sister Christina to look for her. By 26 July 1983 Philda had also heard about the murder victims at Woodlands. Christina identified the body of her sister at the local mortuary.

Forty-eight-year-old Thomas Gabuza was the uncle of 19-year-old Hazel Dladla who lived in his house. On 8 July 1983 Hazel went to her uncle's place of work to collect money for groceries. He gave her the money, adding one rand for her to spend on herself. Hazel was supposed to have met her cousin Clementine, Thomas' daughter, at half past four in East Street. When Hazel did not turn up, Clementine decided to go home, hoping that Hazel had gone home too. But Hazel did not return. On 30 August 1983 Clementine identified Hazel's clothes at the Mountain Rise police station.

In the mean time Sergeant Daniel Khumbula Njilo obtained information that Phillip Magoso was working in the Bulwer area and on 26 July 1983 he found Magoso, whom he had known personally, and arrested him. The following day Magoso took Njilo to his home and showed him various items of women's clothing which Njilo took possession of. Phillip was wearing the sunglasses of one of his victims.

Because he had been in trouble with the police before, Magoso wanted to make a voluntary confession, and when Njilo arrested him he confessed to killing all five of the women found in the Woodlands plantation by strangling them with their pantyhose. He did not confess to raping them, but wooden chips were found inside the vagina of one of the victims. He said that he had sold their clothing.

In 1976 Magoso had been found guilty of the possession of an unlicensed firearm and unlicensed ammunition and was sentenced to forty days' imprisonment and a further ninety days suspended for three years. In 1978 he was found guilty of housebreaking and was given another prison sentence, which was also suspended for five years. For the rape in 1980 he was sentenced to three years in prison and he completed the term. He had also stolen ten rand from his victim and was sentenced to a year's imprisonment, which ran concurrently with the three-year sentence.

A week after his arrest, Magoso's aunt, Gladys Khosini Bhengu, stated that he had stayed with her in Plessislaer since April 1983.

He had been released from prison on 20 January 1983 and found employment with a building contractor at Imbali. At the beginning of June 1983 he left for Bulwer, only to return in the middle of July. On the evening of 21 July 1983 he did not sleep at home, but when he returned the following morning she did not ask him where he had been. This was the night that he had spent in the Woodlands plantation with Winile. Two days later, on 23 July 1983, and three days before his arrest, Magoso told his aunt that he was in trouble and he left her home.

The police managed to trace the women to whom Magoso had sold the clothing of his victims. Rupina Dhlamini said that Magoso had sold her a pair of shoes for two rand during the first week of July 1983; Teresia Siziba had bought a blue striped skirt and a brown hat; Alice Ndlani bought a white jersey. Mapile Elizabeth Dlamini reported that she had known Magoso for three months through his girlfriend, who was a friend of hers. The clothing was sold in Mapile's room. Mapile said that Magoso told her that the clothing belonged to his sister, but it no longer fitted her as she was pregnant, and she needed the money. Mapile had bought a skirt and a leather belt for ten rand. During Magoso's trial Njilo handed in the articles of clothing as evidence.

The remaining two victims were never identified and were buried as paupers.

Phillip Khehla Magoso was charged with five counts of murder, six counts of rape and one count of robbery. His trial lasted from 2 to 9 April 1984 at the Pietermaritzburg Supreme Court. On 9 April 1984 the Honourable Mr Justice W Booysen passed five life sentences for each of the murders, twelve years for each rape and six years for the theft of Winile's eight rand.

Notes

A good detective will have an extensive informer network. Informers are members of the public, usually ex-convicts, who provide the detective with information in exchange for money.

The price of the information is relative. Many people make a living in this way and once an informer is trusted and has proved his worth, the detective will go out of his way to look after him. Informers always run the risk of being identified as *impimpi* and may be killed for their trouble. A detective is under no obligation whatsoever to reveal the identity of his informer, not even in court.

In a 'normal' murder investigation the detective will try to establish the motive for the crime, which often points him to his suspect. Informers also come forward with names of possible suspects. People often reveal their secrets to others, or their behaviour becomes suspicious and is easily noticed by those around them. A person does not have to register as a full-time informer to give information, but will be allocated a number which is used when payment is made. Therefore a member of the public who has never 'informed' before, and who has no intention of doing it again, should have no fear of being exposed.

Serial killer cases are notoriously difficult to investigate. First of all, there is no apparent motive; secondly, there is usually no link between the murderer and the victim – it is a stranger upon stranger crime – and thirdly, serial killers keep their secrets and do not tell anyone about their crimes. It is therefore rare that an informer can be used successfully in serial homicide investigations. When a detective makes enquiries in a serial killer case, he is inclined not to ask people to report something out of the ordinary, but rather to report on the ordinary. Serial killers are ordinary people and take special care not to stand out and be recognised. They do not want to be detected. It is important for the public to know that they should not be on the lookout for a raving lunatic, but rather for a normal man who might fit the psychological profile. People should learn to trust their intuition and not disregard nagging feelings that something is 'not quite right' about a particular individual.

Detectives do identify possible suspects by collecting names of former convicts who operated in the same area and displayed a similar modus operandi. They ask prisons to supply them with the names of recently released prisoners and they rely heavily on the public to come forward with names of people who might fit the psychological profile. This leads to many hours of laborious paper work, which takes up most of the time spent on the investigation. By pointing this out, I am not negating the possibility of rehabilitation. If a person committed a crime, served his sentence and refrains from crime for the rest of his life, he has nothing to fear. As a rehabilitated citizen, he should be satisfied that the detectives are doing their work in a thorough and systematic way. Unfortunately sexual offenders tend to be repeat offenders.

In Magoso's case it was a stroke of good fortune that Winile managed to escape and that she noticed the body of another victim. If she had not, Magoso would have continued killing undetected. It was also fortunate that detective Holby and his colleagues had a good informer system which came up with the name of the suspect. In South Africa, the reward leading to the arrest and conviction of a serial killer is set between R250 000 and R500 000.

JAN ABRAHAM CHRISTOFFEL NEL

Northern Cape, 1984 & 1997-98

Jan Abraham Christoffel Nel, or Chris as he was known to acquaintances, grew up as the oldest child and only son with five sisters. One was his own blood relative, two were half-sisters and two were stepsisters. Nel loved his own father, but after his death his mother remarried and he did not get on with his stepfather. During his adolescence he was sent to a hostel from which he often ran away. He alleged that his stepfather disciplined him and assaulted him with his fist and a belt. He had also watched his stepfather hit his mother, a matter with which Nel had no problem since it was his opinion that a man should put a woman in her place.

When he was sixteen years old Nel left home and went to stay with his grandmother who lived in Benoni on the East Rand, while he tried to complete grade 9. He told his mother that he was going to live with his grandmother and she said that he should go if he wanted to. Although Nel repeated grade 9 he did not manage to pass and enlisted in the army in 1983. In January 1984 he went to Postmasburg, a small town in the Northern Cape, where he worked as a driver for the railways. He lived in the railways hostel and worked shifts. He had no intimate friends and watched about nine videos a day.

On the evening of 3 November 1984, Nel attended a disco at the local showgrounds. He had spent the day visiting acquaintances and watching videos. He had several drinks during the day, but arrived at the disco in a sober state of mind. He asked several girls to dance with him but most refused. To the 18-year-old Nel, this rekindled the rejection he had experienced when a girlfriend had left him for another man three months earlier, and it also reminded him of his mother, who had not only sent him to a hostel but also did not appear to care when he informed her that he was going to live with his grandmother.

At about eleven o'clock that night Nel went outside to relieve himself. Earlier in the evening a friend had given his car keys to Nel to take care of and there was a small pocket knife attached to the keys. He saw two young girls entering the ladies' toilets. He testified later that at that moment he knew that he was going to kill them. He followed the girls inside.

Fifteen-year-old Rika Fouche was standing behind her friend, 17-year-old Miss S and both were combing their hair. The girls suddenly saw, reflected in the mirror, a man with a knife in his raised hand. Miss S grabbed Rika and tried to drag her into one of the toilets, but Nel pulled her away. Miss S ran into the toilet and locked the door. She heard Nel tell Rika to take off her clothes but Rika refused. Miss S heard them struggling. She heard Rika make a rasping noise and then everything was quiet. She climbed on to the toilet bowl and peered over the wall. Nel was washing his hands. He turned around and smiled at her. He had slit Rika's throat and stabbed her about twenty-five times. He had ripped her panties with his knife, but had not managed to rape her. She was lying on the floor in a pool of blood.

Nel climbed on to the wall between the two toilets and when Miss S opened the door in an effort to escape, he stuck his foot between the door and the wall of the cubicle. She ran out, but he managed to catch her. He picked her up and carried her to the nearby stables while she pleaded with him not to kill her. He told her that nobody loved him, that he hated all women, that all women were the same, and that his girlfriend had left him for another man. Miss S answered that the girlfriend could not have loved him. This comment infuriated Nel who stripped Miss S and raped her brutally. Later, as she bent down to pick up her clothes, she bumped into him and managed to get away from him. He ran after her and tackled her. As they fell, the lights of a vehicle shone upon them and Miss S managed to run towards the car. Nel fled into one of the stables, where he was arrested later that night.

When Nel was taken to the police station, he said at first that he had nothing to do with the incident, that he had merely seen the naked girl running from the stables and had held on to her to comfort her. Meanwhile, the knife belonging to Nel's friend had been found at the scene of the crime, and Miss S had made her statement. Nel was interrogated by Major Louis Swanepoel and confronted with the facts. He admitted to killing Rika and was pointed out by Miss S as the man who had raped her. He told Major Swanepoel that he hated women, that he had been dumped by a girlfriend, and that he felt relieved after the murder and had no regrets.

In June 1986 the Honourable Mr Justice Basson decided not to pass the death sentence on Nel because of his youth and the fact that he had no previous convictions. Instead, he sentenced him to a total of twenty years in prison for the murder and attempted rape of Rika Fouche and the rape of Miss S. He reprimanded Nel and told him to use the time in prison to rehabilitate himself and not to bear a grudge against society.

For twelve and a half years Nel sat in jail, but he did not use those years to rehabilitate himself. Instead, his hatred for women grew even stronger. When he was released on parole in January 1997 he settled in Upington, where he worked at CAY Motors as a mechanic. He kept to himself, living alone in a garden flat and going out only with colleagues from work. He had no other friends and did not date.

Up the road from CAY Motors in Roux Street, at the corner of the local secondary school, was the spot where the local prostitutes gathered at night.

On the evening of Friday 10 November 1997, 18-year-old Hermien Maasdorp, a scholar, attended a dance at the Fantasy nightclub, which was also close to CAY Motors in Roux Street.

She left the dance at approximately one o'clock. Friends who saw her last said she was looking for a lift home.

Hermien's body was found the following day in the arid deserted veld along the Lutsput Road, which is an extension of Roux Street. She was wearing only her bra. Hermien had been brutally attacked with a blunt object and she had been raped. She had died of head injuries. Swabs were taken and the Forensic Science Laboratory of the South African Police Service managed to isolate a DNA profile from the sperm found on her body.

Some time during December 1997, 22-year-old Belinda Visagie, a prostitute, was plying her trade on the corner of Roux Street when Nel picked her up. According to the other prostitutes Nel was a regular client, but he called himself Johan. He drove Belinda out to a remote spot in the semi-desert on the Louisville Road, where he had consensual sex with Belinda. He then demanded anal sex, which she refused. Nel lost his temper and began to assault her, striking her on the face and head with a bottle. He threatened to kill her, but she managed to get away from him.

Belinda hid in the bushes while Nel searched for her in the dark. When he did not find her, he left. Belinda walked to the road and managed to get a lift home with a woman driver. She did not report the assault to the police, but she was examined by a doctor who confirmed her multiple injuries.

About three months later, on 18 March 1998, Nel went with his colleagues to a pub and gambling den. Some time during the night he left his colleagues, took the company bakkie and drove to Roux Street where he picked up 30-year-old prostitute Janetta Meintjies. The other women warned Janetta not to go with Nel because he had assaulted Belinda, but Janetta answered that she had a date with the man.

The following day Janetta's body was found in the veld, about 400 metres from the spot where Belinda had been assaulted. She was naked and her face was covered with sand. There were multiple injuries on her face and body. The impact of one of the blows had broken her jaw, which became lodged in her throat, and she died of suffocation. Janetta's body was identified and the prostitutes told investigating officer Sergeant Jacques Visser that she had been picked up by Nel in the CAY Motors bakkie.

Nel was arrested at CAY Motors on 23 March 1998. Visser knew about the unsolved murder of Hermien Maasdorp and requested blood samples from Nel. The DNA matched that identified in Hermien's case. In the mean time the other prostitutes persuaded Belinda to lay an assault charge against Nel.

During July 1999 Nel was charged with the attempted murder of Belinda Visagie, and with the murder and rape of Hermien Maasdorp and Janetta Meintjies. Advocate Johan de Nysschen represented the State and Advocate George Galloway was counsel for the accused before the Honourable Mr Justice Kriek in Upington. Nel pleaded not guilty to all the charges and claimed that he did not even know the victims. He could give no explanation for the fact that his semen had been found at Hermien's crime scene. On 28 July 1999 Nel was found guilty on all the charges except the rape of Janetta. Since she was a prostitute, it could not be proved that she had not given permission for sex. Nel was sentenced to life imprisonment.

Nel showed no emotion throughout the trial. Hermien's father began crying softly in the public gallery when Judge Kriek pronounced Nel guilty of his daughter's murder and rape.

Notes

Nel had already served a twelve and a half year sentence for rape, murder and attempted rape when he resumed his career as a serial killer. He exemplifies the fact that serial killers cannot be rehabilitated and will carry on killing if they are released. He had a long time in prison in which to decide whether to try and change his life, but he chose to kill again. Nel later said that Miss S was one of the girlfriends who had rejected him and that Rika Fouche just happened to be in the wrong place at the wrong time.

I do not know of any instance of a serial killer who has not continued killing after his release from prison. Correctional Services authorities should adhere to a judge's sentence. If a man is sentenced to life imprisonment for these types of crimes he should stay in prison for the rest of his life. After he was released from prison, notorious rapist Skroewedraaier van der Merwe kidnapped two girls, murdered one and was shot by the other. American Ed Kemper was sent to a correctional facility after killing his grandparents at the age of fifteen, but was released into the custody of his mother. Thereafter he killed six young women, his own mother and her friend before giving himself up to the police.

THE STATION STRANGLER

Mitchell's Plain, 1986-94

Twenty-five years for murder and another ten years for kidnapping was the sentence passed by Mr Justice W A van Deventer on 15 June 1995 in the High Court in Cape Town. On 27 March 1998 five judges of the Appeal Court of South Africa changed the sentence to life, and thus concluded the last episode of a tragic tale that touched the lives of the community of Mitchell's Plain, about 30 kilometres outside Cape Town, as well as the lives of many detectives and other personnel of the South African Police Service, attorneys and the media and, of course, that of the accused, Avzal Sarfaraaz Norman Simons.

For the community of Mitchell's Plain the story began on 3 October 1986 when the body of 14-year-old Jonathan Claasen was discovered near the Modderdam railway station. He was the first victim of the Station Strangler, so dubbed by the media because he appeared to lure children from railway stations to their deaths. The next victim, 10-year-old Yussuf Hoffmann, was found on 7 January 1987 in Rocklands, a suburb of Mitchell's Plain, and the third, 13-year-old Mario Thomas, was discovered in the bushes near Kuilsrivier on 23 January 1987.

Although the bodies were badly decomposed it seemed that all of them had been sodomised and strangled with their own clothing. Over the next five years seven more bodies were discovered in similar circumstances. The body of an unknown boy was found on 9 April 1987, again near the Modderdam

Station. The body of 12-year-old Freddie Cleaves was discovered near the Belhar Station on 26 June 1987 and, two months later, on 25 August 1987, that of 15-year-old Samuel Ngaba was also found near the same station. On 1 October 1987 the body of another unidentified boy was discovered at the Modderdam Station, and on 8 February 1988 the body of nine-year-old Calvin Spiro was found at the Unibel Station in Belhar. Eleven-year-old Denver Ghazu's body was found at the Sarepta Station on 11 November 1989. Then almost three years passed before the body of 11-year-old Jacobus Louw was discovered on the Mnandi beach near Mitchell's Plain on 27 October 1992.

On 13 January 1994 a municipal worker came across the body of an unidentified boy in the Weltevrede dunes in Mitchell's Plain. During the following two weeks more bodies were found strewn among the dunes. The killer's pace had accelerated to eleven victims in one month. The body of Elino Sprinkle (11) was discovered on 20 January 1994. On 25 January 1994 the bodies of Donovan Swartz (10) and Jeremy Benjamin (12) were found lying about 20 metres apart. The community of Mitchell's Plain became hysterical after these discoveries and joined members of the South African Police Force in a search party the following weekend.

Their search led to the gruesome discovery of eight more bodies. On 26 January 1994 the body of Jeremy Smith (13) was found, and on 27 January 1994 the bodies of Marcelino Cupido (9), Neville Samaai (14), an unidentified young boy and an adult male were found. The bodies of best friends, eight-year-old Fabian Willowmore and 11-year-old Owen Hofmeester were discovered lying side by side. They had been strangled with each other's clothing. Another unidentified boy, fully clothed, was found in the dunes. He was lying on his back and his hands had been tied with nylon cord. He had been strangled with the same cord. His underpants were found nearby. At this stage the Station Strangler's victims totalled twenty-one.

The community of Mitchell's Plain gathered at the local police station demanding the Station Strangler's head. They formed vigilante groups and any man seen in the company of a young boy feared for his life as angry mobs chased suspicious looking individuals into the dunes. The community stormed the Steenberg police station, broke down fences and demolished private homes if they thought a suspect might be hiding there. They formed units which spent days and nights searching the sewers beneath Mitchell's Plain, and they patrolled school grounds.

Learners were lectured on the dangers of being approached by strangers, and school schedules were changed to enable younger children to be accompanied home by the older children. In the churches congregations prayed for the souls of the victims and for their families. The families of the victims buried their sons and grieved, some in private and some in public. At night, though, police still spotted youngsters walking alone on the streets.

The Mitchell's Plain community turned to the South African Police Force for help and the police responded to their call. A single detective from the Murder and Robbery Unit, Warrant Officer Reggie Schilders had investigated the earlier murders, which started in 1986, but he had since retired leaving the cases unsolved. In February 1994 a fourteen-man special task team, dubbed the Station Strangler Squad, was established. The team was led by Lieutenant Johan Kotze, under the supervision of the commander of the Cape Peninsula Murder and Robbery Unit, Colonel Leonard Knipe.

The team operated from the yard of the Mitchell's Plain police station. Three police caravans parked on the lawn served as offices for the task team. The parade room of the police station was converted into an operations room and its walls were lined with maps, details about the victims, the crime scenes and suspects. It was also fitted out with a computer for processing incoming data. The investigation became more focused and previously unheard of support, such as forensic psychologists, were seconded to the team. These were luxuries that had not been available to Schilders during the 1980s.

The Strangler Squad was inundated with approximately three

hundred calls a day from the community, all of them offering names of possible suspects. Up to two thousand suspects were interviewed and interrogated between February and April 1994. Thousands of criminal records were perused and all the information in the earlier dockets was followed up once more. Detectives even interviewed convicted child abusers to get to know more about their modus operandi.

A psychological profile of the suspect was drawn up by a police psychologist. The profile described the suspect as a coloured man between the ages of 25 and 35 years. He would be bilingual, a single man probably living with his family, and he would be a homosexual. He was described as an intelligent man who dressed very neatly, and he would probably be a teacher, preacher, policeman or a social worker who preferred the company of children to that of adults. He would be a local who lived in Mitchell's Plain and would probably own a vehicle, which he would often have resprayed in a different colour. It was likely that as a boy the suspect would have been sexually abused by a family member. The profile was released to the community by the media.

The Strangler Squad used the profile to eliminate the thousands of suspects who did not match it. The detectives were under tremendous pressure: the community wanted revenge and had to be restrained when they turned violent; politicians tried to use the investigation as a tool in their 1994 election campaigns; and the media watched the police's every move.

During the investigation, detectives visited schools to warn the children, they gave feedback to the families and community leaders and they attended the funerals of the children. They diverted other cases of child abuse to the Child Protection Unit, they listened to psychics and they even halted a robbery in progress which happened to take place in their presence. They patrolled the dunes looking for more bodies and searched for and found missing children. Those who were off duty at weekends brought in food for their colleagues. The fourteen men worked 24-hour shifts for three months. The pace of the investigation did not slacken for a moment. Meetings were held twice daily to keep everyone fully briefed.

On the morning of Saturday 19 March 1994, the call the detectives dreaded most came through. Another body had been found at Kleinvlei, bordering Mitchell's Plain. The detectives gathered at the scene within minutes. There was no doubt that this was another of the Strangler's victims. The body of the young boy was lying face down with his hands tied behind his back and his tracksuit pants were tied around his neck. The task team was devastated. A crowd gathered and someone alerted the press, who spotted the members of the Strangler Squad and drew the correct conclusion.

The body was soon identified as that of 10-year-old Elroy van Rooi from the Strand, a town further down the coast. Elroy's grandmother identified him; she had reported him missing a week before his body was discovered. A witness, Mrs Fouzia Hercules, came forward and reported that she had seen the boy and his cousin Ryno accompany a man from a shopping centre in the Strand to the railway station. The cousin had become uncomfortable with the stranger, who had offered each boy money to carry empty boxes to the station, and had run off. Elroy was not so fortunate and paid with his life. The cousin and Mrs Hercules drew up an identikit, which was released to the press.

Alerted by a nurse at a private psychiatric clinic, the detectives pulled in a suspect on the evening of 12 April 1994, after having kept him under observation for a few days. They warned him of his rights and asked him to accompany them to the caravans at the police station, which he did voluntarily. The suspect was 27-year-old Avzal Sarfaraaz Norman Simons, an unmarried school teacher who lived with his mother in Mitchell's Plain. He was described by his friends as a homosexual, he dressed neatly and owned a car which he had had resprayed.

Simons volunteered to write down his life story and was given a pen and paper. He said he was an inpatient at the clinic but that he could not return to the clinic that evening because the doors were already locked. He did not want to return home either. The detectives offered him one of the caravans to sleep in. At noon on 13 April 1994, Lieutenant Kotze formally arrested Simons in connection with the Mitchell's Plain cases, but not the Kleinvlei case. On 14 April 1994 an identity parade was held and Simons was identified by Mrs Hercules. Ryno said that he also recognised Simons, but was too scared to point him out as the murderer of his cousin. On 15 April 1994 the detectives realised they did not have enough evidence to charge Simons with the Mitchell's Plain cases and released him, but immediately rearrested him in connection with the Kleinvlei case. Simons said that he wished to make a confession and was taken to a magistrate to whom he confessed to having killed children since 1986. He did not elect to have an attorney present.

On Saturday 16 April 1994 Simons was taken to Valkenberg Psychiatric Hospital to see a psychiatrist, since Colonel Knipe was concerned about his mental state. When the Colonel interrogated Simons he had claimed that in killing the children he was acting on the orders of his deceased brother. Simons admitted that he had been sodomised by his older brother when he was the same age as his victims. The psychiatrist found that Simons was not suffering from mental illness, but that he had a personality disorder. Simons then retracted his first confession, and claimed to be innocent. He gave an alibi statement which was proved to be false during his trial.

On Sunday 17 April 1994, Simons called Kotze and said that he wanted to make a second confession. During the interrogation that day, he actually demonstrated to the detectives how he had managed to kill two boys at the same time. He was taken to another magistrate that evening to make a second confession. After the confession he proceeded to point out all the crime scenes to Lieutenant Mike Barkhuizen. This pointing out took place during the early hours of the morning of Monday 18 April 1994, while the community of Mitchell's Plain was still asleep.

The Station Strangler Squad followed Barkhuizen's vehicle at a distance, to provide back-up in case the community woke up and harassed the suspect. Later that morning Simons was charged in court for the first time.

The arrest of the suspect did not herald the end of the detectives' duties. They had to take statements and follow up the background details of the suspect, but mercifully the pressure had abated and they could focus their attention on only one man.

Months later the Strangler Squad was disbanded and one by one they returned to their former stations, except for Kotze, Warrant Officer Div de Villiers and Sergeant A J Oliver who had to prepare the case for trial. For them, the strain ended only a year later when the judge found Simons guilty.

The case was referred to the office of the Attorney-General of the Western Cape. At first it was received negatively because of the lack of evidence in the initial cases. The bodies were badly decomposed and had been lying in the sun between the dunes for months. It is characteristic of organised serial killers not to leave any evidence.

Eventually senior state advocate Mike Stowe and his colleague Anette de Lange volunteered to take on the case. They decided not to charge Simons with the Mitchell's Plain cases, but with the kidnapping, indecent assault and murder of Elroy van Rooi.

The trial began on Monday 27 February 1995. Advocate Koos Louw was appointed by attorney Ruben Liddel to act as defence counsel and Mr Justice van Deventer and two assessors, Mr J Booysen and Advocate C Williams, presided.

The trial was riddled with postponements and dragged on for months. The accused was often late for court because of a strike at the prison. The detectives were grilled under cross examination – Kotze was in the witness box for four days.

During what became a trial within a trial, the admissibility of the confessions and pointings out were put to the test. The accused refused to testify. He sat quietly during the trial, taking notes and giving instructions to his defence counsel. Sometimes he clicked his tongue irritably when he did not agree with the testimony of the detectives. He never claimed to have been abused by any of them.

The case was postponed to 31 May 1995 for final argument. The atmosphere in court was tense. The victim's family, the mothers of other victims, residents and gangsters of Mitchell's Plain and friends and family of the accused sat silently in the court gallery. The press took notes frantically and television crews were waiting anxiously outside the High Court building in the centre of Cape Town.

Throughout the story the media had treated the Strangler case with the sensation they thought it deserved. They splashed pictures of the victims and their bereaved parents on the front pages and created 'Station Strangler case files' which gave a day by day account of the investigation and the trial.

The media haunted the detectives day and night during the investigation, trying their best to elicit a scoop. On one occasion the detectives pulled over to the side of the road to eat their lunchtime sandwiches and the media pulled up behind them and asked whether another body had been found. After the suspect had been arrested the media obtained permission from the Minister of Law and Order to publish his picture. This upset the investigating team because it could seriously have prejudiced the identity parade.

Television news broadcast scenes of thousands of policemen patrolling the dunes searching for bodies, and during the trial they jostled with one another in their efforts to get a good picture of the accused. At times the judge reprimanded them for inaccurate reporting, but on the whole the proceedings were correctly represented. The Station Strangler case also enjoyed international media attention. Everyone focused their lenses on the scarred face of the accused. Simons had burnt his face as a child when he fell on to a heater. The scar was one of the features by which he was identified.

The story of the Station Strangler had begun years earlier for Norman Simons, who later embraced the Islamic faith and changed his name to Avzal.

In his confessions, Simons wrote that he had been born on 27 January 1967 in Green Point, Cape Town. His mother and father were of different ethnic groups. Simons was brought up as a Xhosa, growing up in Queenstown in the Eastern Cape province. He claimed that an old woman had placed an evil spell on him. He said this was a main element in most of his deeds as she had planted the darkness in him. He returned to Cape Town in 1982 and moved into his mother's house. His stepfather was also a Xhosa and he never really knew his biological father. He alleged that he had been sodomised by his older brother while he lived with his mother as a teenager. His brother was murdered in 1993.

Simons said that the killings began in 1986, when he was in his grade 12 year. He said that he had acted in response to the voice of his brother inside him. He often expressed his remorse for the murders in his written confessions. He also thanked the detectives by name for arresting him.

Simons had realised that he needed help and from 1991 he booked himself into various psychiatric clinics and institutions for treatment for depression. His diagnosis was adjustment disorder with depressive moods, personality disorders and depression. There seemed to have been an informal correlation between the times he committed himself to these institutions and the times of the murders. During the trial the defence tried to indicate that he suffered from dissociative personality disorder and hypomania, but they failed to establish this.

Simons had problems with his ethnic, religious and sexual identities, but he was an educated man who spoke seven languages, including French. He liked classical music. He loved his vocation as a teacher and appeared to be good at it. His pupils adored him and he was respected by his colleagues. Although one of his victims was a pupil from his school, the boy was not in any of his classes. Simons was a volunteer at NICRO, an organisation which assists ex-convicts to readjust to society; he helped out in religious groups and he had a few good friends. He preferred the company of children and would often take them swimming in the ocean and treat them to ice cream. On the morning of 11

March 1994, he had his picture taken to enlist as a police reservist to 'help in the investigation of the Station Strangler'. Later that day he murdered Elroy van Rooi.

Had it not been for his dark secret, Simons would have been a respected member of the Mitchell's Plain community who made an active contribution to the upliftment of his fellow men. In his final confession he wished all citizens a successful election and asked for peace for South Africa.

But Simons *did* have a dark secret – he had an urge to kill young boys who reminded him of the victim he had once been.

Avzal Simons irrevocably changed the lives of many and although he was not charged with all the crimes of the Station Strangler, he was brought to court for murder by a team effort, by members of the South African Police Service* and the community who testified, the advocates who prosecuted him and, in the end, justice found him guilty of kidnapping a boy by luring him on to a train and strangling him near a railway station.

Despite his failed appeal, Simons still proclaims his innocence and has written to Elroy's grandmother denying his involvement in the death of her beloved grandson. The mothers of Jonathan, Yussuf, Mario, Freddie, Samuel, Calvin, Denver, Jacobus, Jeremy Benjamin, Marcelino, Elino, Fabian, Owen, Donovan, Jeremy Smith and Neville believe that the murderer of their sons is in prison, but there will never be a trial for them.

Notes

In 1995, after the conviction of the Station Strangler, the South African Police Service established the Investigative Psychology Unit to deal mainly with serial killer cases. Thirty to forty Murder and Robbery Unit detectives are trained annually by the Unit to

---

*The South African Police Force became the South African Police Service after the 1994 elections and the change of government.

combat this growing menace.

In the Station Strangler case the community constructively assisted the police by providing the names of possible suspects. Detectives processed more than two thousand names in three months. Unfortunately people with vendettas against others gave their names, for the sole purpose of taking pleasure in their adversaries being roped in for interrogation. This was a considerable waste of the detectives' time – and time is of the essence in a serial killer investigation, for he might strike again at any moment.

The community participated in the search for the bodies and unfortunately the names of the victims and the dates of the murders were printed in the newspapers. Thus Simons could not be charged with these murders for they were common knowledge and the State would not have been able to prove that he had prior knowledge of them.

The case was also complicated by psychics offering help and information. All information is processed by the police, but they are under no obligation to use that given to them by psychics. Detectives check what psychics tell them against what has appeared in print in the newspapers. A psychic who gives a general description of the suspect or who relates information that is easily obtainable through the media is of no use to the police and is wasting their time. Psychics often want rewards for their information and this alienates detectives. Those who have worthwhile information should contact the investigating officer, make an appointment to see him and try to verify their knowledge. There are people with special talents who can help in this regard and they usually do not charge the police for their assistance.

This case of Avzal Simons clearly illustrates the reversal of the active-passive role. When he was abused by his older bother he was the passive helpless victim. He needed to master this traumatic event by reversing the roles and placing himself in the active aggressive role. He therefore took on the active role of his brother and selected victims who reminded him of himself at the same age and placed them in the passive helpless role, thereby attempting to regain the control he had lost when he was a victim. Although this process can be psychologically explained, it remains just that – an explanation, and not an excuse.

The case of the Station Strangler brings to mind that of Wayne Williams, the Atlanta Child Killer. Between 1979 and 1981 twenty-six children were abducted, sexually molested and killed. One child has never been accounted for. Williams also killed an adult male, Nathaniel Cater, and was spotted when he was dumping Cater's body in a river.

The similarities between Wayne Williams and Avzal Simons are remarkable. Besides the fact that they even look alike, both were respected members of their communities. Williams had his own radio station which he used to promote children with musical talent. Both claimed to be innocent even after being convicted.

The cases were also similar in the way in which the communities became involved, the amount of media hype which the investigations attracted, and the political motivations that surfaced during the investigations. Williams was charged with only two murders, due to lack of evidence, and Simons was charged with only one for the same reason. The murders ceased after their arrests, and both were eventually sentenced to life imprisonment.

DAVID MOTSHEKGWA

Jouberton, 1988

On 23 January 1988, 28-year-old Frank Avontuur was walking from Klerksdorp to his home in neighbouring Jouberton. His route took him past a small hill, the Oudorp Koppie, and it was there that he detected a very bad smell. On investigating, he found the decomposed body of a woman lying between the rocks on the koppie. The post mortem of the unidentified victim indicated that she had died twenty-two days earlier, but so severe was the decomposition that no cause of death could be established. The woman was in her early twenties.

On 5 February 1988 two more decomposed bodies of unidentified women were discovered on the same koppie by the Klerksdorp commando.

On 10 February detectives from Klerksdorp decided to launch a thorough search of the Oudorp Koppie and Constable Majaja and his colleagues discovered the decomposed bodies of three more women. They had been covered with dry twigs and branches. Pathologist Dr J C Steyn determined that two of the women had died two months before their bodies were discovered. The third victim had died seven weeks before she was found. The cause of death could not be established.

On 13 February the body of another unidentified woman was found by a member of the public, 42-year-old Marthinus Christoffel Botha, who was walking on the koppie with friends. And on 16 February a further three bodies of unidentified women were found by the police. By mid-February 1988 a total of ten bodies had been found on the koppie and the Klerksdorp detective unit launched a full-scale investigation. The murders were given considerable coverage in newspapers and on radio.

A police informer supplied information that a woman had told him about a man who had promised her work. She went with him, but when she reached the koppie, she became scared and ran away.

Twenty-two-year-old Evelyn Madibo and her older sister, 25-year-old Mirriam Madibo both lived at No. 7 Jonker Street. On the morning of 9 February 1988, Mirriam left their home to go to Kolonel Nel Street where she worked. She did not return home that evening. Evelyn searched for her sister in vain and then, on 13 February, she went to Kolonel Nel Street only to find that the owners of the house where Mirriam had worked, had moved. The house was empty and no one in the vicinity had any idea where Mirriam might be. On 16 February Evelyn went to the Klerksdorp police station to report Mirriam as missing. They took her to the mortuary, where she identified her sister's body.

On Friday 19 February, Elisa Moilwa of Klerksdorp heard on the radio that bodies of women had been discovered on the koppie. She went to the mortuary in Klerksdorp and asked to see the bodies. She identified one of them as a friend of hers, 31-year-old Wilhelminah Hukunyane Mathiba. Elisa stated that Wilhelminah had visited her on 5 January 1988 and told her that she was on her way to meet her sister, Honey Mathiba, in the industrial area. Wilhelminah was wearing a cream-coloured dress with a floral pattern on 5 January and she was still wearing this dress when her body was discovered.

The victim's sister, Honey, said that she and Wilhelminah had gone to Klerksdorp during December 1987 to look for work. Wilhelminah stayed with her boyfriend Guava on one of the plots at Adamayview, and Honey stayed with her boyfriend in Jouberton.

On Sunday 10 January 1988, Honey met Guava who told her that Wilhelminah had been missing since 5 January. On 19 February 1988 Honey received a message from Elisa that her sister had been murdered and that her body was in the mortuary. Honey also identified her sister's body. Guava was interrogated, but cleared of suspicion.

On 19 February 1988, 22-year-old Dinah Merahe also went to the mortuary where she found the body of her older sister, 44-year-old Mosadiwapula Sophia Merahe. Dinah said that Mosadiwapula had met her on 5 February and told her that she had taken the day off work to go to Rustenburg to fetch her possessions. As she did not have enough cash to get to Rustenburg, she was planning to go first to Mrs Maria Lephaleha in Orkney to borrow money. Dinah saw her sister get into a taxi which was bound for Orkney. Mosadiwapula told Dinah that she planned to return on 7 February. When Dinah had not heard anything from her sister by Monday 8 February, she went looking for her at her place of employment. She was told that Mosadiwapula had not returned.

On 11 February 1988 Dinah went to Orkney to see Maria Lephaleha. Maria confirmed that Mosadiwapula had arrived there on 5 February, but that she had left on Monday 8 February to return to Klerksdorp. She had not been seen alive since then.

Fifty-year-old Petrus Rakgosi of Jouberton had also heard about the bodies that had been found on the koppie. On 25 February 1988 he went to the mortuary to look for his girlfriend, 34-year-old Semanga Grace Dedeka, whom he had last seen alive on 1 February when he left her at their shack in Jouberton while he went to look for work. When he returned she was gone. Three days later a friend informed him that Semanga had told him, on 1 February, that she had found work in town. At the mortuary, Petrus was able to identify Semanga's body by her red shoes and underwear. Although decomposed, he could still recognise her face.

Twenty-five-year-old Pauline Makhunga, who lived in Jouberton, also went to the mortuary on 25 February 1988 and identified the body of her older sister, 41-year-old Eva Makhunga. Paulina stated that Eva had arrived at her house on 4 February and said that she was looking for work. The following morning Paulina left Eva at her home. She did not see her alive again.

For some months no more bodies were found on the koppie and the police continued to follow up the leads that they had. Then, on 9 June 1988, 29-year-old Samson Mazantsana took a detour from the footpath on the koppie to relieve himself. As he approached a tree, he saw skeletal remains sticking out of the undergrowth. Samson alerted the police. Dr Steyn found that the victim, an unidentified woman, had been killed six months before her body was discovered. This brought the total number of victims to eleven.

At about 7 am on 30 June 1988, 30-year-old Simon Dikupe left his home in Jouberton to go to work. His wife Sarah was going to Jouberton to collect her salary. When Simon returned home that night, his wife was missing. Simon asked his grandmother Maria whether she had seen Sarah that day, for Sarah had to collect her salary at the same place where Maria worked. Maria told Simon that Sarah had said that a man had found work for her at the tennis courts. Maria had seen the man when he fetched Sarah that afternoon. She described him to the police as having a 'lazy' left eye, some of his teeth were missing and he wore blue overalls. Simon had also reported to the police that his identity book was missing.

On 18 July 1988 Sergeant Tebello Lazarus Ramarou, the investigating officer in the Dikupe case, was keeping surveillance on activities on the koppie. At about lunchtime he noticed a man on the far side of the koppie. The man walked over to him and started talking to him. Tebello realised that the man matched the description of the suspect in Sarah Dikupe's disappearance. He immediately arrested him and read him his rights. Tebello found an identity book in the suspect's pocket. The man said it belonged to his brother, but the name he gave did not match the name in the book. Tebello identified the man in the book as Simon Dikupe.

Tebello took the suspect back to the detective headquarters where he was identified as 45-year-old David Motshekgwa.

Motshekgwa said that he wanted to point out a crime scene and Captain Evert Joubert was asked to officiate at the pointing out. Motshekgwa gave the police officers directions to the koppie. On the way he told them that he had been a patient at Weskoppies mental institution, but that he had absconded because he thought he was well again. He lived next to a bridge in the veld alongside the koppie and did piece work as a gardener wherever he could.

Motshekgwa also recounted how he had murdered his last victim and said that he burnt her clothes. When they reached the koppie he pointed out where he had burnt the clothes and he then led the detectives to the body of his last victim. Motshekgwa told Constable Kubedi, who accompanied them, that he knew that he had done very bad things and that he had murdered several women on the koppie. Joubert asked Motshekgwa how many women he had killed and Motshekgwa held up all his fingers. He said it could even be more. At that stage Motshekgwa's tally was twelve victims, for some time between March and July 1988 another body was discovered on the koppie. Simon Dikupe identified this victim as his missing wife Sarah.

The following morning Warrant Officer Richard Henry Rossouw interrogated Motshekgwa. Motshekgwa said that he wanted to make a confession to a magistrate and was taken before Magistrate Claassens. Later that afternoon Motshekgwa called Rossouw to his cell and told him that the interpreter who had been with him when he made his confession to the magistrate had not allowed him to talk enough and that he wanted to make a further confession to a police officer. Rossouw asked Major Visser to take the confession.

On 21 July 1988, 26-year-old Stompie Phika came forward and made a statement to the effect that she had met a man on 1 February 1988 who had promised her employment. She followed him to the koppie where he attacked her and tried to rape and strangle her. She had put up a fight and managed to get away. Luckily, there was another woman on the koppie at the time and when the man saw her, he let Stompie go. Stompie and Simon Dikupe's grandmother Maria, as well as another woman who had been with Maria, all identified David Motshekgwa at an identity parade on 21 July.

On 13 August 1988 Lieutenant Andre Myburgh was again called out to the koppie where the thirteenth victim had been found. According to the pathologist, she had been killed six weeks earlier, which meant that Motshekgwa could have been the murderer. On 20 August Sergeant Schalk van der Sandt was called out when the decomposed body of yet another unidentified woman was found on the koppie. Dr Steyn determined that she, too, had died six to seven weeks before she was found.

On 30 January 1990 David Motshekgwa was sentenced by the Honourable Judge W J Hartzenberg to fourteen life sentences for fourteen murders and to ten years for the attempted murder of Stompie Phika. Motshekgwa said that he had lured the women to the koppie with the promise of finding them employment. He wanted only to have sex with them but afterwards they asked him to pay them ten rands and since he only had one rand, he decided to kill them in case they reported him to the police. His excuse that he killed them because he did not have enough money to pay them is a feeble attempt at avoiding responsibility.

Notes

Serial killers often lure their victims by promising them employment. Women should be warned never to accompany an unknown man alone anywhere, no matter how promising the prospects sound. Serial killers are sophisticated manipulators and can be very charming. When the police alert a community that a serial killer is operative, women should take special precautions. Remember, serial killers target innocent strangers – it could be you. Never trust a stranger. Women should always tell someone where they are going, when they expect to arrive, and should also let them know that they have arrived safely.

Our mortuaries are full of Jane and John Does and these unclaimed bodies are buried in unidentified paupers' graves. It is very difficult later for a detective to help a family identify a missing person or even to trace the grave once a person has been buried as a pauper. The family would have to request an exhumation and pay for it, as well as for the transfer and reburial of the victim. This is a costly and emotionally stressful process, which could be unnecessary if people keep tabs on their friends and family and report missing persons without delay. A person does not have to be missing for twenty-four or forty-eight hours before the police start to investigate. This is a myth. They have to open a case immediately.

Detectives usually try to recover the clothing the victim was wearing to aid in identification, but this can be problematic as the victim could have left her home weeks or months before and bought or borrowed new clothing. One of Willem Grobler's victims (see page 241) was wearing a borrowed blouse. During the trial the defence will often contest the manner in which the victim was identified, and clothing might not be enough.

The police will often give details of the clothing a victim was wearing to the press. Any member of the public who notices someone wearing the clothing, regardless of whether they actually know the person or not, should alert the investigating officer. For example, someone could notice that the clothing on a woman sitting next to him in a taxi matches the description released by the police. If he alerts the police, they will at least be able to start tracing the last movements of the victim and this may lead them to the suspect. Should this information lead to the arrest and conviction of the suspect, the observant passenger who contacted the police with what he might have thought was trivial information could earn himself a reward of R250 000.

Identifying a loved one is a traumatic experience and it is best to select a family member with a strong emotional constitution to fulfil this sad duty. It is preferable for that person to be able to identify the body by some distinguishing feature, rather than relying on the clothing.

JACOBUS GELDENHUYS

Johannesburg & East Rand, 1989-92

Jacobus (Kobus) Geldenhuys grew up in a rigid, conservative Afrikaner home, but the difference between his home and other typical Afrikaner homes of that era was that in Geldenhuys' home, his mother wore the pants. According to court records, she was a zealot, who also believed that her home was possessed by the Devil.

Geldenhuys' parents described him as a quiet, well-behaved child. He remembered his childhood as extremely lonely. Because of illness Geldenhuys missed most of grade 5. He was forced by his mother to repeat the year and it was during that year that he began stealing. He was a prefect in grade 7, but failed the year. He was however promoted to the next grade because of his age. His secondary school years passed without incident, except for the fact that his mother liked to wrestle with him. This was unusual behaviour for a woman who refused to discuss sex with her child. Geldenhuys' pattern of loneliness continued.

After passing matric, Geldenhuys wanted to join the navy, but was turned down. He applied to the Post Office and to the South African Police Force, who also rejected him. Eventually he was accepted by the Railway Police and worked at Johannesburg International Airport. When the Railway Police and the South African Police Force were amalgamated, Geldenhuys stayed on at the airport, but was later transferred to the Internal Stability Unit at Alexandra. He experienced his time of working in the townships as boring and not at all traumatic.

Geldenhuys attended church regularly with his parents and it was at church that he met his girlfriend, Nadine. He apparently pricked her backside with a pin one day and that was how their relationship started.

On the morning of 12 May 1989, Geldenhuys was bored with the video games he was playing in his parents' house at No. 12D Railway Road, Benoni. He went outside, took a ladder and placed it against the wall of the garage. He climbed on to the roof of the garage and then jumped into the neighbour's backyard. His intention was to burgle the house but then he spotted the housekeeper, 21-year-old Franiswa Tundzi, coming out of her room in her pyjamas. She screamed when she saw him. Geldenhuys later admitted that he wanted to rape the woman. He pushed her into her room and tore her clothing. He hit her in the stomach to try to stop her from screaming. He took a brick from under her bed and hit her again on the stomach and neck. Then he strangled her. Whether or not she was raped could not be established, for Geldenhuys set some papers on fire and the burning paper fell on to her body. He went home and had a shower for the incident had made him feel dirty. He later admitted that he expected to be arrested and said that he would have confessed.

Geldenhuys and Nadine had set a wedding date for October 1991, after an eighteen-month engagement. Shortly before the wedding, Nadine's father phoned to confront Geldenhuys about his lack of ambition. He wanted Geldenhuys to write his sergeant's examinations and to obtain a police flat for him and Nadine. Geldenhuys had by this time moved out of his parents' home to the Norwood police barracks in Johannesburg. He became angry with his future father-in-law and slammed down the phone. Nadine's father called off the wedding.

A month after this fallout, on 2 November 1991, Geldenhuys became bored watching TV in the barracks and went out for a walk. He passed Grantwood Close Flats and noticed an open window. When he realised that no one was about, he climbed through the window. He stole thirteen CDs and went back to his room.

The following night, 3 November, his need for adventure and relief from boredom compelled him to go outside again. This time he chose a block of flats right next door to the barracks. He climbed through an open window and stole four CDs, a CD player and two speakers. The flat was occupied by 37-year-old Miss F. He also took her BMW car keys and took the car for a joy ride. The next day he returned the car to its parking place and threw the keys through the window.

On the evening of 6 November, Geldenhuys returned to Miss F's flat. He entered and made his way to the bedroom where he found Miss F in bed. He took off his clothes and when the woman woke and asked him what he wanted, he threatened her with his 9 mm service pistol. Miss F told Geldenhuys that he did not seem like a violent person and begged him to put the gun down. He retaliated by struggling with her to show her how violent he could be and then he raped her. Geldenhuys had trouble getting an erection. Miss F asked him why he had raped her and he replied that he did it for fun. He turned the gun on her once more, and again she begged for her life. He threw the duvet cover over her and got dressed. He told Miss F to pull the duvet cover over her head, which she did. He then ripped out the telephone and left through a window. Just before he left, Miss F asked him if he was scared, and he answered that he 'didn't care'.

Twenty days later, on 26 November, Geldenhuys was bored once more. He strolled around the neighbourhood and noticed a handbag through the window of a ground floor flat in Grant Close. He climbed through the window and stole fifty rand from the handbag. There was a woman sitting in the lounge but she did not notice him. He left the flat silently and went back to his quarters.

Later that same night Geldenhuys returned to the flat. Sixty-eight-year-old Mrs M woke up to find him in her room. When she screamed he hit her on the head with his service pistol and began to undress her as well as himself. He raped her and then asked her for money. She told him that the money was locked away. He kissed her and raped her again. Then he got dressed and threw a blanket over his victim. He wished her a good night, told her to sleep well and left the flat through a window.

Twenty days later, on 16 December, Geldenhuys kept surveillance on the house of 27-year-old Julia Margaret Hitge in Shipstone Lane. He knew the house was occupied by two women and a man. He walked past the house a few times that night, but there were always people about. At last the house was quiet and Geldenhuys entered through the unlocked sliding door of the lounge. He went first to the man's room only to find it empty. He walked down the passage to one of the other bedrooms and noticed a purse on a table. He could not see properly and switched on the light. Julia awoke and saw him and this was when he decided that she would have to die. She asked him what he wanted and he started to struggle with her. He hit her on the back of the head with his pistol. He raped the stunned woman and then shot her in cold blood through the temple when he was finished. He took the notes from the purse, but left the change. He left by the same door through which he had entered.

Two weeks later, on 30 December, Geldenhuys entered a second floor flat in a complex next to the barracks. He went to the bedroom, switched on the light and found 27-year-old Jennifer Matfield in her bed. She screamed when she saw him. Geldenhuys hit her on the head with his pistol, ripped her pyjamas and raped her. When he had finished she asked if she could go to the toilet. He agreed, but accompanied her. He told her to take a bath, which she did. He then returned to her room and dressed himself. He went back to the bathroom and stood in the doorway smoking a cigarette. He then calmly drew out his pistol. Jennifer turned her head away and he shot her in the back of the head and left. The next morning she was found by her flatmate who called the police. The police found footprints leading from the block of flats to the wall separating the barracks and the complex. Fresh footprints were found on the barracks side of the wall and a mould was taken.

Geldenhuys later said that he would play video games after the murders to take his mind off them. He showed no signs of stress and there were no changes in his eating or sleeping habits between murders. News of the Norwood serial rapist/serial killer had hit the media by then. Geldenhuys had watched the news on television and was afraid that he would be arrested. He kept his pistol next to his bed at all times, ready to commit suicide should the dreaded knock on the door come. But no knock came and it was only a matter of time before he began killing again.

After the fourth case, the murder of Jennifer Matfield, all the men in the barracks were told to assemble in the TV room to have their fingerprints taken, since fingerprints had been found in her flat. Geldenhuys decided that he would give himself up then, but no one arrived to take the fingerprints and he felt safe again.

For four months, Geldenhuys managed to control the 'thing', as he called it, and he did not commit any murders.

On 7 May 1992 74-year-old Susanna Elizabeth Wandrag was alone in her flatlet in Brakpan. She lived in the same complex as Nadine's parents, just two doors away. Geldenhuys (who was presumably in Brakpan to visit his fiancée) entered Mrs Wandrag's home through a sliding door and went to her bedroom. He switched the light on and off and then went to another room where he found a torch. He returned to the main bedroom and found a handbag. He opened it and took the change which he found there. Mrs Wandrag woke up when he switched on the light. She screamed and he hit her with his pistol. She grabbed his hands, whereupon he shot her in the face. Geldenhuys sat in the lounge for three hours before he left the scene.

The case was being investigated by Warrant Officer Miles of the Norwood detective unit. Miles was certain that his suspect was a resident in the Norwood barracks. The thought that one of his colleagues was a murderer horrified him. Most of the flats where the murders were committed were visible from the roof of the barracks. Obviously the case and its progress was also discussed in the barracks. Geldenhuys decided that things were getting too hot for him and asked for a transfer to his parents' home town of Benoni.

The attacks had terrified the women of Norwood. Those who could moved away temporarily, and the sales of burglar bars, security systems and firearms soared.

On the afternoon of 15 July 1992 Geldenhuys was again bored and climbed over a few fences into a neighbour's yard. The house belonged to a Mrs Taylor who shared it with her 16-year-old daughter Veronica. The back door was open and Geldenhuys saw this as an invitation to enter. As he approached the door Veronica came outside. She asked him what he wanted and he pointed his pistol at her. She screamed and ran inside, but Geldenhuys followed. He dragged her to her room and stripped off her blouse. He told her to take off her jeans, which she did. When she asked him what he wanted, he demanded money. Veronica told him that the money was in her mother's room and offered to take him there. She asked him if she could put a gown on but he refused. Veronica gave him R150 from her mother's cupboard. He told her to lie on the end of the bed with her legs on the ground. Geldenhuys could not manage to penetrate her, but he ejaculated. Then he shot her in the forehead. He picked up the ballistic casing and on his way out noticed a purse in the lounge. He stole the six rand in the purse and left the house.

This case was investigated by Warrant Officer Leon Nel of the East Rand Murder and Robbery Unit. As it happened, the post mortem on Veronica Taylor was performed by pathologist Dr Vernon Kemp, who had also performed the post mortems on the victims of the Norwood rapist. Dr Kemp had a suspicion that Veronica had been murdered by the same man. Warrant Officers Miles and Nel got in touch with each other. They decided to check on all policemen from the Internal Stability Unit who had been transferred to the East Rand during the past month. Geldenhuys was one of two names which came up, but he was not regarded as the main suspect, since the blood group identified from the semen on the crime scenes was O+ and his blood group was A+.

On 21 July 1992, Miles went to the Internal Stability Unit in Benoni. He had meant to speak to the other person on his list, but that man was out on duty. However, Geldenhuys was there. When he heard that Miles was on his way, he deviously swapped his service pistol for another from the station's armoury. Miles called Geldenhuys in and asked him where he lived. He said that he lived at No. 12D Railway Road with his parents. He seemed very nervous. Miles asked him if he knew anything about Veronica's murder since it had taken place close to his parents' house. Geldenhuys refused to answer and Miles took possession of his firearm. Miles asked what his blood group was and Geldenhuys answered that it was A+. Miles asked Geldenhuys if he knew anything about the Norwood murders but he refused to answer.

Geldenhuys' behaviour aroused Miles' suspicions and he arrested him and took him to the Norwood police station where he took a full set of fingerprints. His prints matched those found at Jennifer Matfield's crime scene. Miles informed Geldenhuys of the match, whereafter he confessed and also agreed to make a full confession to a magistrate.

Geldenhuys told Miles that he had swapped his pistol in Benoni and Miles sent both pistols to the Forensic Science Laboratory in Pretoria. Geldenhuys' pistol matched the ballistic evidence found at some of the crime scenes. As far as the discrepancy in the blood groups was concerned, it was eventually established that Geldenhuys was one of the very few people whose blood group as identified in the semen differs from that identified in the blood. When samples were taken of his semen, the blood group was O+ – the same as that of the killer.

Although a criminologist testified that Geldenhuys suffered from a schizoid personality disorder and that biophysical factors could have influenced the serotonin levels in his brain, the psychologists who examined him could not confirm the diagnosis and discounted the biophysical dysfunction as unproven speculation. Geldenhuys was found fit to stand trial.

On 24 September 1993, the Honourable Judge R Cloete passed five death sentences on Jacobus Petrus Geldenhuys for the murders, three life sentences for the rapes, twelve years for robbery, and thirty-five months for theft and for using a vehicle without the owner's permission.

Geldenhuys told the criminologist that he did not know why he had committed the crimes, that he knew that it was wrong, but that he had enjoyed the adventure. He said that he had started his 'career' stealing money from his mother's purse. His former fiancée Nadine reported that she had had a normal relationship with Geldenhuys and that their sex life was normal. However, most of the time he had difficulty getting an erection for the rapes. When asked if he had anything to say at the end of his trial, he replied that he knew that he was a sinner and asked people to forgive him.

The death sentence was abolished before Kobus Geldenhuys faced the noose. He is currently serving a life sentence.

Notes

The notorious Russian serial killer Andrei Chicatillo and the British serial killer Patrick Duffy both shared with Geldenhuys the rare phenomenon of a difference in their blood grouping as determined in their semen and their blood.

Kobus Geldenhuys probably fixated in the Oedipus phase and, of course, in the latency phase. Apparently he said that his mother was not affectionate during his childhood, but became more so when he was a teenager. This initial lack of affection could have been experienced as rejection. On a subconscious level, Geldenhuys was probably experiencing castration by his mother. He had to prove his manhood by raping but he had difficulty doing this as he could not maintain an erection. He had no problems in his intimacy with Nadine, for she posed no threat to him. According to court records, Geldenhuys' father was emotionally absent and was dominated by his wife, which meant that Geldenhuys did not identify with a strong male role model and did not develop a conscience or superego. This is fixation in the latency phase.

It could be debated whether Geldenhuys was a serial rapist who killed his victims to prevent them from identifying him, or whether he was a serial killer who killed because he liked doing so. The fact that he told a criminologist that he enjoyed seeing the star shape wound that a close-up shot caused confirms to me that he was a serial killer.

BRYDONE BRANDT

Port Elizabeth, 1989-97

Brydone Brandt was born on 15 April 1964 in Welkom in the Free State. He was the sixth of seven children. He maintained that he was breastfed up to the age of nine. He alleged that his father was an aggressive man who often encouraged his sons to fight with each other. Brydone, being the youngest son, did not come off too well during these fights. His father would tie the children over a chair and hit them with a sjambok when they were naughty. He also abused his wife.

Brandt claimed that when he was ten years old his second eldest brother began molesting him sexually and that the eldest brother forced the younger brothers to commit incest with the sisters. He said the family was isolated and that they were not allowed to make friends with other children.

Brandt was sent to an industrial school by the Department of Welfare, where he claimed that he was sodomised by other boys. He also assaulted a teacher. He completed grade 10 and went into the army where he said that he was a member of the military police.

In March 1984, at the age of twenty, Brandt's criminal career took off. He was arrested in Kroonstad on a charge of crimen injuria and received a four-month suspended sentence. In October that year he was caned for stealing jewellery. In 1986 he stole a bicycle and received a three-month suspended sentence or a fine of R300.

In 1987 he relocated to Port Elizabeth with his brother and

Left: The Station Strangler, Avzal Simons, is escorted from court during his trial in the High Court in Cape Town in 1995. The Mitchell's Plain schoolteacher is serving a life sentence.

Below: Many of the Station Strangler's victims were found in the vast and desolate dunes near Mitchell's Plain.

(*Sunday Times*)

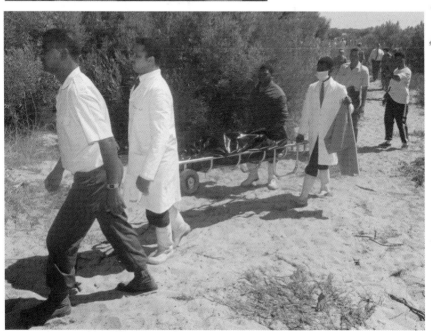

Van Dyk Mine on the East Rand, September 1995. When police processed this crime scene, a total of 10 bodies were found, all of them victims of Moses Sithole. (*Sunday Times*)

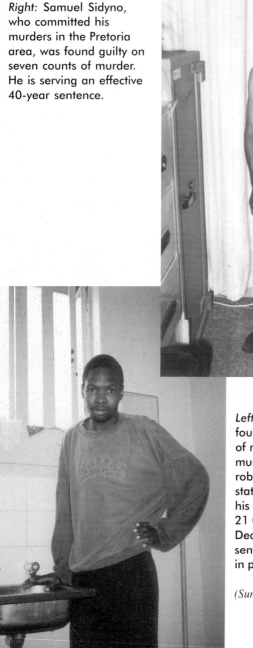

Right: Samuel Sidyno, who committed his murders in the Pretoria area, was found guilty on seven counts of murder. He is serving an effective 40-year sentence.

Left: Moses Sithole was found guilty on 40 counts of rape, 38 counts of murder and 6 counts of robbery. More than 350 state witnesses testified at his trial, which began on 21 October 1996. On 31 December 1997 he was sentenced to 2410 years in prison.

(Sunday Times)

Norwood serial killer Jacobus Geldenhuys is serving a life sentence.
Detective Leon Nel was one of the investigating officers.

(Sunday Times)

(Sunday Times)

Above: Velaphi Ndlangamandla, the so-called Saloon Killer, terrorised a squatter village in the Piet Retief area in 1997-98. He killed 20 people and wounded a further 11. He received 20 life sentences, plus 135 years.

Right: One of the most cold-blooded serial killers in South African criminal history, Cedric Maake employed five different modus operandi in committing his appalling murders. He faced 133 charges, including 27 counts of murder, and was sentenced to 1835 years' imprisonment.

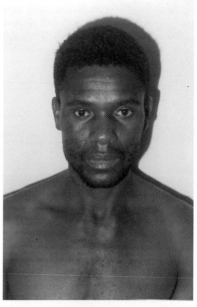

Stewart Wilken was charged with 6 murders, including that of his own daughter. He was given 7 life sentences in 1998.

(Sunday Times)

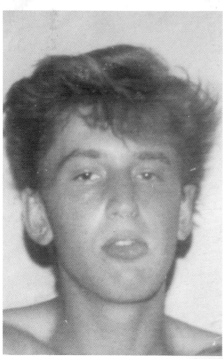

Cross-dresser Jacques Coetzee who, with his partner John Frank Brown, was charged with five counts of murder. Coetzee committed suicide in prison during the trial.

(Sunday Times)

in that year he was fined R50 for assaulting someone with a brick. In 1988 he was fined R100 for malicious damage to property when he broke a mirror in a hotel. In 1989 he received a sentence of R250 or fifty days' imprisonment for driving under the influence of alcohol. In that year he committed his first murder, but this went undetected. In 1990 he was convicted again on a charge of malicious damage to property when he kicked down a front door. He was sentenced to a fine of R300 or ninety days' imprisonment. Later that same year he was found guilty of fraud and sentenced to a fine of R120 or sixty days' imprisonment.

No one knew that Brandt committed his second murder in 1990, the year in which his father died. In 1991 he was sentenced to one year's imprisonment for stealing furniture. Later that year he was released and again charged with theft, rape and assault with grievous bodily harm. The case was dropped because of insufficient evidence. In 1992 he was found guilty of house-breaking and attempted murder. He was sent to jail in 1992 and released in 1996. His mother committed suicide while he was in prison.

As an adult Brandt worked for the Parks division of the Welkom municipality. When he and his brother moved to Port Elizabeth he invented for himself an identity as a private detective and worked as a bouncer and bodyguard. He claimed that he was raised as a racist and that he was involved in Satanism, but that he converted to Christianity later in his life.

To return to Brandt's murders: On 9 December 1989 he met Jean Natlazo, a prostitute, at the Palmerstone Night Club. He took her to the Port Elizabeth municipal buildings where they had sex. He claimed that they had an argument about the price and he lost his temper and killed her with a knife. She was found on the stairs of the building, lying half-naked on her back. Her private parts were exposed and there were lacerations in her vagina. The case remained unsolved for eight years.

In his confession Brandt said that he had fallen in love with a woman who belonged to a racist religious group and that this group had influenced him to kill Jean Natlazo.

A month after Jean Natlazo's murder, on 5 January 1990, Brandt met Sarie Schoeman and two other prostitutes at the Station Bar. He drove the three women to the Marine Drive near the University of Port Elizabeth. They got out of the car and sat at roadside tables discussing prices for sex. Brandt and Sarie got into the car, leaving the other two women alongside the road. He drove further along the Marine Drive. A short while later the other two prostitutes saw him drive past them alone. There was a dent in the car's bumper.

The women went looking for Sarie and found her body in the shrubs off the Marine Drive. A wine bottle had been inserted in her vagina. The cause of death appeared to be a fractured skull, caused by a blow from a rock. They removed the bottle, but left the body where it was and did not alert the police. A while later the body was discovered again by vagrants, but this time it had been moved further into the bush, was naked, lying face down and a stick had been inserted into the vagina.

It was only much later that the police managed to trace the two prostitutes. They then showed the police where they had first found the body; it was not the same place as where it was found the second time. Brandt later alleged that he had gone back to the scene, had picked up the body and driven around with it in his car. Then he went back and dumped it deeper in the bushes.

Between 1991 and 1996 Brandt was in prison for house-breaking and attempted murder. When he was released in 1996 he went to live in a boarding house in Port Elizabeth. He worked as a bodyguard for a doctor. He alleged that he was asked by this doctor to kill a certain man and his girlfriend, but instead he invited them to move in with him. He kicked out the boyfriend because he was unhygienic.

Brandt alleged that on 9 December 1996, a young boy running away from his father came to him. He and the boy were sleeping when Julia got into the bed. He said she was drunk and he asked her to leave. She refused and they had a fight. In his confession, Brandt said he could not remember how it happened, but she had fallen and broken her neck. He said he paid an ex-Satanist to remove her body and that this man had placed it in a green plastic bag and dumped it behind the Feather Market Hall. The body was discovered, but the case remained unsolved.

On 17 September 1997, Brandt was living at another boarding house. He shared accommodation with a 52-year-old man named Glenton Dean Morris. They were drinking buddies. Brandt alleged that he had a fight with Morris about money, during which Morris attacked him with a shifting spanner. They were both drunk. Brandt retaliated and killed Morris. The cause of death was strangulation. Brandt cut up the mattress that Morris had died on and stuffed it into plastic bags which he placed in the dustbins outside the boarding house. He also dumped Morris' body, upside down, in one of the dustbins. A blood-soaked Brandt was picked up by an ambulance and taken to a hospital where he was arrested for the murder of Glenton Morris. Other residents had heard the fight and found Morris' body.

It is ironic that Brandt was finally brought to justice for a murder which was unrelated to his serial murders. His victims of preference were prostitutes, whom he raped, assaulted aggressively and mutilated, but Glenton Morris died as a result of a drunken rage.

On 22 September 1997, Brandt made a full confession to a magistrate. He claimed that he had killed another prostitute and left her body in the Donkin Park, but no evidence could be found to support this. In May 1999 he was sentenced to four life sentences for the four murders.

Notes

Brydone Brandt said that his brother was diagnosed as a psychopath, but he himself showed many characteristics of antisocial personality disorder. One of the major characteristics of such a disorder is lack of remorse and lack of responsibility for one's actions. For instance, Brandt said that as a child he 'accidentally' strangled chicks, and he also found excuses for his murders, blaming the racist religious group, self-defence, and so on. He claimed he was brought up as a racist, yet he was engaged to a woman of another race.

Another characteristic of psychopaths is that they will often contradict themselves and utter barefaced lies, even though they may be aware of the fact that you know they are lying. Brandt reported that he hit his ex-girlfriend when she swore at her son. A little later in the same conversation, when asked why he had inserted a bottle and a stick into the vagina of one of his victims, he answered that he would never so much as strike a woman.

Running away from home, physical violence towards other people and animals, no respect for others' property or possessions and fire-setting are signs of psychopathy during childhood. Brandt had all of these characteristics.

Brandt claimed that he had become a Christian. It is not for anyone to judge whether or not a man has truly found God in his life, but what is interesting is that when he spoke about religion, Brandt was more concerned about convincing others of how good a Christian he was, than actually spreading the word of God. Like other psychopaths, the word 'I' featured much more than the word 'God' in his religious conversations.

'I don't believe in conning the public', 'I love to sing and give sweets to little children', 'I just want to make people happy', 'My heart goes out to all the men and women who have been rejected by their loved ones without reason . . . to the women who have to take so much from their cowardly men (assault, drunkenness, etc) while there are so many men who will love and comfort them of which I am one', 'Maybe I am too sensitive, too lovable and too protective . . .' said the man who had fourteen criminal offences to his name and who was eventually convicted of four brutal murders.

STEWART WILKEN, ALIAS 'BOETIE BOER'

Port Elizabeth, 1990-97

Stewart Wilken had a raw deal as a child. He was born on 11 November 1966 in Boksburg on the East Rand. Six months after his birth he and his older sister, only a toddler herself, were discovered by a domestic worker in a telephone booth in Boksburg. Apparently their biological mother had abandoned her children.

The domestic worker took both children to her employer, known to Stewart only as 'Doep'. While in the care of Doep, Stewart was severely abused. He alleged that his private parts were burnt with cigarettes, his food was taken from him and fed to the dogs and he had to eat from the dogs' bowls. He also alleged that he often had to watch while Doep committed bestiality with the dogs and that he had to lick Doep's penis after these incidents. During this time Stewart's sister disappeared and he never knew what happened to her.

Doep's neighbours, the Wilkens, took pity on the child and adopted him when he was two years old. Stewart was infested with lice and suffering from malnutrition. He recalls that his biological mother visited his adoptive parents when he was two years old and that she brought him a packet of sweets, which he rejected. He did not realise at the time that she was his biological mother and he did not see her again after that. According to Mrs Wilken, this took place at the time when she and her husband decided to adopt Stewart and they needed the biological mother's consent.

Stewart was a difficult child and did not do well at school. He failed grade 1 and consequently his adoptive mother withheld his Christmas present, a toy milk truck. Seven-year-old Stewart was devastated and vowed never to be interested in his school work again. He kept his promise, failing grade 3 three times and being transferred to a special class. According to Stewart, his teacher encouraged the other children to tease him about his adoptive status. This was the first time he realised that the Wilkens were not his natural parents. When he went to school the next day, Stewart assaulted his teacher by hitting her in the face. The principal retaliated by beating Stewart all over his body with a cane in front of the other children. Stewart alleged that on another occasion a teacher incited one of the other boys to attack him. When he retaliated he was sent home. His adoptive mother did not take his side and Stewart decided from that day to be his own 'mother, father, sister and auntie'.

Stewart started smoking dagga at the age of eight and Mrs Wilken described him as a problem child who she could not control. He recalled being physically abused by his adoptive older brother, being put into an ice-cold bath at night because of his sleep walking, and being punished by his adoptive mother for wetting his bed at night.

He remembered being sodomised at the age of nine by a deacon of the church, who invited him home one day after Sunday school. Mrs Wilken turned to the Department of Welfare who placed Stewart in an industrial school, where he alleged he was sodomised by the older boys. Stewart ran away from the school to the home of his adoptive mother's sister. He stayed there for a month. On his birthday the aunt gave him a parcel and some money and told him to return home. He hitch-hiked back to Port Elizabeth where his adoptive parents were living. Stewart was taken to a magistrate who told him that he would give him a letter stating that no one was allowed to punish him, on condition that he completed grade 11.

Stewart kept his promise and completed grade 11, after which he went into the army. He was discharged after four months because of an attempted suicide. He moved in with his adoptive mother in Despatch near Port Elizabeth and enrolled for a course as a joiner. He injured his hand during this training and thereafter received a disability pension from the state.

Wilken met his first wife, Lynne, at a nightclub. Lynne already had a daughter from a previous relationship and on Christmas Day in 1985, Wilken and Lynne's daughter Wuane was born. Wilken alleged that soon after the birth of their child Lynne began working as a prostitute, leaving him alone at home to tend to the children. He would inspect her underwear when she returned home.

Lynne stated that shortly after the birth of Wuane, Wilken never again had normal sex with her, but always insisted on anal sex. He decided to marry Lynne when the welfare authorities threatened to remove her older daughter. Wuane was already five years old when her parents married.

Their marriage, which lasted nine years, was riddled with problems. Lynne would repeatedly have Wilken locked up for smoking dagga and he would repeatedly assault her. For a while he was admitted to the Elizabeth Donkin Psychiatric Hospital where he was diagnosed as a psychopath. On his return home, Lynne phoned the police again, but Wilken saw them arrive and took an overdose of pills. He recovered in hospital and divorced Lynne soon afterwards. She remarried and he found work as a fisherman.

In the early 1990s he met Veronica, a woman of a different race, who became his second wife. Wilken vowed that he would never sleep with a white woman again for fear that she might be his lost sister. Two daughters were born of this marriage and Veronica already had two boys from a previous relationship. Wilken had many problems with his in-laws and his new wife. For a while, he, Veronica and their children moved in with Lynne and her new family. When Wilken's in-laws alleged that he had sodomised Veronica's two boys he left home. He lived in the veld behind Happy Valley, a recreational park close to the Holiday Inn in Port Elizabeth. He said that his only happy memories as a child were of being was taken to Happy Valley to play. The charges of sodomy were dropped on 23 January 1997, but soon afterwards Wilken was arrested for murder.

On 31 January 1997 Sergeant Derrick Norsworthy of the Port Elizabeth Murder and Robbery Unit was asked by the Child Protection Unit to question Stewart Wilken about the disappearance of his daughter Wuane and a boy, Henry Bakers, with whom Wilken was acquainted. The Child Protection Unit suspected that Wilken was their man, but they had no proof. And so Norsworthy was approached because he had been trained to investigate serial homicide.

Norsworthy was informed that Wuane Wilken had disappeared two years before, on 29 September 1995, and was last seen in the company of her father. Henry Bakers disappeared on 22 January 1997 and was also last seen in Wilken's company.

Norsworthy called Wilken to his office. Wilken introduced himself as 'Boetie Boer', an alias he ascribed to a second personality. Norsworthy had a framed photograph of his own daughter, who was a little younger than Wuane, on the wall of his office. His framed certificates verifying his training in the investigation of serial homicide were also on the wall. Norsworthy left Wilken alone for a short while. When he returned he found Wilken staring intently at the photograph of Norsworthy's daughter. Norsworthy drew his attention to the certificates and told him that he had been trained to investigate serial killings. He told Wilken that he knew that he had killed both the children and that he would return to the bodies to commit necrophilia. Wilken was quiet for a moment. Then he realised that he had met his match and confessed to Norsworthy that he had killed the children and that he had actually gone back to Henry's decomposing body that very morning to have sex with it.

A long night followed during which Wilken made the two confessions and pointed out the remains of the children. He had kept his daughter's body at his hideout in the veld where he slept. After her body had decomposed he covered the skeleton with a tarpaulin and spread her clothes out on the ground every night when he slept beside it. Wilken alleged that Wuane had been sexually abused by her stepfather and that he wanted to save her from a life of hell, such as he had had as a child.

In the early hours of that morning Norsworthy and Wilken returned to the offices of the Murder and Robbery Unit. Both men were exhausted. Wilken sank down into a chair and Norsworthy watched him wearily. Then Norsworthy followed his intuition and asked Wilken how many other people he had murdered. Wilken replied that it was probably at least ten.

Wilken made a full confession – using the most foul language – to his lawyer, Mr Griebenouw. His confession was as follows:

On the night of 3 October 1990, when he was still married to Lynne and after an argument with her, Wilken met a prostitute, Virginia Gysman, in Russel Road, Port Elizabeth. She asked him for fifty rand for sex. He showed her the money and took her to the nearby Dagbreek School. He had sex with her and then proceeded to have anal sex, about which she complained. He strangled her with a piece of clothing while he climaxed and then he left her body in the school grounds.

On 10 January 1991 he met Mercia Papenfus, also a prostitute, at the Red Lion hotel. She propositioned him. He took her to St George's Park where she demanded the money before the sex. This enraged Wilken, who was of the opinion that he should not have to pay for sexual pleasure, since God had freely given that pleasure to women and men. He strangled her with her clothing and then had sex with the corpse.

On 21 October 1991 Wilken met a 14-year-old street child. He propositioned the boy who, according to Wilken, consented to sex. He took the boy to St George's Park where the boy demanded fifty rand. Again, Wilken became enraged and the boy tried to flee. He then sodomised the boy and strangled him with clothing while he climaxed.

Some time between June 1993 and 21 September 1993, when the decomposed body was eventually discovered, Wilken met another street child of about 14 years at the Norwich building.

He asked the boy if he would masturbate him for money. The boy allegedly agreed. Wilken took the boy to the Fort Frederick Museum in midtown where the boy masturbated him. He then sodomised the boy. When the boy threatened to inform the police, an angry Wilken strangled him with his belt and hid the body in the bush.

On 27 July 1995 Wilken met Georgina Zweni, a prostitute, at Sydenham Primary School. She asked him for thirty rand for sex. He took her to Sydenham Park and proceeded to sodomise her, after which he strangled her with her clothing. He then took his knife, inserted it into her vagina and cut it open. He sliced off her nipples and ate them, and threw her clothing into a fish pond. He later admitted to Norsworthy that he had been present when some of his victims had been discovered in the parks and that he had watched the police process the scenes. He noticed that they collected hairs from the body and realised that he should get rid of the victims' clothing to prevent the police from finding hairs.

On 29 September 1995 Wilken went to visit his daughter Wuane. He claimed that she complained to him that her step-father was sexually abusing her. He took Wuane, who was ten years old at the time, to his hideout on the opposite side of town. There he strangled her and kept her body. When Norsworthy asked him whether he had had sex with Wuane, Wilken answered only that he had inspected her vagina and found that she was no longer a virgin. In all probability Wilken had sex with his daughter's body for a while after he killed her.

Wilken admitted to Norsworthy that he would often return to the bodies of the boys he had hidden to have sex with their corpses. He would insert newspaper into their anuses to prevent maggots from infesting the orifices.

On 25 May 1996 Wilken met another prostitute, Katriena Claassen, at the Albany Road interchange. He strangled her while he was reaching a climax. He also forced a plastic bag down her throat. He found it ironic that he had left her body next to a wall with graffiti which stated that people should not steal.

Wilken was of the opinion that whores stole money from people and he hated them for it.

Some time between May 1996 and 9 August 1996 Wilken met another street child whom he took to the Cilliers Secondary School. He sodomised the boy, strangled him and left the naked body in the school yard. He said that when he sodomised children he recalled the time that he had been sodomised by the deacon.

On 22 January 1997 Wilken met 12-year-old Henry Bakers, the child of a woman with whom he was acquainted, alongside a road in Algoa Park. He alleged that Henry asked him to teach him about sex. He took Henry into the nearby veld and told him to undress, which the boy did. Wilken masturbated the boy and forced him to have oral sex. Then he sodomised the screaming child and strangled him while he climaxed.

Wilken preferred to climax as his victims passed their last breath. He called this the 'jellybean effect'. He said that when they were being strangled their lips would swell and their tongues protruded. It was this 'jellybean effect' which caused him to climax.

Wilken was charged with ten murders. Attorney Alwyn Griebenouw and Advocate Gideon Huyshamen represented him and the state prosecutor's team was led by Advocate Leon Knoetze. Mr Justice Chris Jansen presided. Wilken was convicted on seven of the murder charges on 23 February 1998. He is currently serving seven life sentences in the St Albans Prison in Port Elizabeth. He suffers from nightmares and claims that the ghosts of his victims are persecuting him in prison.

Norsworthy traced Wilken's biological mother just before he was sentenced. She expressed the wish to make contact with her son and claimed that she had never wanted to abandon him but was forced to do by his father, since she was expecting another child. She had reclaimed Wilken's older sister. After sentence was passed Norsworthy informed Wilken that he had found his biological mother and relayed her message of love to him. He burst into tears. When his biological mother spoke to him on the phone, he called her 'mommy'. This was the first time in his life that he could recall using the word.

Notes

Wilken obviously fixated in both the oral phase – evidenced by his eating the nipples of one of his victims – and in the anal phase – evidenced by his perfectionism and preference for anal sex, which points to sadism. He had no role model with whom to identify and therefore fixated in the latency phase as well.

Like Avzal Simons, Wilken chose young street boys to reverse the passive/active role in order to try to overcome what had happened to him. When a killer strangles someone, he becomes the active aggressor and the other person is the passive victim. This seems to relieve the serial killer's own pain of having previously been the victim.

Sadists have a preference for anal sex, for it hurts and humiliates the victim. One of the most notorious sadists and cannibals was American Albert Fish. Fish was born in 1870 and by 1934, when he was arrested, he had violently assaulted more than one hundred girls and killed twelve of them. One was 12-year-old Grace Budd, whose body he kept in a derelict house. Fish returned regularly to the house and cut off pieces of Grace's flesh, which he ate. Fish also derived masochistic pleasure from inserting burning tissue into his own anus. He was found not to be insane, was tried and found guilty and electrocuted on 19 January 1936.

American Ed Gein was another cannibalistic serial killer. Gein's mother refused her sons access to any female company and when Ed's brother died in 1944 and his mother died the year after that, he was a middle-aged virgin living alone on a farm at Plainstead, Wisconsin. Gein visited the local graveyard where he dug up women's bodies and removed their facial skin. He made masks from these, keeping the skin soft with motor car oil. In

1954, local resident 54-year-old Mary Hogan disappeared, and in 1957 elderly Bernice Worden also vanished. While making their enquiries the police called at Gein's farm where they found the decapitated body of Bernice in the barn, strung up and gutted like a slaughtered buck. In the house they found several masks made of human skin. Gein had also made lampshades and other articles from human skin. The fridge was stocked with intestines. Ed Gein was found fit to stand trial, and was declared guilty but insane. He was committed to a state hospital.

Jeffrey Dahmer, the Milwaukee serial killer who murdered eleven young men, ate the muscles of his victims. During an interview, FBI agent Robert Ressler asked Dahmer if he ate the flesh raw and Dahmer answered: 'Mr Ressler, I'm not that sick. I cooked it first.'

Stewart Wilken was not as sophisticated as Dahmer. He ate the nipples and flesh of his victim there and then, at the crime scene. He said he was still filled with lust after he had strangled and sodomised his victim and he therefore stuck the knife into her vagina and ripped open her flesh. It was an act of substituted penetration. He mutilated the breasts and ate the nipples as a symbolic action, 'to get to the missing mother's milk'.

ANTONIE WESSELS & JEAN-PIERRE HAVENGA

1991

Edward Perlmutter was an American traveller who hitch-hiked across Africa in 1991. He had an agreement with his parents that he would phone them once a week to let them know exactly where he was and where he was going. When his parents had not heard from their son for two weeks, they contacted the Knysna police, for this was the last place Edward had told them he was going to. Knysna is a quaint coastal town situated on the border of the Western and Eastern Cape provinces, lying on a seaside lake. It is backed on the landward side by thousands of hectares of indigenous forest.

A case of a missing person was opened by Warrant Officer Lawrence Oliver, who placed Edward's photograph in the newspaper. A short while later, Oliver was contacted by a Mr and Mrs Baxter from Cape Town. They had recognised Edward's photograph and told Oliver that during October 1991 they had walked the Millwood trail in the Knysna forest and that Edward had joined up with them. They all slept in the Millwood House and the following morning Edward said that he would go ahead and wait for the couple at the end of the trail. When the Baxters reached the end of the trail, there was no sign of Edward. They assumed that he had moved on without them.

Oliver organised a search party of as many policemen as he could muster and police dogs were also brought in. The area they had to cover was 20 square kilometres of dense Knysna forest – a daunting task. Only when they were covering the trail for the fourth time did they pick up the scent of a decomposing body. Had the wind not been blowing in their direction they might never have found it. In the dense bush about 12 metres off the trail, Oliver discovered Edward's decomposed body. His hands were tied behind his back, his skull was fractured and it was obvious that his throat had been cut. Twigs and branches were neatly packed over his body in a diagonal pattern. According to the pathologist's report, Edward Perlmutter died on 25 October 1991.

Oliver made enquiries in the area and foresters told him that they had noticed two men in the vicinity who did not seem to fit in. Both men wore black clothing. Mr and Mrs Baxter confirmed that they had also seen the men who had, in fact, stolen food from them at Millwood House the evening before Edward's disappearance.

Oliver made enquiries in Knysna in an attempt to trace the two men, but found himself at a dead end. Eventually he decided to contact the Satanist high priest in Knysna, who was known to the police, since both the men he was looking for had been wearing black clothing and might conceivably be Satanists. Oliver's hunch paid off. The high priest confirmed that both men had stayed with him after Perlmutter's murder. One of them called himself Norris and said he was a bouncer, but the priest was sure that they were using false names. They had stolen money from him. The priest told Oliver that both men had worn T-shirts with the words 'Sand Pebbles Disco' on them.

Oliver traced a woman in neighbouring Belvedere, who confirmed that the men had stayed with her for a short while. He also tracked down a man who lived on a farm between Plettenberg Bay and Knysna who had taken the two men in. They left behind at the farm a spool of film which belonged to Edward Perlmutter. The men had stolen from all the people with whom they had stayed.

Oliver was convinced that these men were his suspects. He assembled all the people who had had anything to do with the men and they drew up identikits. One of the men was tall and older than the other who was smaller and a juvenile.

By chance, Oliver read a newspaper report of the attempted murder of Clive Newman, a gay man from Port Elizabeth. He had been found in the dunes at Blue Water Bay. His hands had been tied with his tie and his throat had been cut, but he survived. Newman's car – a maroon Monza – had been stolen. Oliver phoned Warrant Officer Whale of the Port Elizabeth Murder and Robbery Unit who was investigating the case. They met and came to the conclusion that there were so many similarities between the cases that they should work together.

In the mean time Oliver had established that Sand Pebbles was a club on the Durban Bluff. When Oliver phoned the owner he confirmed that a person named Norris worked as his bouncer, but said that Norris had not left Durban.

Oliver, Whale and the Knysna commander, Captain Zeelie, went to Durban to look for leads. If their suspect was not Norris then they surmised that he must have frequented the Sand Pebbles club. They established that all the club's bouncers were hired from Ford's Gym. The owner of Ford's Gym recognised the suspect from the identikits, but told Oliver that he would not show his face in Durban, since the Child Protection Unit was looking for him.

Oliver, Whale and Zeelie met officers from the Child Protection Unit who took one look at the identikits and identified the suspects as 30-year-old Antonie Louwrens Johannes Wessels and his lover, Jean-Pierre Havenga, who was sixteen years old and thus under age. The Child Protection Unit was looking for Wessels because of his relationship with the under age Havenga. Wessels was in trouble with the local mafia as well and it was most unlikely that he would return to Durban. The detectives at the Child Protection Unit gave Oliver the name of a friend of Wessels who lived in Buccleuch, Johannesburg.

The three detectives went to Johannesburg. They clocked in at the Brixton Murder and Robbery Unit where they posted a lookout for Clive Newman's Monza. Captain Piet Byleveld of Brixton assisted them. They kept surveillance on the house in

Buccleuch and when the owner returned home they confronted him. He acknowledged that he knew Wessels and told the police that he was probably in Johannesburg, as a petrol card had been stolen from his attaché case and Wessels knew where he kept his attaché case. The detectives contacted the bank concerned and established that Wessels had used the petrol card on the way to the Kruger National Park. He had changed the number plates of the vehicle. A new lookout for a maroon Monza with false plates was posted. The bank kept the detectives informed about the locations where Wessels had stopped for petrol, but they were always a week behind.

One night the detectives got a call from the Boksburg Flying Squad who had spotted the Monza parked outside the Masonic hotel. The detectives asked the Flying Squad to keep the car under surveillance, warning them that the suspects were to be considered dangerous. They left for Boksburg immediately. When they arrived the Flying Squad arrested Wessels and Havenga. The two suspects were taken to the Boksburg police station for interrogation.

Oliver asked Wessels whose car he was driving and he answered that it belonged to a friend. He was clearly under the impression that he was being arrested only in connection with the stolen car. When Oliver informed him that he was from Knysna and that he had been on his trail for weeks, Wessels' expression changed and he refused to talk. Oliver went into the next room where Havenga was being held and confronted him. He broke down and told Oliver that the firearm of a man they had murdered in Pretoria was under the seat of the car.

Oliver and Byleveld confronted Wessels once more and he told them that apart from killing Edward Perlmutter and Clive Newman (Wessels did not know that Newman had survived), they had murdered 15-year-old David Sehmels in the Drakensberg, and Jacobus Petrus Joubert, a retired prison warder in Pretoria.

David Sehmels lost his parents when he was a young child. After his adoptive parents died he was placed in the care of several foster families. He ended up in the Excelsior Place of Safety for Juveniles, where he met Jean-Pierre Havenga. Both David and

Jean-Pierre ran away from Excelsior to join Wessels. David was murdered at Giant's Castle in the Drakensberg Mountains. The detectives could not understand the motive for David's murder but Wessels later told them that he killed him because he became a liability. Wessels apparently went back to David's body and cut off a piece of his thigh, which they ate. He said they did this only because they were very hungry.

Wessels said that he killed Joubert because Joubert 'came on' to Havenga. They had met Joubert in a gay pub and he took both of them to his home, but when he showed an interest in Havenga, Wessels became enraged and killed him. Wessels and Havenga had painted the words 'fuck the whites' on a wall in Joubert's house in an attempt to confuse the police. They said that they had left the Monza at a taxi rank in Johannesburg, full of petrol and with the doors unlocked and the keys in the ignition, hoping that it would be stolen and that the thief would be accused of Newman's murder. But when no one had stolen the car after a week, Wessels and Havenga took it back again. Wessels said that he had killed Newman because he paid too much attention to Havenga.

Wessels said that his mother had told him that his natural father and namesake had been a murderer. Antonie Louwrens Wessels senior had apparently killed 66-year-old Barney Uronowsky and his 55-year-old wife Fanny on their smallholding in Turffontein in 1962. Wessels claimed that his stepfather and stepbrother abused him sexually during his adolescence and that his mother believed in poltergeists and spiritualism.

The trial took place in Cape Town in December 1992. Mr Justice Gerald Friedman sentenced Wessels to death and Havenga to twenty-five years in prison. Wessels threatened to kill one fellow convict a day if he was separated from Havenga. In 1994 the death sentence was abolished and both men are still in prison. Wessels had a criminal record for stealing five rand worth of pills from a pharmacy, before he embarked on his career as a killer. He maintained that he killed to protect Havenga.

Wessels and Havenga were split up after their convictions.

Havenga turned to religion and Wessels is reportedly still interested in the occult.

Notes

Wessels and Havenga were not the only gay couple to commit serial murder in South Africa. In 1996 John Frank Brown and Jacques Coetzee (page 193), a deadly duo who preyed on gay men, were arrested. They had a tally of five male victims and were particularly brutal in their attacks.

Wessels obviously did not have a positive male role model with whom to identify. If a child's natural father is absent or abuses the boy in any manner, he still has the opportunity to form an attachment to a male relative, teacher, etc, but after the age of twelve to thirteen years it is virtually impossible to help a young boy who has murderous fantasies. Besides, who could he tell about them? Those who work closely with children need to be sensitive towards those who have problems and encourage them to talk about them.

MOSES MOKGETI

West Rand, 1991-93

Some time during May 1993, a four-year-old girl and two friends, two-year-old Rearabetswe Kgoleng and four-year-old Dinton Isaac Nkwe, were playing in the streets of Mohklaheng, a township outside Randfontein. A man approached them and offered to buy them sweets from a spaza shop. But instead he took them to a bluegum forest and there he tortured, raped and murdered Rearabetswe and Dinton.

During the trial of Moses Mokgeti, the surviving four-year-old girl told how Mokgeti had raped and tortured the children and pulled out their teeth with pliers. He then strangled the three children, laid their bodies side by side and covered them with dense vegetation. The four-year-old, however, was not dead. She dug herself out and was found the next morning, naked and bleeding, alongside a road. She was taken home. Her parents and her community had been searching for her all night, as she was not the first child to have disappeared from the community in recent years.

The little girl pointed out the scene where the crimes took place and the police dug up the remains of six children, including those of Rearabetswe and Dinton. Some of the bodies were badly decomposed, but eventually seven-year-old Julia Sithole and eight-year-old Gladnest Senoedi were identified. It is believed that the other bodies were those of Shirley Saulus and ten-year-old Robert Kgosimang. Their bodies had also been mutilated. Several more skulls were found, but could not be identified.

Robert and Gladnest had disappeared in the same township on 29 August 1991. Mokgeti, an appliance repairman, had visited Robert's home that afternoon to repair the television. He was a regular visitor at the house. A month earlier he had raped a nine-year-old girl after buying her sweets and luring her away. Mokgeti had been arrested in connection with this rape, but escaped from custody. Apart from the rape, Mokgeti was also found guilty of sexually molesting a 17-year-old girl.

When Mokgeti was arrested in neighbouring Carletonville, he told Warrant Officer Sampie Venter of the East Rand Murder and Robbery Unit that he had mutilated the children and removed the body parts for *muti* purposes. He sold their genitals and hearts and livers. He would go back to the crime scene the day after the murder to harvest the body parts and he was paid R300 for each part.

Not much is known about Mokgeti. He had a common law wife and two children and he lived with his parents. He was a handyman who had built his own helicopter, which could actually fly, although he only completed grade 7 at school.

Mr Justice M J Strydom sentenced Mokgeti to life for the murder of each of the six children and to twelve years for raping the young girl and six years for her attempted murder.

Notes

As in the case of Phillip Mogoso (page 110), had it not been for the fact that a victim escaped to tell her story, Mokgeti would have been classified as a *muti* killer and not a serial killer. In Africa, traditional doctors use herbs as medicine and this is called *muti*. Certain witchdoctors use body parts as medicine. A *muti* killer is someone who harvests body parts for the witchdoctor. The fact that Mokgeti raped his victims and mutilated them indicated that he did not kill them for financial gain only, but also for his own pleasure. This makes him a serial killer who made an extra profit out of the murders. The main motive was not financial profit, but pleasure.

Although serial killers' main motive is psychological gain and pleasure, some of them profit financially from the murders by stealing from their victims or, as in the case of Mokgeti, selling body parts. However, not all *muti* killers are serial killers.

THE CAPE TOWN PROSTITUTE KILLER

1992-96

Prostitutes are easy prey for serial killers, because they go anywhere with anyone. When they do become victims of serial killers, the profiler has to decide whether they were selected because of their profession – which would classify the killer as mission-motivated – or whether they were just easily available.

During early 1996 a serial killer terrorised the prostitutes of Cape Town, specifically those doing business along the Voortrekker Road strip. This is a long main road, running through the centre of a number of middle-class suburbs. It is lined with bars, shops and businesses and the side streets are mostly residential.

Sergeant Piet Viljoen of the Peninsula Murder and Robbery Unit was initially in charge of the case. By February 1996 he had concluded that someone was targeting the local prostitutes. These women were streetwise and would have no qualms about pulling a knife on a customer if they suspected that they were being taken for a ride. They would not easily leave their territories, as that would mean missing out on quick tricks. But despite this, their bodies were found on remote farm roads about 50 kilometres from their beats.

Viljoen assembled a task team to assist him with the investigation. He also requested that all previous dockets of prostitute murders in the Peninsula be forwarded to him. Sixteen similar cases were identified, dating back to 1992. Viljoen and his team visited the crime scenes and spoke to relatives and acquaintances of the victims. Together, the team reconstructed the basis of the killer's modus operandi.

The killer would wait for a rainy day and then, during the afternoon, drive out to the farm roads to search for a safe location to dump the body of his potential victim. Viljoen and his team arrived at this deduction because there was no way the killer could have found those particular places on a dark night. He must have preselected the spots during the daylight hours.

The killer would then cruise the Voortrekker strip in his vehicle that same night, pick up his victim and park his car in a parking lot. Since it was raining, no one would pay much attention to what might be happening in a parked car. He would instruct his victim to undress and would then hit her in the face with his fist. All the victims had assault wounds on their jaws. The stunned victim would fall forward and the killer would pull her over on to his lap and strangle her. Once she was dead, he would drive out to his preselected spot and dump her body. The rain would wash away his tyre tracks.

This killer tried to 'stage' the crime scenes in an attempt to prevent the detectives from linking them to one murderer. Sometimes he half buried his victims and sometimes he posed them as if they had been raped. No semen was found and there were no signs of forced penetration, which indicated that the killer was probably impotent. The victims were scattered all over the Peninsula, as the killer tried not to succumb to a pattern of habit. But he made a mistake by deliberately trying to throw the police off track, for this very fact became his signature. Although the locations were dispersed, he ran out of ideas and repeated previous attempts at staging, which immediately linked the scenes.

One victim, Gloria, was found naked with a Coke bottle inserted into her vagina. Her body was very decomposed when it was eventually discovered.

Detectives and prostitutes worked together to try to solve the case. As in the case of Cornelius Burger (page 63), detectives protected the prostitutes. The prostitutes cooperated by giving

174

their fingerprints to Sergeant Viljoen and his team and having their photographs taken. This would help with identification of bodies. Posters with emergency telephone numbers were posted on all the streets and prostitutes and pimps wrote down the registration numbers of the vehicles that picked them up.

Information flowed in at a steady rate. One prostitute told Viljoen of a customer who had a fantasy about inserting a Coke bottle into a woman's private parts. He was an elderly unemployed man who drove a blue truck. He was mostly impotent and could get an erection only if the woman had a lot of patience with him. This corresponded with information that a man fitting the description and driving a blue truck had been seen in the vicinity where Gloria's body was found, and on the day she went missing.

It did not take Viljoen long to identifiy the suspect. He lived in a caravan in the suburb of Parow, just off the Voortrekker Road strip. Viljoen interviewed his ex-wife who told him of her ex-husband's habit of disappearing for hours without being able to explain where he had been. She said he would claim to have had blackouts and that he then suffered from amnesia. He had been admitted to the Tygerberg Hospital for this problem. Viljoen checked the hospital records and found that the suspect had been booked in for 'amnesia' the day after Gloria was murdered. The doctors did tests but could find nothing wrong with him; it seemed to them that he had faked the symptoms of amnesia.

When the suspect was brought in for questioning in April 1996 he played games with the detectives, telling Viljoen that he could have killed the women, but that he had no memory of it. He said it would be up to the detectives to prove his guilt. His vehicle was searched and although the fingerprints of one of the murdered women were found, as well as a few pieces of cheap jewellery, this was not enough evidence to secure a conviction.

The suspect was released but kept under surveillance. Unfortunately he sometimes managed to give the detectives the slip – and then another body would be found. Eventually the police did not have enough manpower to keep him under full-time surveillance. Viljoen and his team were called out to more crime scenes, but this time the victims were not prostitutes; they were domestic workers. The killer had realised that it had become too difficult for him to pick up prostitutes.

Viljoen was transferred and the case was handed over to Inspector George Lochner who diligently continued with the investigation.

Eventually the suspect made a bad mistake. He phoned the local police radio control room on 21 June 1996, threatening that as soon as his truck was in working order, more women would be killed. The conversation was taped and the voice matched that of the suspect. He was taken into custody by Lochner. By this time nineteen murders were included in the investigation. The suspect was sent to the Valkenberg Psychiatric Hospital for observation and then transferred to Pollsmoor Prison as an awaiting trial prisoner. Coincidentally, in prison he became a friend of Avzal Simons, the man who was arrested for the Station Strangler killings (page 122).

The suspect often threw tantrums, hired and fired his legal team, and refused to appear in court. His case was remanded every time.

Eventually in September 1997, the Attorney General of the Western Cape decided that there was not enough evidence to formally charge the suspect with murder. An inquest into the deaths of the women was held and the case was closed. The suspect was a free man.

In the mean time, another prostitute killer struck in the Western Cape, but as this was an ongoing investigation at the time of going to press, no details can be released. Now and then another murdered prostitute was found, with evidence of the same signature as the Cape Town Prostitute Killer. The police simply do not have enough manpower to keep this man under constant surveillance and, moreover, it would be an infringement of his rights. Most prostitutes in the area know his name and face.

Lochner has since retired.

Notes

During interrogation the suspect revealed that he had shared his mother's bed until he was sixteen. This was also the age, he alleged, when he first had sex with an older woman who had seduced him. His father had died and his mother had many young boyfriends, which upset him terribly. He did not have a steady job and after his divorce he lived in his caravan which was parked outside a boarding house. His ex-wife paid for his meals at the boarding house. He regarded his mother as a whore and felt severely rejected by her behaviour. His mother was involved in the occult and died when he was an adult.

The suspect's ex-wife told the detectives that he had contracted a venereal disease. One can therefore suppose that he was mission-orientated, set on taking out his hatred for his mother on the prostitutes. He was also impotent and blamed the prostitutes for the fact that he had contracted a venereal disease.

'Staging' is the term used to describe a crime scene when the criminal has tried to introduce changes in order to mislead the police. This is usually a mistake, as the police have many hours in which to process a crime scene and there are many of them present. Someone will be sure to notice something out of place or out of sequence.

Unfortunately, the family of a victim may also be responsible for changing the crime scene. In sexually related murders in particular, victims may be found in degrading and shocking circumstances and family members try to cover the victims, thereby disturbing the crime scene. It is understandable that the family would not want strangers – the police – to see their loved ones in such positions, but the police are accustomed to this and will think no less of the victim for it. A pristine crime scene gives the police a better chance of identifying the criminal.

In the 1980s an unknown killer, dubbed 'The Bergie Killer' murdered thirteen vagrants within a two kilometre radius of the Caledon Square Police Station in central Cape Town. All the victims were killed on Thursday evenings at point blank range with a .22 calibre firearm. Vagrants in Cape Town are called 'Bergies', a reference to destitute people who live in the veld on Table Mountain. No one was arrested and a principal suspect is known to have fled the country.

Like the case of the prostitute killer, these murders seem to have been mission-orientated, and both cases remain unsolved.

NORMAN PIETER HOBKIRK

Johannesburg, 1992-97

Pyromania is a rare sexual disorder in which a person is sexually stimulated by fire. In 1997 there were two overlapping cases of pyromania in Johannesburg and Pretoria, where the perpetrators were not only sexually stimulated by fire, but also set their victims on fire.

During the early hours of the morning of Saturday 30 August 1997, 35-year-old William Crichton walked across a park in Bertrams, a sub-economic suburb of Johannesburg, on his way home. Crichton, a divorcée who lived with his parents, was an alcoholic. He worked at a local hardware store and was due to receive his pay later that Saturday. Crichton had almost crossed the park when he was approached by a young man. They had a short discussion, after which after the young man attacked Crichton with a brick. He was sexually molested and his attacker then strangled him with a belt. The attacker dragged an abandoned mattress on to Crichton and set it alight. He then left the scene. Children discovered Crichton's almost completely burnt body underneath the burnt mattress the following day. His pants and underpants had been torn off and his shoes and wallet were missing. His spectacles, a brick and a cigarette lighter were found on the scene.

Many of the local residents watched as the police processed the scene. Captain Mike van Aardt, the investigating officer from the Jeppe Detective Unit, had no idea that his suspect was among the crowd. And he did not know that the suspect lived across the park and had watched the body burn from his veranda.

Three days later, during the early hours of Wednesday 3 September 1997, 69-year-old Clarence Albert Pretorius stepped out of his ground floor unit in the Bertrams Retirement Village to smoke a cigarette. He had problems sleeping and would often stand outside in the early morning having a cigarette. The flick of his lighter attracted the attention of a young man lurking in the grounds. He approached Pretorius and struck up a conversation. Pretorius knew the young man because his girlfriend lived with her mother in the Retirement Village. The young man had helped him with an errand a few days before.

The last thing Clarence Pretorius expected was that the young man would suddenly attack him with a brick. He ran towards his unit but his assailant followed and inside the room he was brutally attacked and then his throat was slit with a knife. He was also sexually molested. The assailant set the mattress alight and threw a duvet cover over Pretorius, which he also set alight before he left the scene. Pretorius' half-burnt body was discovered the next day. His pants and underpants had been torn off. A shoe found outside the apartment and blood splattered on the ground told Van Aardt where the attack had originated. The Retirement Village was located opposite the park where William Crichton had been killed three days before.

The investigation proved a difficult one for Van Aardt. He knew the residents of Bertrams well and realised that it was unlikely that anyone would come forward with information. According to Van Aardt, many of the people who lived in Bertrams were involved in crime in one way or another, and his concern deepened when a profiler from the South African Police Service told him that another murder could be expected soon if the killer was not apprehended. Van Aardt activated all his informers in the area.

Twenty-four days later, on 27 September 1997, middle-aged Alexander Willem Landsberg was enjoying a drink in a bar in Pretoria when he was approached by a scrawny young man who asked him for a drink. Landsberg bought the drink and talked to the young man. When the young man told Landsberg that he had no place to stay, Landsberg invited him to his Wespark apartment. He offered the young man a bath and then had one himself. Sexual intimacy took place between the two men. The young man then took a knife from the kitchen and stabbed Landsberg forty-seven times. He stole some household goods, loaded Landsberg's dog into Landsberg's bakkie and set the apartment alight. When the police arrived on the scene they discovered the mutilated and burnt body inside. Amongst the rubble were several sex toys and pornography.

A detective pressed the redial button on the phone and it was answered by a Mrs Anna-Marie Venter, who lived in Kimberley in the Northern Cape. She told the detective that her son, 24-year-old Jan Adriaan van der Westhuizen, had phoned her earlier and told her that he had done something terrible.

Van der Westhuizen drove to his mother's house that night and asked her to look after the dog. He then went to Johannesburg for a few days before leaving for Durban. Detectives of the Durban Murder and Robbery Unit arrested Van der Westhuizen soon after his arrival at a beachfront hotel and he was escorted back to Pretoria. He confessed to the murder, saying that Landsberg had forced him into sex. He sold the stolen goods to pay for petrol and abandoned the bakkie.

Van der Westhuizen was also interrogated by Van Aardt to try to establish a possible connection with the two Bertrams murders. It seemed likely that Van der Westhuizen had also committed these murders, as there were many similarities, especially between the murders of Landsberg and Pretorius. Van der Westhuizen steadfastly denied that he was involved in the Bertrams murders.

Van Aardt was highly frustrated by his denial, especially since Van der Westhuizen fitted the profile that had been drawn up of the pyromaniac. As predicted in the profile, Van der Westhuizen had scars on his head and hands where he had previously set himself on fire. He also had an extensive criminal record and had started a blaze in the Kimberley prison. He escaped when he was admitted to hospital suffering from burns.

Van der Westhuizen was an old hand at escaping from custody and managed to escape again from the police cells in Pretoria West. He hitch-hiked to Johannesburg and was picked up on the way by a 25-year-old motorist. Van der Westhuizen persuaded the man to give him a job and the man gave him his business card and asked him to phone him the following day. Later that evening the motorist's father was reading aloud a newspaper report about Van der Westhuizen's escape from custody. The man froze when he realised that he had picked up Jan Adriaan van der Westhuizen. He contacted the police and together they set a trap for Van der Westhuizen, who was rearrested.

Van der Westhuizen was again questioned by Van Aardt and he again denied involvement in the two Bertrams murders. Van Aardt reasoned that he might be telling the truth. Van der Westhuizen knew that he would probably receive a life sentence for the Landsberg murder, and that he would have nothing to lose if he confessed to the others as well. The fact that he did not confess indicated to Van Aardt that there might be another pyromaniac on the loose. The thought chilled him, but he diligently kept digging for information in Bertrams.

Eventually, Van Aardt's hard work paid off. In June 1998 an informer told him of a man who had been murdered in 1992 in a park opposite the one where William Crichton was killed. The male victim had been attacked with a brick and stabbed to death with a broken bottle. His pants had been removed, but there was no fire. Van Aardt's informer said that a certain Norman Pieter Hobkirk had committed that murder, but that no one knew about it. Van Aardt searched for the murder docket and found it lodged at his unit in Jeppe. The suspect had not been traced and the case had remained open. A fingerprint on a piece of broken bottle-neck and a bloodied footprint had been collected from the scene as evidence.

Van Aardt began to trace Norman Hobkirk through state channels and found out that he lived with his parents at Carr

House, the apartment block right opposite the two parks. He made enquiries and discovered that Hobkirk had been sentenced to a prison term of eight years for manslaughter and theft shortly after Pretorius' murder. Hobkirk's fingerprints matched the ones found on the bottleneck.

Van Aardt traced 25-year-old Hobkirk to Diepkloof prison and decided to pay him a visit. Hobkirk told him that in 1992 he and a friend were walking through a storm water drain in the park opposite the one where Crichton was killed when they came upon a group of men who accosted them. They managed to get away, but Hobkirk returned later to find one of the men who had accosted them on his own. He picked up a stick and beat him. He left the man in the ditch and phoned the police himself. The man had died of his injuries. In prison, Hobkirk was trying to qualify as a welder. He told Van Aardt that the blue flame of a welding iron held a particular attraction for him.

Van Aardt interrogated Hobkirk about the Bertrams murders. At first he denied all knowledge of them. Eventually when he was confronted with the evidence of the 1992 murder he confessed to it. When he realised that he would spend his life in prison for committing this murder, he confessed to the others as well. He told Van Aardt in detail what had happened on the nights of the murders. He had watched William Crichton burn from his veranda and the next morning he had actually stood next to the police photographer observing the police processing the crime scene.

In September 2000 Hobkirk was charged with the three murders. He appeared before Mr Justice Nigel Willis in the Johannesburg High Court. Advocate Don Thinane acted for the defence and Advocate Mahlala acted on behalf of the State. Hobkirk denied setting the fires. He said he had killed Crichton but that vagrants must have placed the mattress on top of him. Van Aardt had however found a witness who had seen Hobkirk drag the mattress on to Crichton. In the case of Pretorius, Hobkirk alleged that a candle had accidentally fallen over, but an arson expert, Mr Breyten Vuuren, testified there was no evidence of a candle and that two fires were in fact set – one on the bed and another on the duvet covering Pretorius' body. Persons suffering from sexual disorders such as pyromania are typically unlikely to admit to their involvement.

Hobkirk was sentenced to two life sentences for the murders of William Crichton and Clarence Pretorius and to a twenty-year sentence for the murder of the unidentified victim in 1992.

Notes

Pyromanic serial killers are very rare. A typical profile would indicate a male of about twenty-five years. In Hobkirk's case, as well as Van der Westhuizen's (although the latter killed only one person), the murders had the characteristics of a disorganised serial killer, indicating that they happened spontaneously, that the killer did not use a vehicle and that he lived within a one kilometre radius of the murder scene. He would live on his own or with one or both of his parents. He would have been a juvenile delinquent and have a low level of education. He would be a loner and nocturnal in habit. He would have unhygienic habits, would skulk and avoid eye contact. He would be unable to form long-term relationships with others and would feel himself isolated from human contact. Since the victims in these cases were male, the profile specified that the suspect would probably have spent time in reformatories or prison where he was sexually molested. He would be passive, lazy and have a low frustration tolerance, which would lead to aggressive temper tantrums. He would also often take his anger out on himself, by physical self-mutilation. He would have a fascination for fire.

Hobkirk fitted the profile perfectly. He grew up in a dys-functional family, with an alcoholic father, who had been to prison, and a domineering mother. His father and cousins had molested him sexually as a boy. Hobkirk often got into trouble for petty theft. He once set a veld fire and watched as the fire brigade extinguished it. He also set things on fire in big drums.

When he was seven years old, the Welfare Department removed him from his parents and he was sent to an orphanage. He attended an industrial school from grade 8 and at the age of seventeen he was sent to a reformatory in Cape Town. As a young adult he spent three and a half years in Leeuwkop prison for theft. He was sexually abused by fellow learners and inmates in these institutions and would often cut himself with a blade.

Hobkirk's case typically illustrates the pattern of an abused child who grew up unprotected and unloved by his family. He became introverted and as a child he would take his anger out on himself. Physical pain, such as cutting oneself with a blade, relieves emotional pain. He was too young and too small to direct his anger against others.

When he was finally released from prison he felt that the only way he could relieve his anger was to project it on to vulnerable victims. As an adult, Hobkirk was strong enough to overpower other men. His victims were vulnerable in the sense that they were either intoxicated or too old to defend themselves. Although Hobkirk alleged that his victims approached him for sex and that this caused him to lose his temper, there was no evidence that any of the men he killed had homosexual tendencies. The victims did nothing to antagonise Hobkirk, they were simply in the wrong place at the wrong time. He did not plan the murders; he happened to come upon the victims and saw his chance to avenge his anger and pain.

Hobkirk was sexually stimulated by the sight of fire. Fire has an ancient hypnotic effect and represents power. Typically a pyromaniac will masturbate while watching the fire. No traces of semen were found on the crime scenes for it would have been burnt. It is possible that semen might have been spilled on the bed in Pretorius' room and that was why the bed and the duvet were set on fire.

Jan Adriaan van der Westhuizen's life had followed the same pattern as Hobkirk's. They could have been brothers. Both men liked to hitch-hike and were often picked up by motorists – mostly by men who would have thought it safe to pick up a young man, never suspecting that they were giving a ride to a serial killer.

David Berkowitz, the 'Son of Sam' serial killer who tallied fourteen victims between 1976 and 1977 in New York, set more than 1 400 fires in his life. He was twenty-five years old when he was arrested and sentenced to 365 years in prison.

CHRISTIAAN DE WET

East Rand, 1993-94

Eight-year-old Ewa Nosal, a pretty blonde child, phoned her mother Martha from their home in Goudnip Street, Boksburg, at about half past one on the afternoon of 26 January 1994. Ewa had taken the bus home from school that day and, as was her habit, she collected the mail from the post office before she walked the few blocks to her house. She must have noticed a red car parked in front of the house when she arrived, but she went inside and locked the front door as her parents had taught her.

Ewa, her 12-year-old sister Beata and their parents had emigrated to South Africa three years earlier from Poland. On this particular afternoon Ewa was excited because in the mail was a slip indicating that a parcel was awaiting collection at the post office. The parcel was from Poland, and Ewa knew there would be a surprise in it for her. So she phoned her mother and asked her if she would collect the parcel on her way home.

Martha told her daughter that she would not be able to pick up the parcel that day and asked her to phone her father, Richard. Ewa phoned her father at two o'clock but he was unavailable. However, at two minutes past two he phoned her back. He listened to her request and told her that he would pick up the parcel the following day. At about half past two Martha phoned Ewa back and told her she would be able to fetch the parcel that afternoon after all. Ewa was very excited about this. That was the last time her parents spoke to her.

At a quarter to three, a mere fifteen minutes after Ewa had

spoken to her mother, Beata arrived home from school. As she approached the house she noticed immediately that something was wrong. The front door, the window next to the front door and the back door were open. Ewa's school blazer was lying next to the front door where she always dropped it, but Ewa was nowhere to be found. Beata searched the house, but could not find her sister. She phoned her father and he arrived home at half past three.

He phoned the Child Protection Unit and the first detective arrived on the scene at ten minutes past four. Martha had also rushed home. The detective called the radio control room, who alerted all police vehicles in the area. But none of them could know that Ewa was already dead.

Fingerprint and crime scene experts arrived at the house, but no evidence was found. Richard explained to the detectives that the window next to the front door was open, because Ewa would first have spoken to the stranger through the window as her parents had taught her. He could not understand why she had opened the door.

The commander of the Child Protection Unit, Captain Visser, arrived at six o'clock and the area commander, Colonel Schwartz, arrived half an hour later. Policemen were dispatched to search the neighbourhood and make enquiries. Neighbourhood children told the detectives that they had seen a red car in front of the house. A friend of Ewa's added that he had noticed a red car following the bus on their way home. But the car did not continue following the bus after Ewa had alighted.

Ewa's disappearance was broadcast on radio.

The following day the search was extended to the park and the wetland in the area. The disappearance of the eight-year-old was also broadcast on national television news that evening.

On the second day, 28 January, when Ewa had still not been found, 280 policemen, eleven police dogs and one helicopter were deployed to continue the search. The case was transferred to Captain Frans van Niekerk of the East Rand Murder and Robbery Unit. Members of the police water wing searched all the dams and underwater sewerage systems in the area.

The investigation intensified and many leads were followed up by Van Niekerk and his team. Ewa's parents had posters printed and these were distributed throughout Boksburg. Newspapers and magazines carried the news of Ewa's disappearance and published her photograph, but to no avail. Her father offered a reward of R200 000 and the police added another R50 000 for anyone with information about the missing child. Amidst the media hype, Van Niekerk worked according to a plan. He asked for dockets of all similar cases to be forwarded to him and checked through the records of known paedophiles in the area.

One docket caught Van Niekerk's attention. Seven months before Ewa's disappearance, on 13 May 1993, 12-year-old Helena de Villiers of Boksburg was abducted from her school. Her body was found under a pile of stones at the Ginderville Dam. She had been raped and stoned to death. Helena and Ewa resembled each other in appearance and to Van Niekerk the modus operandi seemed similar. No suspect had been arrested in Helena's case.

Van Niekerk's research into known paedophiles in the area paid off. This was an unofficial list kept by the Child Protection Unit of people who had been convicted of crimes against children. He worked diligently through the list, bringing suspects in for questioning. One suspect was 25-year-old Christiaan de Wet. He had a record for indecently assaulting a child, but denied having anything to do with the murders. De Wet was engaged to be married and managed to convince Van Niekerk that he was not a paedophile. Van Niekerk let him go, but he had a nagging feeling he was on the right track. He decided to follow his intuition and obtained a search warrant for De Wet's house which was close to the Ginderville Dam.

During the search, De Wet broke down and confessed to both murders.

Some weeks afterwards Ewa's decomposed body was discovered hidden in the reeds at the dam in the neighbouring town of Benoni. She had been raped and strangled to death.

De Wet was charged but the case was postponed. While he was awaiting trial at Diepkloof prison he arranged with his fiancée and two other women to help him escape. Van Niekerk got wind of this and arrested him during the escape attempt. De Wet was taken back to the cells where he committed suicide that night.

Notes

The United Kingdom has a policy whereby paedophiles are identified to the community in order to protect children. There is no official record of paedophiles in South Africa. After their release from prison no tabs are kept on their whereabouts. Children's rights are protected by the Constitution and the South African Police Service has a 24-hour Childline to which anyone can report a crime against a child.

The amount of attention paid to Ewa's disappearance was exceptional. The Child Protection Unit has since been incorporated into the Domestic Violence and Child Protection Unit. The integrated unit is seriously understaffed and its detectives now have responsibility for all cases of domestic violence as well as crimes against children. But although they are understaffed, they are well trained and dedicated.

Missing persons can be reported to any police station and there is no waiting period before the police initiate an investigation. In the United States of America there is a Missing Children's Bureau, but there is no differentiation between missing children and missing adults in South Africa. There is also a national Crime Stop number (0800 11 12 13) to which any crime or missing person can be reported.

Statistics show that missing children are usually murdered within twenty-four hours of abduction. This includes cases where family members are responsible for kidnapping the child.

During 1988 and 1989 a Pretoria resident named Gert van

Rooyen and his girlfriend Joey Haarhoff abducted six young girls, mostly in the Gauteng province. The girls were Anne-Marie Wapenaar, Odette Boucher, Tracey-Lee Scott-Crosley, Fiona Harvey, Joan Horn and Yolanda Wessels. Yolanda was Haarhoff's niece, but no one suspected her of anything untoward at the time of Yolanda's disappearance. A huge investigation was launched into the abductions.

On 11 January 1990 Haarhoff spotted teenager Joan Booysen waiting for a bus on Church Square in Pretoria and offered her a lift. Joan later said that her parents had warned her against accepting lifts from strange men, but no one warned her against someone who looked like a friendly granny. She got into Haarhoff's car and Haarhoff told her she had to go first to her brother's house before she dropped Joan off at school.

Van Rooyen and Haarhoff locked Joan in a cupboard at his house at 227 Malherbe Street, Capitol Park, Pretoria. They then went out. Joan managed to escape and the police were alerted. Van Rooyen and Haarhoff left for Durban, but when they returned the police were waiting for them. Unfortunately Van Rooyen spotted the police and a car chase ensued. Van Rooyen stopped his car and shot and killed Joey before turning the gun on himself. The police found evidence that some of the missing girls had been in the house. The house was subsequently razed and several excavations were made on the property, but no bodies were found.

Although it seems as if the answer to the disappearance of the six girls was lost with Van Rooyen's death, the case is still under investigation and new leads as to the girls' whereabouts are still being followed up. Captain Carel Cornelius is the investigating officer. The families of Ewa Nosal and Helena de Villiers may be able to come to terms with the fate of their beloved daughters, but the parents of the six missing girls are still hoping that their daughters will be found, whether dead or alive.

Ewa's parents had taught her not to open the door to strangers but to speak to them first through the window. Somehow

Christiaan de Wet managed to talk his way into the house. The Child Protection Unit recommends that parents rehearse several situations with their children and drill safety precautions into them. Parents could ask friends who are not known to their children to knock on the door and to give different reasons why the children should open, to test and strengthen their ability to resist.

Children are never safe, but it is impossible for a parent to keep a child under watch around the clock. Children should be taught how to look out for themselves and not to be intimidated, threatened or persuaded into anything by anyone.

JOHN FRANK BROWN
& SAMUEL JACQUES COETZEE

Johannesburg area, 1995

At the age of three, Samuel Jacques Coetzee, known as Jacques, lost his father. At six, Jacques refused to play with other little boys and preferred playing with his sister's dolls. His mother was concerned about her son's behaviour and consulted a psychologist who told her this was natural behaviour for a boy who had lost his father.

But Jacques secretly dreamt of becoming a girl and when he began developing breasts at the age of thirteen, he was delighted. Jacques left school in grade 10 and ran away from home when he was seventeen. He returned for a short time and was then called up for service in the army.

The effeminate Jacques could not cope with army life and attempted suicide in 1989 by taking an overdose of pills. While he was recovering in hospital he told his mother that he wanted to be a woman. Jacques moved out of home and in 1993 he met his nemesis, 30-year-old John Frank Brown.

Jacques Coetzee solicited John Brown for sex and soon afterwards the two moved in together. The men frequented gay clubs in Johannesburg and neighbouring Germiston. Coetzee delighted in cross-dressing and assumed the aliases of Kimberley, Debbie and Gail. As a woman, he was ravishingly beautiful and very seductive. As a male, he used the aliases Deon, JC and Jakes. Brown was consumed with jealousy when Coetzee prostituted himself, but he profited from the venture as he was unemployed, having recently lost his job at a bank. He frequently assaulted

Coetzee. It was an ill-fated affair of sadomasochistic sex and physical abuse which culminated in the murder of four men and an under age boy and, ultimately, in Coetzee's suicide.

By October 1995 Brown was serving a prison sentence for stealing a 6.35 pistol from Miss Cheryl van Straaten and for housebreaking. Both men had lived with her, but Coetzee moved out after the arrest. While in prison, Brown told Inspector Ronald Spanjers of murders that Coetzee had allegedly committed.

The murder cases were referred to the East Rand Murder and Robbery Unit, to Captain Frans van Niekerk – who had investigated the Christiaan de Wet serial killer case (page 187) and also later investigated the Atteridgeville serial killer case (page 198) – and to Captain Leon Nel.

The detectives gathered information on the murders and were eventually able to fill in the missing pieces of the jigsaw puzzle.

On 30 August 1993, the couple met 35-year-old Chris Anderson, a drifter with no fixed address. Anderson had sex with Coetzee while Brown watched, but Brown became enraged when Coetzee apparently allowed Anderson to 'do things to him' which he never allowed Brown to do. During the trial Coetzee said that Brown had stabbed Anderson in the neck with a drill bit and then strangled him with a tie. They dumped Anderson's body on a gravel road at Skurweberg near Atteridgeville.

On 4 November 1993, Brown and Coetzee met a 30-year-old man and a 15-year-old boy in a café in Johannesburg. The strangers asked them for money and the couple took them home where they had sex with them. Afterwards they took the man and the boy to Tamboekiesfontein farm near Heidelberg where an argument about money took place. Both the man and the boy were shot, stabbed and strangled and left in the veld.

On 1 September 1995, 27-year-old Avhewngi Robert Bele, a gardener, watched through the window as Brown and Coetzee engaged in sex in a house in Roodepoort. Brown spotted the gardener and invited him in. Coetzee had sex with him. Then Brown became angry and strangled Bele and cut off his genitals. They dumped the body in the veld at Mindalore, Krugersdorp, dropping the mutilated genitals not far from the body.

Three weeks later, 32-year-old Robert Farrel Richter picked up Brown and Coetzee in a park and took them to his home in Constantia Court, Edenvale, Johannesburg. Coetzee had sex with Richter. According to Coetzee, Richter asked to be tied to his bed, and the couple complied with his request. Then they strangled him with a karate belt and stole his car, a firearm and other household articles.

The detectives released photographs of Coetzee to the media and he was identified by members of the public. On 13 April 1996 he was arrested at a house in Turffontein, Johannesburg. At that stage he was on parole for car theft, but this was revoked when he was charged with murder. Coetzee and Brown appeared in the Germiston magistrate's court and were referred to Sterkfontein Psychiatric Hospital for observation. Both were found competent to stand trial.

The trial started on 21 April 1997. Advocate L Swanepoel appeared for Coetzee and Advocate H Knopp for Brown. The State Prosecutor was Advocate Gerhard Nel and Mr Justice J Coetzee presided.

The men were charged with five counts of murder, one count of robbery with aggravating circumstances and four charges of illegal possession of firearms and ammunition. Both pleaded not guilty. Coetzee's mother attended the trial every day.

During the trial both men accused each other of committing the murders.

Ten days after the trial commenced, Coetzee committed suicide in his cell in Boksburg prison by taking an overdose of pills. He wrote a suicide note to Brown telling him he did not want to live any longer.

Brown's trial continued. After Coetzee's suicide he changed his plea to guilty of the murder of Robert Richter, guilty of being an accessory after the fact in the murder of the other four victims, guilty of robbery with aggravating circumstances and guilty on two charges of illegal possession of firearms and ammunition. He told the judge that during August to November 1993 he was working night shift and when he returned home in the morning he found the bodies in his bedroom. He said that Coetzee had blackmailed him into helping him get rid of the bodies. He had committed petrol card fraud at the bank where he had worked and Coetzee threatened to tell his employers if he did not help him dispose of the bodies.

On 15 May 1997, Mr Justice Coetzee sentenced Brown to life for the murder of Robert Richter, to sixty years for being accessory after the fact to the other four murders, fifteen years for the robbery and four years for being in possession of illegal firearms and ammunition. The judge said he did not believe Brown's testimony, but could find no evidence that he had been directly involved in the other four murders.

Notes

So ended the passionate and disturbed love affair of Jacques Coetzee and John Frank Brown. In court they turned on each other as viciously as they had attacked their victims.

Their case is reminiscent of a case in Pasadena, California, USA, in 1973.

Seventeen-year-old Wayne Henley was the young lover of Dean Corll. Henley played a role in the relationship similar to that of Jacques Coetzee, and Corll a role that paralleled that of Brown. Henley and Corll raped, tortured and killed thirty-two young men. The victims were vagrants and hitch-hikers whom Henley had picked up. They were taken to Corll's house where they were treated to drink and drugs. Once the victim was unconscious, Henley and Corll would tie him to a board, sodomise and torture him and then kill him. Victims were tortured by inserting glass rods in their penises and bullet-like instruments in their anuses.

On 8 August 1973, Henley called the Pasadena Police and told them he had just killed Corll. The police arrived on the scene to find Corll's bullet-riddled body. Henley told them that he had brought two friends, a teenage girl and boy, to the house. Corll was furious about the girl's presence and fed drugs to all of them. When Henley came to, he was tied to the torture board. He pleaded for his life and Corll only set him free when Henley promised he would rape and kill the girl. Both the boy and girl were tied to the torture board but at that point, Henley turned the firearm on Corll and killed him. The police recovered seventeen bodies in the boat shed on the property and the sites where the other bodies were buried were pointed out by Henley.

Henley implicated another friend, David Brooks, as a co-conspirator. Henley claimed that Corll was the main instigator, and he and Brooks tried to blame each other for the crimes. Henley was sentenced to six terms of ninety-nine years' imprisonment and Brooks was jailed for life.

Most lovers who collaborate in committing crimes tend to turn on each other when they are fighting for their lives.

MOSES SITHOLE

Cleveland, Atteridgeville & East Rand, 1994-95

Moses Sithole was the fourth of the six children of Simon Tangawira Sithole and his wife Sophie Mnisis. Simon died when Moses was a child, and Sophie and her family lost their home in Vosloorus, east of Johannesburg, and were left destitute. Sophie had no option but to hand the children over to an orphanage in Benoni, rather than leave them to grow up on the streets. Moses said his mother took them to a police station and left them there, threatening to kill them if they told the police that they knew her. The boys were transferred to a home in Dingaanstad, KwaZulu-Natal, where Moses spent three years before running away. He maintained that the boys in the home were ill-treated.

Moses Sithole eventually boarded with his older brother, who had bought a house in Vosloorus, and found employment in Boksburg. The brother lost his job and home and decided to move to Venda. Sithole stayed behind, finding employment wherever he could. Sometimes he worked on farms and travelled around the country, but most of the time he lived and worked on the East Rand. He was believed at one stage to have stayed at a hostel in Rosherville, next to Cleveland in Johannesburg.

At thirty-eight years of age, Patricia Khumalo found herself in the same predicament as many other women in South Africa. She was unemployed and desperately looking for work. On 14 September 1987, Patricia believed her luck had changed. While in Boksburg with her sister, she met a man who called himself

Martin. He was handsome and charming and told Patricia and her sister that he had found work for two women in Cleveland, but that they had not turned up. He invited Patricia to accompany him to Cleveland so that she could take the job.

Patricia was delighted and boarded a train with Martin. They alighted at Geldenhuys Station and Martin told her that they could take a short cut through the veld. When they were out of sight of the station, Martin's demeanour suddenly changed. He turned on Patricia and demanded her earrings and her set of wedding rings. Then he undressed her, tied her hands behind her back with her bra and raped her repeatedly. When he had finished he threw a garment over her head, tied it and drew her dress over her head. He left her in the veld.

Patricia was lucky to escape with her life. She had unknowingly become the first victim of Moses Sithole, one of South Africa's, and the world's, most notorious serial killers.

The attack on Patricia seems to have been a trial run because she was not killed and a year passed before Moses attempted another attack. Most serial killers have 'dry runs' or rehearsals when they act out parts of their murderous fantasies, just to see how far they can go.

A year later, on 28 September 1988, Dorcas Kedibone Khobane (26) of Vosloorus was also looking for employment. She was visiting a friend's workplace when she met a man called Moses who promised her work in Cleveland. As with Patricia, he asked her to accompany him and she was only too pleased to do so. They boarded a train, alighting at a station close to Cleveland. They followed a footpath leading into the bush. The charming Moses' behaviour changed and he hit her in the face. He began to strangle her with his hands and then raped her repeatedly. He robbed her of her money but fled when another man approached them. Dorcas survived.

During this time, Sithole had a relationship with the sister of Lindiwe Nkosi (24), also of Vosloorus. She knew him either as Moses or as Martin. On a Saturday in October 1988, Sithole invited Lindiwe to go with him to Soweto to visit her sister. They took a taxi to the Dunswart station, where they boarded the train to Geldenhuys, where they alighted. As they were walking through the veld, Sithole threatened Lindiwe that he would set her on fire with a bottle of petrol he was carrying if she refused to have sex with him. He slapped her and then raped her. He throttled her until she lost consciousness. When she regained consciousness, Sithole accompanied her back to Vosloorus, threatening to kill her and her niece if she reported the incident.

Again, it seemed as if Sithole was rehearsing his fantasy, all the time getting closer and closer to actually killing someone.

In February 1989, Buyiswa Doris Swakamisa was on her way to Germiston to look for work when she met a man who called himself Lloyd Thomas. Like the other women, she went with him on the train to Cleveland. Again, they took a route across the veld. The man pulled out a panga that he had concealed in a newspaper and threatened her. He robbed her of her money and raped her. He tied her hands and feet with her underwear and tied an overcoat over her face. He said he would kill her if she reported the attack. Sithole was not charged with this case during his trial, but it was mentioned in evidence because of the modus operandi.

When Sithole's brother moved to Venda, he illegally sold his brother's house. A charge of theft and fraud was laid against him. In 1989 Sithole was sentenced to ten years for rape. He became a member of the choir at Pretoria Central Prison. He loved reading and was fond of classical music. While in prison he met his common-law wife who was visiting her younger brother. Sithole maintained throughout his time in prison that he was innocent of the rape and that he had been pointed out at an identity parade by a woman he had never encountered in his life. Sithole was released on parole for good behaviour in 1993. He had completed seven years of the ten-year sentence.

The last time her family saw Maria Monene Monama (19) alive was on 14 July 1994, when she left her home in Mamelodi, east of Pretoria, to go to Visagie Street in central Pretoria. Her body was found two days later in the veld behind a hostel in Rosherville, close to Cleveland. Maria had been raped and strangled. The following messages were written on her thighs: 'She a beach [sic]' and 'I am not fighting with you please' and 'We stay here as long as you don't understand'. Maria was not identified until 10 November, when photographs of the crime scene were published in the press.

Sithole had become a vicious serial killer.

About two weeks later, on 2 August 1994, Amanda Kebofile Thethe (26) of Krugersdorp was on her way to a school in the Winterveld north of Pretoria, where she was employed as a teacher. Amanda had met Sithole a while before and had introduced him to her parents as her boyfriend. Amanda's body was discovered in the mine dumps at Cleveland on 6 August 1994, with her pantyhose and panties in her mouth, and a jersey over her head. She had been raped and strangled with a piece of clothing. It was established that Sithole had used Amanda's credit card to withdraw cash on several occasions between 2 and 4 August. She was identified from photographs on 17 October 1994. Sithole attended Amanda's funeral.

A week later, on 9 August 1994, Joyce Thakane Mashabela (33) of Yeoville, Johannesburg, left her home to visit her sister in Pretoria. On 19 August her body was found near Lotus Gardens in Pretoria West. She had been assaulted, raped and strangled with her pantyhose. Clothing was tied around her eyes and nose. She was identified by her fingerprints.

Amanda Refilwe Mokale (24) was excited at the prospect of becoming a student. Some time between 5 and 7 September 1994 she left her home in Soshanguwe on her way to the Technikon in Pretoria. Her body was discovered on 18 September in Cleveland. She had been assaulted and raped and strangled with her bra. She was identified from photographs on 2 November.

On 15 September 1994, Rose Rebothile Mogotsi (22) of Mabopane had an appointment with Sithole, who had promised to find her work. Her body was also found on 18 September behind the Angelo hotel in Boksburg. She had been raped and strangled with her underwear. She was identified by her fingerprints.

At this stage the murders of Maria Monene Monama, Amanda Kebofile Thethe, Amanda Refilwe Mokale and seven others – namely Daphne Papo, Hermina Papenfus, Betty Phalahadi, Dorah Moleka Mokoena, Margaret Ntombeni Ledwaba and two unidentified women – were being investigated as the 'Cleveland serial killer' case by Brixton Murder and Robbery detectives. Two bodies discovered in Atteridgeville, Pretoria – namely Joyce Thakane Mashabela and Peggy Bodile – were also included in this series because of the similar modus operandi.

Acting on information given to them by an informer, the Brixton Murder and Robbery detectives arrested David Selepe as their suspect on 15 December 1995. Selepe confessed to killing fifteen women in Johannesburg, Boksburg and Pretoria. He pointed out crime scenes to the police and it was while he was pointing out the crime scene of Amanda Refilwe Mokale that he attacked the police in an attempt to escape and was fatally wounded by a detective.

Like Sithole, David Selepe lived and worked mainly on the East Rand. Before he was killed he had told the detectives that he did not commit the murders on his own. The detectives were never able to trace his accomplices as Selepe referred to them only by their first names, which could have been aliases.

On 4 January 1995 the decomposed body of an unknown woman was found near the Phomolong squatter camp at Saulsville in Atteridgeville. She had been raped, but due to the advanced state of decomposition of the body, the cause of death could not be established.

Some time during January 1995, Beauty Nuku Soko (27) went to visit her sister in Klipgat. Her body was discovered on 9 February, west of Saulsville. She was naked, but her clothing had been placed on top of her badly decomposed body and stones were packed on top of the clothing. The cause of death could not be established. She was later identified by fingerprints.

On 3 March 1995, Sarah Matlakala Mokono (25) left her parents' home in Hammanskraal to meet Sithole who had promised her work at Loftus Versveld. On the morning of 6 March when municipal workers, who were digging trenches in Atteridgeville, arrived at work they noticed a woman's breasts protruding from the soil in one of the trenches. They uncovered Sarah's naked body. She was identified by her fingerprints.

Just before the start of the Easter weekend in April 1995, Letta Nomthandazo Ndlangamandla (25) and her young son Sibusiso left their home at Ivory Park to meet Sithole in Pretoria North. He had promised her employment. Letta's body was found on 12 April in Saulsville. She was fully dressed, but her hands were tied with her bra. She had been raped. The body of Sibusiso was discovered only on 20 April, not far from where his mother had been killed. Although it could not be established exactly how they had died, Letta was probably suffocated and Sibusiso had head wounds.

On 7 April 1995, Nikiwe Diko (24) left her home in Tweefontein, KwaNdebele to meet Sithole in Pretoria. Following his by now established modus operandi, he had promised her employment. Her body was discovered on 24 June west of Saulsville. Her arms had been tied up with underwear and she had been strangled with her pantyhose. A stick had been wound into the pantyhose to form a garrotte. Dogs had already ripped her body apart. It seemed as if a stick had been inserted inside her vagina.

Sithole was becoming increasingly sophisticated in his methods of murder. By using the garrotte method he could release and tighten the ligature, thereby allowing his victims to gain and lose consciousness as he pleased. This is an exceptionally cruel manner in which to take a life. Nikiwe was identified by her fingerprints.

On the evening of 12 May 1995, Esther Moshibudi Mainetja (29) was last seen alive at the Sunsetview café near plot 48,

Uitzicht, Hercules, in Pretoria West. She set off to walk to her nearby home. Her body was found the next day in a mealie field close to her home. She had been assaulted, raped and strangled.

On 23 May 1995, Granny Dimakatso Ramela (21) left her parents' home in the Winterveld to go to Pretoria to fetch her identity document. Her decomposed body was discovered on 17 July in a wattle forest near Westford Hospital in Pretoria West. A garrotte was found around her neck and she had been raped. Her fingerprints were used to identify her.

Elizabeth Granny Mathetsa (19) originally came from Kimberley, but she worked at a café in Wonder Park, Acacia, north of Pretoria. Her employer dropped her off in neighbouring Nina Park on the night of 25 May 1995. Her naked body was found on 16 June in open land in Bergland, Rosslyn. She had been raped. Elizabeth was identified in the police mortuary by her family.

Francina Nomsa Sithebe (25) left work at about midday on 13 June 1995. That same day her body was discovered on the koppie in Atteridgeville. She had been raped and then strangled with her panties and the strap of her handbag. The strap had also been tied to a tree. The contents of her handbag were found scattered on the koppie, including her identity document.

On 22 June 1995, the body of Ernestina Mohadi Mosebo (30) was discovered next to Rand Airport Road in Rosherville. She had been raped and strangled. She had left her sister's home in South Hills earlier that month to search for employment. Her identity document was found on the crime scene.

Josephine Montsali Mlangeni (25) left her home in Germiston on 17 July 1995 to accompany Sithole who had offered her employment in Boksburg. Near Davidson Street in Boksburg North, he lured her into the veld, raped her and strangled her with a belt. Her body was found shortly afterwards.

On this day, 17 July 1995, a team led by Captain Vinol Viljoen of the Pretoria Murder and Robbery Unit was established to investigate the Atteridgeville serial killings. Viljoen collected all the dockets from the different police stations in Atteridgeville, Pretoria West and neighbouring stations in which the killer had used a similar modus operandi. It was also on this day that the team was called out to Granny Dimakatso Ramela's murder scene at the Westford Hospital.

At this stage the team did not include the Cleveland murders in their investigation for it was assumed that they had been committed by David Selepe; he had, after all, confessed to them and pointed out some of the crime scenes. Selepe had a DNA grouping of 1212 and at that time the Forensic Science Laboratory of the South African Police Service was unable to identify polymarkers of DNA.

On 12 September 1995 the body of an unknown adult woman was discovered near Heidelberg Road in Cleveland. She had been assaulted, raped and strangled. She has never been identified.

Sithole probably felt safe committing murders in Cleveland and the East Rand for the death of Selepe had taken the heat out of the Cleveland investigation. He was probably uncomfortable about continuing to murder in the Atteridgeville area, for the investigation received huge media coverage. So he moved his killing field further north to the Onderstepoort/Bon Accord areas.

Mildred Ntiya Lepule (28) was elated when Sithole offered her a job as a social worker at his bogus organisation, Youth Against Human Abuse. On 30 May 1995, her husband, a taxi driver, dropped her off in Vermeulen Street in Pretoria to meet Sithole. Sithole took her to Onderstepoort where he raped her and strangled her with her pantyhose next to a railway line. He drew her panties over her head and neck. Her body was not found until 26 July in the cement ditch next to the railway line. She was identified by her fingerprints.

On 14 July 1995, Elsie Khoti Masango (25) left her home in the Winterveld to meet Sithole at Afrox in Pretoria. He had promised her a job. Sithole was a casual worker at Afrox and he also helped his common-law wife's brother-in-law repairing cars at their home in Atteridgeville. Elsie's body was discovered on

8 August in Onderstepoort. She had been raped and strangled with the strap of a handbag. Her hands were tied behind her back and a cloth was tied over her eyes. Her handbag was discovered the next day and she was identified by documents found in the bag.

On the same day that Elsie's handbag was found the charred remains of an unknown woman were discovered in the same area. This woman must have been killed some time in 1994 or 1995. One can imagine that Sithole showed this corpse to Elsie with the intention of terrifying her. It is not known whether he set the corpse on fire; it is more likely that it was burnt during a veld fire.

On 28 August 1995 the body of an unknown woman was found in the veld at the Bon Accord Dam, not far from Onderstepoort. Her arms had been tied with underwear and she had been strangled with the strap of a handbag. Clothing was tied around her head. She was never identified.

Two days later, on 30 August 1995, the body of yet another unidentified woman was discovered in Onderstepoort. She too had been raped and strangled. She had probably died six months before her body was found.

By this time the detectives were very active in the Onderstepoort area and Sithole moved back to the East Rand to commit his murders. He had had a row with his common-law wife, and left her and their daughter in Atteridgeville. Apparently he slept and lived at Park Station in Johannesburg where he was often seen approaching women. He also helped street children.

Oscarina Vuyokazi Jakalase (30) left her home in Dobsonville on 8 August 1995 to meet Sithole at the Horizon Station. He had promised her work in a supermarket. He took her to the Van Dyk Mine on the East Rand where he assaulted, raped and strangled her. She was discovered on 23 August 1995 and identified by her fingerprints.

On 16 September 1995, Mr Solomon Kungwane took his dogs for a walk in the veld at Van Dyk Mine. They led him to the decomposing body of a woman. He alerted the police. On 17 and 18 September 1995 the police processed the crime scene and found a total of ten bodies in various stages of decomposition spread all over the veld. Unfortunately the gruesome discovery was leaked to the media, who published the story on the front pages the next day. Had this story been kept under wraps for just a few days, the police could have kept surveillance and Sithole might have been caught red-handed. The lives of five women might have been saved. Sithole read the newspapers and thereafter moved his operations back to Benoni, Germiston and Cleveland, where he felt safe. The following bodies were discovered during those two days at the Van Dyk Mine scene:

Amelia Dikamakatso Rapodile (43) lived in Krugersdorp, but worked at Johannesburg International Airport. Sithole, who she knew, had told her that he had found her a better job at Shell House in Johannesburg. At about two o'clock on the afternoon of 7 September 1995 she left her place of employment in the company of Sithole. Amelia's hands had been tied to her neck with pantyhose and the garrotte method was used to strangle her. She had also been raped. On the same night that he murdered her, Sithole withdrew cash from Amelia's bank account on three separate occasions in Germiston. Although her purse and identity document were discovered some distance from the crime scene, she was also identified by her fingerprints.

Monica Gabisile Vilakazi (31) had left her home in Wattville, Benoni on 12 September 1995 to seek employment in Germiston. She had been raped and the garrotte method was used to strangle her. Sithole attempted to withdraw cash using her credit card in Boksburg and Germiston. She was identified by her fingerprints.

Makoba Tryphina Mogotsi (27) worked at Kidshaven in Benoni. Sithole volunteered to work there and met the proprietor, Mrs Moria Simpson. He told the women employed at Kidshaven about his Youth Against Human Abuse organisation and gave them forms to fill out, to apply for employment. He thus had the names and addresses of these women in his possession. Sithole's sister's telephone number in Wattville was on this form and he phoned often to collect his messages. Makoba made an appointment to meet Sithole at 7 am on 15 August 1995 at the Benoni station. She was never seen alive again.

When her mother, Ntomkhulu Mogotsi, arrived at Kidshaven to enquire about her missing daughter, Makoba's friend Esther told her about her daughter's appointment with Sithole. Mrs Simpson phoned the police and gave them Makoba's and Sithole's details. A photograph of Makoba was published as a missing person in the newspaper. Nothing was heard from the police for a long time. When Makoba's body was discovered at the Van Dyk Mine scene her hands were tied with her panties, she had been raped and strangled with her bra. Her watch had been stolen. Had the police followed up on this information and been able to trace Sithole, many lives could have been saved.

On 4 September 1995, Nelisiwe Nontobeko Zulu (26) left her sister's home in Primrose, Germiston, to look for work. Her hands had been tied with her pantyhose. Part of the pantyhose was tied around her neck and she had clearly been strangled. She had also been raped. She was identified by her fingerprints.

Hazel Nozipho Madikizela (21) left her parents' home in Germiston to go to Randfontein. She was also found with her arms tied to her neck with underwear. She had been assaulted and raped and was identified by her fingerprints.

Five of the victims remained unidentified. One was possibly Thoko Vilakazi (27) of Denver, Johannesburg. Another might have been Julia Booi (27) of the West Rand who had also been raped, but her body was so badly decomposed that the cause of death could not be established. The third was possibly a woman named Tsidi from Lesotho, who had been raped and strangled with underwear, and the fourth could have been Jabulile Mathathe (25) of Krugersdorp. She had also been strangled with her underwear.

Captain Frans van Niekerk of the East Rand Murder and Robbery Unit was in charge of this investigation. Because of the similarities between these murders and those in Atteridgeville, the two investigation teams joined forces and worked together. It was established that the DNA grouping of the latest killer was also 1212. This troubled the detectives. Although it is quite possible that many people may share the same grouping, it was difficult to put this down to coincidence.

When the detectives found Amelia Rapodile's identity document on the crime scene, they were able to trace her place of work. Her colleagues told them that she had had an appointment with Moses Sithole who had offered her work and the detectives also got hold of one of Sithole's Youth Against Human Abuse application forms, which had his sister's telephone number in Wattville on it. Captain Leon Nel of the East Rand Murder and Robbery Unit was a member of Captain van Niekerk's team. He remembered the photograph of the missing Makoba and asked the Criminal Record Centre at police headquarters in Pretoria to check the fingerprints of the bodies against Makoba Tryphina Mogotsi's records. A few days later the report came back. The fingerprints matched. Thus was Makoba's body identified and another link to Moses Sithole established. The investigation now became extremely urgent. The address of his sister, Kwazi Sithole, was checked out, but Moses no longer lived there.

On 25 September 1995 Agnes Sibongile Mbuli (20) of Kwa-Thema on the East Rand went to visit a friend in Katlehong. Her body was discovered on 3 October at Kleinfontein Station in Benoni. She had been strangled with a belt, which was also tied around one of her ankles.

Then, on 3 October 1995, a man calling himself Joseph phoned a journalist, Ms Tamsen de Beer, at *The Star* newspaper. He claimed to be the serial killer and said he wanted to give himself up. He spoke about many of the crime scenes, but it was possible that he had gained this information from newspaper reports. He claimed to have killed the women because they reminded him of the woman who had sent him to jail for a rape he claimed he had not committed. 'Joseph' said he would phone again later.

Ms de Beer contacted the investigating detectives and when Joseph phoned again a meeting was arranged between him and the detectives at a railway station. Sithole later maintained that he had arrived for the appointment, but when he saw the policemen he took fright, got on to a train and fled.

Sithole phoned another journalist, Charles Mogane of *City Press*, and asked to meet him one night at Stap en Rus station on the East Rand where he said he would hand himself over. Mr Mogane did not inform the police of this appointment. Sithole asked that his common-law wife Martha should also come to the meeting. But the family decided it would be better if Sithole's brother-in-law went instead of Martha. When Mr Mogane and the brother-in-law arrived at the designated spot at midnight, they saw a green Golf parked a short distance away. A man approached the car and the men inside jumped out and frisked him, but then let him go. Mr Mogane was convinced that the men in the green car were policemen who had followed them. The police regarded Mr Mogane's behaviour as irresponsible, for Sithole could have abducted him and held him to ransom.

On 9 October 1995 the body of yet another unidentified woman was found under a sheet of corrugated iron at the mine dumps near Jupiter Station on the East Rand. She had been raped and strangled with the strap of a handbag.

Beauty Ntombi Ndabeni (31) left her home in Meadowlands, Soweto, on 10 October 1995 to go to Johannesburg. Her body was discovered on 11 October in a ditch next to the railway lines behind Tongaat Foods in Germiston. She had been raped and her pantyhose were tied around her neck in garrotte style. A comb had been used to tighten the garrotte. Her hands had also been tied with pantyhose. Her identity was established by means of her fingerprints.

On 14 October 1995 the body of an unidentified woman was discovered in the veld near Village Main Reef Mine, John Vorster Plain, Johannesburg. She had been raped and strangled with shoelaces that were tied around her neck and to a tree.

Moses Sithole's last victim was an unidentified woman

discovered on 6 November 1995 at the Gosforth Park mine dumps in Germiston. She had also been raped.

In the mean time the detectives were hard at work. They released a photograph of Moses Sithole to the media on 13 October 1995, and appealed to the public only to give them information and not to confront the man. Sithole had used the following aliases: Charles Mokgomo, Martin Sithole, Moses Mdluli, Moses Ndlovu, Moses Abednego Sithole and Moscow Brown.

Sithole eventually phoned his sister Kwazi's husband Maxwell and asked him to bring him a firearm. Maxwell arranged to meet Sithole on 18 October 1995 at a certain factory in Benoni, and he informed the detectives. Inspector Francis Moluvhedzi was planted as a security guard at the factory. Sithole arrived, but became suspicious and fled. Moluvhedzi pursued Sithole, following him into an alley. Sithole attacked him with an axe. Moluvhedzi fired at him in self-defence, wounding him in the leg and stomach. Sithole was arrested and taken to hospital. As soon as the doctors gave the go-ahead, the interrogation process began.

Sithole told the detectives that he had masturbated on the crime scenes when the victims took too long to die. He also masturbated whilst being interrogated. He said Peggy Podile told him she was a karate expert. He told her that she had a chance to defend herself, but if she failed, she would die. She paid with her life.

A profile had been drawn up for the original Cleveland serial killer. This profile was not very accurate, but it should be borne in mind that at the time the profiler was unaware of the fact that at least two men were leaving their psychological fingerprints on the crime scenes. During the Atteridgeville investigation it became clear that at least two people were involved and the original profile was revised. There was still uncertainty about which victims had been killed by which killer, and some of the characteristics predicted by the profiler overlapped between David Selepe and Moses Sithole.

The following predictions were made:

- *The killer would be a male aged between late twenties to early thirties.* Both Selepe and Sithole fell into this group.
- *He would be self-employed and have access to a lot of money.* Both Selepe and Sithole considered themselves self-employed. Selepe had business interests in a school that trained secretaries and Sithole was the 'director' of the Youth Against Human Abuse organisation. Both at times had access to money, either legally or illegally gained.
- *He would drive an expensive car.* Selepe was driving a Mercedes when he was arrested. Sithole claimed he could not drive, that he had never owned a vehicle and nor did he have a licence. Not having a car or a licence does not necessarily preclude one from being able to drive. Also there were unconfirmed reports in the media about women recognising Sithole as a man who had offered them lifts in a car. Sithole used trains and taxis to convey his victims for he had no access to a vehicle. He had driven tractors on the farms he had worked on.
- *He would wear flashy clothes and jewellery.* Selepe was a well-dressed man and Sithole's sister confirmed that he liked clothes, particularly smart shoes. It is unclear whether either of them ever wore jewellery.
- *He would be socially adept, charming and would consider himself a ladies' man.* Neither of these men lacked girlfriends and both could charm their victims into trusting them. Bear in mind that most of the victims, although unemployed, were middle-class women. Some were highly intelligent and employed. None of them were prostitutes who would be inclined to accompany a man more readily.
- *He was probably married or had been married.* Selepe was married and Sithole had a common-law wife.
- *He would frequent shebeens and pubs and enjoy social gatherings.* Sithole apparently did not drink, and it is unconfirmed whether Selepe did.

- *He would probably be involved in fraud and theft.* Selepe had previous charges for fraud and weapons smuggling and Sithole had charges for theft and fraud.
- *He might boast of being a killer, but would speak of the killer in the third person. He would play cat and mouse games with the detectives.* Sithole alleged that he phoned the detectives several times during the investigation, but that they did not take him seriously. He phoned several newspapers including *The Star* and he told his victims that he was the Atteridgeville killer before murdering them. He also showed the victims the bodies of previous victims before killing them. Sithole was videotaped in prison by fellow inmates, boasting about the murders. In prison, Sithole realised that he had a sort of 'celebrity' status and that students as well as the media would like to interview him. He used this to manipulate them. The Department of Correctional Services has a policy that no prison inmate may be interviewed by the media for the precise purpose of countering this notion of 'celebrity' status.
- *He would be up to date on current news events and would follow the investigation in the media.* Selepe had a newspaper with a front-page article on the Cleveland serial killer in the boot of his car when he was arrested. Sithole had close contact with journalists, read the newspapers every day and watched television coverage of his case.
- *He would abhor women, even though he was very charming to them. Although originally rejected by the mother figure, an incident in his adult life in which he was hurt by an adult woman could have sparked the murders. The victims would somehow represent this adult woman.* Sithole said he killed the women because they reminded him of the woman who sent him to jail for rape. He also experienced being placed in an orphanage as a child as rejection by his mother.
- *Post-crime behaviour would be masturbation, collecting souvenirs and later discarding them.* Sithole masturbated on the crime scenes, he took his victims' jewellery and later gave it away.

- *He would have a high sex drive and probably read pornography.* Sithole raped his victims several times, as those who survived testified. It is not known whether he ever read pornography, but he was aroused by women's thighs and masturbated while watching them die.
- *He was exposed to violent sex, maybe as a child.* Sithole lived in orphanages where it is possible that he could have been sodomised. According to a previous cell mate, he was severely sodomised in prison while serving his sentence for rape.
- *He would be highly intelligent and streetwise.* Sithole liked to read English literature, was fond of classical music and was a member of a choir. He also survived on the streets.

Most of the characteristics in the profile fitted Sithole, but Selepe died before more information could be gathered about him. Sithole denied that he fitted the profile at all, reiterating the fact that he did not drive a car and that he did not have money. He denied using his victims' credit cards to draw large sums of money.

The trial of 32-year-old Moses Sithole began on 21 October 1996. By this time the SAPS Forensic Science Laboratory could identify DNA polymarkers and Sithole's DNA was linked to several of the bodies, as well as to some of those victims who were originally ascribed to David Selepe. He was charged with forty counts of rape, thirty-eight counts of murder and six counts of robbery. Advocates Retha Meintjies and George Baloyi prosecuted for the State and Advocates Eben Jordaan and Lena van Wyk defended Sithole. More than 350 state witnesses were called to testify. Sithole had earlier been assessed by state psychiatrists who had found him sane and fit to stand trial. Their report was handed in to the court by Advocate Meintjies.

During the trial it became evident that Sithole used some of the jewellery stolen from his victims to entice and impress future victims and girlfriends. Some of these girlfriends contacted the detectives after Sithole's photograph had been published and returned the jewellery which was subsequently identified by members of the victims' families.

Sithole's common-law wife Martha brought his daughter, who was then approaching her third birthday, to court one day. This was the only day on which Sithole's by then trademark smile was not on his face. He was visibly upset when the mother refused to let him hold his daughter.

On 5 December 1997, more than a year after the trial started and on his daughter's third birthday, Mr Justice Curlewis sentenced Moses Sithole to 2410 years in prison. He was found guilty on all charges and will spend the rest of his life in C-Max facility at Pretoria Central prison. None of the sentences are to run concurrently. Sithole's sentence was a world record. The fact that the court presented the judge with a report stating that Sithole had contracted AIDS made no difference to the sentence. It was predicted that Sithole would have between five to eight years to live.

Sithole said he committed the crimes because of the injustice done to him when he was sentenced to a jail term for a rape he alleges he did not commit. He also held the government responsible for 'bad administration'.

Notes

Moses Sithole was a typical serial killer. Too little is known about his childhood to determine his fixations and the source of his fantasies. One can only surmise that there must have been some Oedipal conflict and a sense that he was rejected by his mother. Like most serial killers, if one encountered this charming, handsome, intelligent man who liked literature and classical music, who sang in a choir, who was kind to his wife and who adored his baby, one would never suspect that he could be a vicious killer. This is where the danger lies. A serial killer could be anyone's husband, anyone's brother, anyone's doting father, anyone's neighbour – which is exactly what Sithole was.

Typically, he never accepted responsibility for the murders, although he liked to boast to the detectives. He loved attention and an audience, and had the makings of a megalomaniac. This is probably also the reason why he denied ever knowing David Selepe. He did not want to share his notoriety with anyone else.

Time frame and summary

Victim	Last seen	Body found	Crime scene
*Maria Monene Monama (19)	14/07/94	16/07/94	Cleveland
*Amanda Kebofile Thethe˙ (26)	2/08/94	6/08/94	Cleveland
*Joyce Thakane Mashabela (33)	9/08/94	19/08/94	Pretoria West
Amanda Refilwe Mokale (24)	5-7/09/94	18/09/94	Cleveland
Rose Rebothile Mogotsi (22)	15/09/94	18/09/94	Boksburg
Unknown		4/01/95	Atteridgeville
Beauty Nuku Soko (27)	Jan. 1995	9/02/95	Atteridgeville
Sarah Matlakala Mokono (25)	3/03/95	6/03/95	Atteridgeville
Letta Nomthandazo Nglangamandla (25) and son Sibusiso	April 95	12/04/95 20/04/95	Atteridgeville
Nikiwe Diko (24)	7/04/95	24/06/95	Atteridgeville

---

*Cleveland serial killer series, investigated by Brixton Murder and Robbery Unit, together with the following cases: Daphne Papo, Hermina Papenfus, Betty Phalahadi, Dorah Moleka Mokoena, Margaret Ntombeni Ledwaba, two unidentified women, and Peggy Bodile.

Esther Mashibudi Mainetja (29)	12/05/95	13/05/95	Pretoria West
Granny Dimakatso Ramela (21)	23/05/95	17/07/95	Pretoria West
Elizabeth Granny Mathetsa (19)	25/05/95	16/06/95	Rosslyn
Francina Nomsa Sithebe (25)	13/06/95	13/06/95	Atteridgeville
Ernestina Mohadi Mosebo (30)	June 95	22/06/95	Rosherville
Josephine Montsali Mlangeni (25)	17/07/95	? July 95	Boksburg
Unknown	?	12/09/95	Cleveland
Mildred Ntiya Lepule (28)	30/05/95	26/07/95	Ondersteprt
Elsie Khoti Masango (25)	14/07/95	8/08/95	Ondersteprt
Unknown	?	9/08/95	Ondersteprt
Unknown	?	28/08/95	Bon Accord
Unknown	?	30/08/95	Ondersteprt
Oscarina Vuyokazi Jakalase (30)	8/08/95	23/08/95	Van Dyk Mine
Amelia Dikamakatso Rapodile (43)	7/09/95	17-18/09/95	Van Dyk Mine
Monica Gabisile Vilakazi (31)	12/09/95	17-18/09/95	Van Dyk Mine
Makoba Tryphina Mogotsi (27)	15/08/95	17-18/09/95	Van Dyk Mine
Nelisiwe Nontobeko Zulu (26)	4/09/95	17-18/09/95	Van Dyk Mine
Hazel Nozipho Madikizela (21)	?	17-18/09/95	Van Dyk Mine

5 unidentified victims, possibly
    Thoko Vilakazi
    Julia Booi
    'Tsidi'
    Jabulile Mathathe
    + one other
	?	17-18/09/95	Van Dyk Mine

Agnes Sibongile Mbuli (20)	25/09/95	3/10/95	Benoni
Unknown	?	9/10/95	Jupiter
Beauty Ntombi Ndabeni (31)	10/10/95	11/10/95	Germiston
Unknown	?	14/10/95	Village Main Reef Mine
Unknown	?	6/11/95	Germiston

MHLENGWA CHRISTOPHER ZIKODE

Donnybrook, 1995

Mhlengwa Zikode was born in Umzimkulu, a rural area in KwaZulu-Natal, on 8 November 1965. He had an older sister and two older brothers. Later the family expanded when three younger brothers were born, and a younger adopted brother and sister joined the family. Of all these children, Zikode's older sister played a major part in his life, for she was his principal caretaker and he adored her.

At the time of Zikode's childhood, faction fights were rife in the rural communities of KwaZulu-Natal and the Zikode family moved many times in an attempt to escape the violence. As a small boy Zikode spent most of his days in the veld, tending to his father's goats. These were lonely years for a young boy who passed his time fantasising about being a fierce warrior who would participate in the faction fights.

Zikode had a good relationship with both his parents. His father was paralysed and Zikode was the child who took care of him. He disliked his older brother, whom he alleged bullied him. Zikode's father did not allow his children to play with other children, for fear that they would come under bad influences. Up to the age of twelve Zikode's world consisted only of his nuclear family and the goats.

When he was ten years old, tragedy struck the Zikode family when the father died, but just before that something very terrible happened to Zikode himself. His sister left the family and he never saw her again. Zikode saw this as rejection and blamed her for the multiple murders he committed later in his life.

At the age of thirteen he went to live with his grandmother, who sent him to school for the first time in his life. Zikode suffered from the handicap of never having been exposed to other children and he therefore could not socialise with them, especially not with girls. At the age of sixteen he went to Durban for a vacation and had his first sexual experience, following the Zulu custom of having sex between his partner's legs in order not to impregnate her. After this encounter he returned to Donnybrook, where he stayed with his mother and younger siblings. He did not have sex again until the age of nineteen, when he began raping his victims. The only other woman that he spoke to, apart from his family members, was the daughter of his neighbour and he imagined himself in love with this girl. His affection was unappreciated and not reciprocated.

Zikode joined the African National Congress and recruited fellow pupils as military cadres. He was expelled from school as a result of his political activities. Maybe Zikode's childhood dreams of being a faction fighter found resonance in his militaristic interest in the ANC. After being expelled from school, Zikode helped his mother to collect firewood, which was her only source of income, and he also found a job at the local trading store in Bulwer. In April 1994 and in March and April 1995 Zikode was allegedly involved in the murder of four political opponents and the attempted murder of another in nearby St Charles. The victims were all males. He had acquired a taste for killing, but these were politically motivated crimes.

Psychologically, Zikode experienced an awakening of sexual desires at the age of nineteen, while his peer group had already experienced this during their puberty years. He had the sexual desires and body of a virile 19-year-old, but the emotions of a shy and awkward 13-year-old. He knew what he wanted, but he did not know how to get it.

Unfortunately, his mother unknowingly provided the catalyst that started Zikode on his career as a serial killer. While collecting wood in the forest one day she came upon some debris left behind by soldiers who had camped there. There were some *Scope* magazines – a men's magazine adorned with semi-naked pin-ups of women – and she brought these home to her son. Zikode specially selected the pin-ups in which women were depicted in poses with chairs and put these up in his hut. These pin-ups activated his sexual desires.

Soon after he had received the magazines, at about six o'clock on the evening of 13 April 1995, Zikode was finishing his shift at the Bulwer trading store when he saw 18-year-old Thandi Gwala and her friend Makhosi Lushaba alight from a taxi. The women were waiting for Thandi's boyfriend, who was Makhosi's brother. Summoning all his courage, Zikode approached the two women. Not having had the opportunity to develop any social skills with regard to communicating with the opposite sex, Zikode told Thandi, without preamble, that he wanted to have sex with her. Thandi was shocked and refused, whereupon Zikode grabbed her arm. Makhosi came to Thandi's rescue, but Zikode produced a firearm and shot Thandi in the left shoulder. She fled into the night but Zikode followed her. He caught up with her on a footpath and ordered her to bend over and touch her toes. He raped her and ran off.

Seven days later, on the night of 19 April 1995, Sibongile Mkhize (20) and her boyfriend, Sbongiseni Hendrik Ngcobo (22), retired to bed in Hendrik's house at the Nkwezela location. Zikode, who had smoked dagga, donned a balaclava, armed himself with a 9mm pistol and walked into the night. As he approached Hendrik's hut he felt his erection rising in anticipation. He kicked open the door of the hut and fired at the two occupants, killing both of them. Hendrik was hit in the head and died instantly. Sibongile was struck in the neck. Unfortunately no forensic tests were done on her body to establish whether or not she was sexually molested post mortem. Zikode returned to his own hut and went to sleep.

The members of the community would not leave their dwellings if they heard gunfire, for faction fighting and political unrest over the years had reduced them to a state of terror.

On 14 May 1995 the body of a woman was found in the Bulwer forest. She had a bullet wound in her head and was naked except for her shoes. Her legs were spreadeagled and kept apart by two wooden pegs driven into the ground next to her ankles. Her face, scalp, eyes, front neck area, right breast and part of her vagina had been removed. Grass and small twigs had been inserted into the vagina, indicating that the killer had a schoolboy curiosity about women's private parts. He had spent a long time on the crime scene, which meant that he knew the area well enough to know that he would not be disturbed. The victim had also been raped. (Zikode was later found guilty of this murder, although he never confessed to it. He was probably too ashamed to admit that he used the opportunity the inspect a woman's private parts, of which he knew so little, at his leisure. The victim was never identified.)

During the evening of 9 June 1995, Mzozayo Phoswa (34) of St Charles went to visit the homestead of his sister-in-law, Ntombi Phoswa (33). Both adults and Ntombi's children were in the kitchen of the hut when the door was suddenly kicked open by a man wearing a balaclava. He pointed a 9mm pistol at them. Mzozayo attempted to disarm the intruder, but he was wounded in the chest and fled from the hut. The intruder was Zikode, who then fired several shots at Ntombi. She died as a result of wounds to her liver and loss of blood.

During the early hours of Saturday 24 June 1995, Caroline Memela (29) and her nine-year-old daughter were asleep in their hut at Seaford when Zikode kicked open the door and fired a shot into the dwelling. He raped Caroline for several hours, using a chair in the way he had seen women posed in the magazines. He then turned his attention to the child who was hiding in the bed and raped her too. In the mean time Caroline managed to escape from the hut and called the neighbours, whereupon Zikode fled from the scene.

On the morning of Monday 26 June 1995, Phumeleni Ngubo (30) and her friend Amos Gxubane (47) were walking to their place of work in St Charles. Zikode approached the couple, drew his firearm and fired several shots at them. Amos was struck in the neck and Phumeleni was wounded in the right leg, which caused her to stumble. Zikode dragged her off the road. He told her that he wanted sex and touched her private parts. Fortunately for Phumeleni a car approached and Zikode fled. Both victims were taken to hospital but Amos died of his wound.

During the early hours of 1 July 1995, Siphiwe Zuma (40) and his wife Annacleta (38) were asleep in their hut at Tafuleni location. Again Zikode kicked open the door of the hut and shot Siphiwe in the temple. He dragged Annacleta outside and kicked her. She screamed so much that the neighbours woke up and she managed to break free from Zikode, who fled immediately.

Seven days later, Zanele Khumalo (27) was sleeping in her house at Kwezela location when Zikode forced his way in. He shot Zanele in the head and then her dragged her out into the neighbouring plantation where he raped her. She died of her injuries.

Early on the morning of 27 July 1995, Beauty Zulu (43), the neighbour whose daughter Zikode fancied himself in love with, was walking to work. Zikode, wearing a balaclava, appeared in front of her with a firearm in his hand. Beauty screamed and attempted to flee, but Zikode fired a shot which hit her in the temple. She was taken to hospital, where she recovered. She had recognised Zikode but was at first too scared to point him out as the killer who had been terrorising the community for the past four months.

During the early hours of 5 August 1995 middle-aged Locatia Madlamini and Cornelia Dlamini were sleeping in their house in Tufaleni location. Relying on his usually successful modus operandi, Zikode kicked the door open and told both women that he wanted sex. They pleaded for their lives. He struck Locatia and forced Cornelia out of the hut, but she managed to break free and ran back past him into the hut. The women barricaded the door and, in frustration, Zikode fired several shots through the door. He wounded both women, but they survived.

Beauty Zulu eventually made a statement to the police who arrested Zikode on 10 August 1995 for attempted murder, but he was released on bail of R300 on 13 August. At this stage the police at Donnybrook did not connect Zikode with the person who had attacked the homesteads at night, for he attacked Beauty during the day when she was on her way to work. While out on bail, Zikode carried on with his killings.

He had to reappear in court on 23 September 1995, when the case was postponed. Because of the agitation of the community, members of the Port Shepstone Murder and Robbery Unit were requested to assist in the investigation. The case was given to Sergeant Dionne van Huyssteen. Inspector Theo Goldstone, who had been trained in the investigation of serial homicide, assisted Van Huyssteen and moved temporarily to Donnybrook.

During the early hours of 25 September 1995, Fikeleni Memela (42) was asleep in her hut at Seaford location when an armed Zikode burst through the door. Fikeleni threw a blanket at him, but he turned on her and fired a shot, wounding her in the jaw. He then raped her and shot her fatally in the chest.

For five months the community had been terrorised by a vicious serial killer. The areas in which he operated were within a range of seven kilometres. On 23 April, 10 June, 19 June, 25 June, 3 July, 6 July and 8 July 1995 identical incidents took place, but Zikode was not charged with these due to lack of evidence. The members of the community had in the mean time stoned to death two other men suspected of being the killer and forced a third to hang himself.

Van Huyssteen established that all the cases were linked and began the long, tedious work of searching for evidence and retaking statements. Some of the bodies had to be exhumed since they had been buried with the bullets still inside them. On 29 September 1995, Van Huyssteen and other members of the Port Shepstone Murder and Robbery Unit rearrested Zikode at his home. Several balaclavas were found in his possession and Goldstone also collected the pin-ups on Zikode's wall. During the trial the relationship between these pictures and Zikode's sexual preferences was brought to light.

The morning after his arrest, Zikode confessed to five of the murders and pointed out some of the crime scenes. Bail was not granted and he remained in custody. He never revealed where he had hidden his firearm.

He told Goldstone that he was a Catholic and would often select his next victim in church. He would follow the woman home to see where she lived. Zikode was not afraid of men and quickly and efficiently got rid of his male competition simply by shooting the men who happened to be in the huts he attacked. He said he would get an erection when he approached the huts and always smoked dagga beforehand to give himself courage. After one of his victims was found, Zikode's mother returned home and took her son back to the crime scene, where most of the community had gathered. He helped the police to lift the body into the mortuary van.

Zikode blamed his sister for the murders. He said it was her duty to teach him how to relate to girlfriends and if he had had the necessary social skills he would not have had to kill for sex. One of the victims had already died of her wounds when he had sex with her. He told the detectives that he did not mind since the body was still warm. Zikode never showed any regret for his crimes and said that it was his mother's duty to apologise to the community. His mother rejected him completely when she realised the truth about her favourite son. Zikode was never abused as a boy, although he was unintentionally neglected.

While awaiting trial Zikode managed to escape with some other prisoners. He committed a housebreaking but was rearrested soon afterwards. On 30 June 1997, about two years after the murders, Mhlengwa Zikode was sentenced to five life terms, totalling 140 years. Advocate Dorian Paver led the State's prosecution. Mr Justice Broom recounted Zikode's savage attacks on innocent people, commenting that he regarded women with contempt and that the murders were appalling.

Notes

Mhlengwa Zikode was an ego-syntonic serial killer. Although he lied about the murders during initial interrogations, this was only to try to escape the law. When he eventually spoke about them he showed no remorse; he felt he had a right to rape the women. He blamed his mother and sister for the murders, typically avoiding responsibility. He said it was his sister's responsibility to provide him with girlfriends and to teach him how to relate to women, and that it was his mother's responsibility to apologise to the community on his behalf.

It would have been easy to make the mistake of classifying Zikode as a disorganised serial killer for he walked everywhere, did not plan much, left the bodies where he murdered them and left evidence all over the crime scenes. However it is important to take other circumstances into consideration and not to follow the 'book' too rigidly. The murders were committed in a rural area, where the level of education is low. Although Zikode is an intelligent man, he did not have the opportunity to read about sophisticated criminal investigation procedures and did not realise that he was leaving evidence. There is little employment in the area where he lived and he could not afford to own a vehicle. Taking these circumstances into consideration, Zikode was clever enough to use different balaclavas in an attempt to conceal his identity and he struck at night when the community was asleep.

THE RIVER STRANGLER

Pinetown, 1995

The KwaZulu-Natal province on the east coast of South Africa is a tropical paradise. The air is humid and the temperatures high, tempered now and then by a light sea breeze. Wild tropical plants, dense shrubbery and vines line the pavements, but behind the exotic splendour death lurks in the form of lethal insects and venomous snakes. Like these animals, a dangerous serial killer used the beautiful, lush green scenery as a cover.

Kim Bodington was a teenager who lived with her divorced mother in Pinetown, Durban. On the afternoon of Sunday 12 February 1995, Kim escaped the sweltering heat of their apartment and walked the short distance to the river behind the building. She made herself comfortable against a tree and began reading her book. Kim never even saw her attacker, who came from behind and covered her mouth to prevent her from screaming. She struggled with him, but he managed to rip her shorts open and rape her. Then he strangled her. He stripped off her Hi-Tech trainers and stole her book and necklace. He dragged her body into the river and left the scene.

When Kim did not return home that evening her distraught mother called her ex-husband. But it was not until the Wednesday that he discovered Kim's body floating in the stagnant river.

Just over a month later, at 7.10 am on Friday 17 March 1995, another young woman was walking to work in Pinetown when she noticed a man crossing over to her side of the road. He was walking ahead of her, but suddenly disappeared behind a wall.

When she passed the wall, he jumped out and dragged her into the bush lining the pavement, pulling her towards the river. The young woman managed to shock her attacker with a small stungun, but when he forced her face into the river, she dropped the weapon. She put up quite a fight when he attempted to rape her, attracting the attention of nearby builders. When the men came running to help, her attacker fled into the bush. The young woman reported the incident to the Pinetown Murder and Robbery Satellite Unit.

Warrant Officer Andy Budke of this unit was in charge of the investigation. He discovered that a case had been reported during the previous year with a similar modus operandi. At about 11.30 on the morning of Friday 9 August 1994, a young woman was walking down Pastel Road, Pinetown, when she became aware of a man following her. He grabbed her from behind and pulled her into the dense shrubbery lining the pavement where he attacked her. He attempted to rape her but fled when pedestrians approached them.

Ten days after the second attempted rape, on 27 March 1995, teenager Kate Wiley was walking home from school in Caversham Road at about 3.20 pm. A woman motorist drove past Kate and when she glanced in her rear-view mirror, she saw a man dragging her down the embankment. The woman turned her car around and returned to the spot where she had seen Kate being attacked. By the time she got there and looked down the embankment, Kate was already dead. The woman rushed home and called the police. They arrived on the scene ten minutes after the incident. Kate had a terrible wound to her head; it looked as if her attacker had used a hatchet on her. She had been raped and there was a bloodstain on her leg and blood on her T-shirt where he had wiped his penis. There was a river close to the scene.

Budke recognised the modus operandi and dubbed the killer the River Strangler. He interviewed both the surviving victims, who described the suspect. It appeared that he might be Rastafarian for he had dreadlocks and smelled of marijuana. An identikit of the suspect was drawn up and given to the media.

Budke established an investigating team and all leads were followed up. A few suspects were interrogated, but to no avail. Eventually the investigation team was disbanded. There is much speculation as to what happened to the suspect, the most reasonable being that he must have died. Serial killers never stop killing, and similar murders did not occur again in that area. It is possible that the suspect was killed during the ongoing faction fighting in KwaZulu-Natal at the time. It is also possible that he had no permanent abode in the area and simply moved on.

The case remains unsolved, but a murder case is never closed. Kim and Kate's parents have not yet seen justice done. It is unnerving to realise that young women walking along a pavement in normal afternoon traffic are not safe.

Notes

The River Strangler provides us with a good example of a disorganised serial killer. The attacks were not planned, but happened spontaneously. The killer was impulsive and opportunistic. The attack was committed in a blitz style, with sudden violence, stunning the victim as quickly as possible. No form of restraint was used. No ruse was used to gain the victims' confidence and hardly any conversation was entered into. The killer had utter contempt for his victims, regarding them merely as objects to gratify his sexual needs. He left them both in exposed and degrading positions and wiped the blood off his penis on Kate's blouse, as one would wipe a knife on a dish cloth.

The murder scenes were messy and he left much evidence. The blood and semen collected could have been used for DNA matching if he was caught.

He took a risk by attacking in broad daylight with possible witnesses nearby. The fact that he attacked at different times during the day indicated that he had no permanent day job. The surviving victims described his clothes as dirty and said that he smelled of sweat and marijuana. This would point to his not having daily access to water to wash himself or his clothes. He could have been a vagabond who lived in the bushes. This would have made his capture more complicated, although usually it is easier to apprehend a disorganised serial killer than an organised one. Organised serial killers cover their tracks; disorganised killers leave evidence and usually live not far from their crime scenes. They can also be recognised by their derelict appearance.

The River Strangler came from the bush, and disappeared into it, never to be found again.

The case is reminiscent of the Green River Strangler in Seattle, USA, although the Green River Strangler's crimes were of a greater magnitude; he tallied at least forty-nine victims between 1982 and 1984. About fifteen million dollars was spent on the investigation into his killings but, like KwaZulu-Natal's River Strangler, he was never apprehended.

VUYANI KENNETH MPENZO

Mdantsane, 1995

Vuyani Kenneth Mpenzo was devastated when he discovered his wife was committing adultery with men in parked cars in the Mdantsane district in the Eastern Cape province. Her treachery was what triggered him to act out the vengeful fantasy that had been smouldering inside him for years. He divorced her and she got custody of their daughter.

Mpenzo shared his two-roomed house in Mdantsane with his ageing mother. In 1995, at the age of thirty-four, the unemployed and lonely Vuyani set out to vent his anger and avenge his honour on innocent people. He targeted couples in the district who had sex in parked cars because they reminded him of his wife and her lovers. Only by killing them could he restore the power imbalance in his psyche.

On 2 March 1995, Khululekile Jonisile and his girlfriend Nombulelo Mbande drove in his Cortina truck to the veld in the Ezinkomeni area near Mdantsane. The couple parked the car, got out and lay down in the veld. Mpenzo saw them and approached silently. He shot Khululekile in the head and he died instantly. Vuyani robbed him of his firearm, a 9mm pistol. He had drawn pantyhose over his hands to avoid leaving fingerprints. He ordered the shocked Nombulelo into the truck and drove further in the bush. He stopped the car and raped her, and then he told her to go.

Two days later, on 4 March 1995, Mbuyiselo Bodla, a policeman from East London, and his girlfriend were sitting in his parked car near the Cementile factory. Mpenzo, who spent his days loitering in the area waiting for couples, stalked them and shot Mbuyiselo in the side. But the wounded policeman put up a fight and struggled with his attacker. Mpenzo tried to get hold of Mbuyiselo's firearm but he shouted to his girlfriend to grab his service pistol and shoot Mpenzo. She shot him in the buttocks. He dropped his firearm – the one which he had stolen from Khululekile – and managed to flee. Mbuyiselo survived.

On 24 April 1995, Mpenzo broke into the house of Tanatu Elliot Keli at No. 2 Golden Highway, Mdantsane, and stole another 9mm pistol as well as a suit, clothing, groceries and money.

The following day, at about five o'clock in the afternoon, Wiseman Mtanase Tukute and his girlfriend Thineka Hina were parked in his Toyota Venture in the Ezinkomeni area. Vuyani approached them and fired five shots. He fatally wounded Wiseman and robbed him of his firearm, wallet, cash and a belt. He drove the car into the bush, raped Thineka three times and then let her go. He set the Venture alight and it burnt out completely.

On 18 May 1995, Mpenzo went berserk near the NU12 section, Mdantsane. He shot Mncedisi Norman Mayeki, hitting him in the leg. He shot at his girlfriend, Ntombizanele Mnikelwa, but missed. Both victims managed to flee. Mpenzo was furious and moved along the road to fire shots at Khumalo Maphathisa Mvambi, Lucas Zenzile, Monica Mnikelwa and Nandhipha Mnikelwa. He forced Nandhipha into Lucas' Ford Cortina and drove away. He raped her and then let her go.

All these cases were investigated by Inspector N T Matoti of the Mdantsane Murder and Robbery Unit, under the guidance of his commander, Captain N Sabana. The surviving victims had helped to draw up an identikit of the suspect. Matoti recognised Mpenzo, but he could not find him.

On 21 May 1995, Mpenzo attended a gathering at NU12 section, Mdantsane, where liquor was served. He became drunk and fired a shot at Taruni Gonyela. He was overpowered by members of the community, who called the police. Matoti was first on the scene. The firearm that Mpenzo had used on this occasion was the one he had stolen from Wiseman Tukute.

Initially Mpenzo refused to cooperate with the detectives but eventually, on the night of 25 May 1995, when confronted with all the evidence, he broke down and confessed.

The trial began in December 1997. Mpenzo faced two charges of murder, eight charges of attempted murder, five counts of rape, five counts of robbery, two counts of attempted robbery, two counts of illegal possession of a firearm and two counts of illegal possession of ammunition, one count of illegally discharging a firearm, one count of housebreaking, one of theft and one of malicious damage to property.

On 12 December 1997 Mr Justice Ebrahim sentenced Mpenzo to a cumulative sentence of 143 years. He was not to be eligible for parole at any time.

Notes

Mpenzo's case brings to mind that of David Berkowitz, alias 'Son of Sam', of New York, who also attacked couples in vehicles. Berkowitz wounded nine people and killed six others between 1976 and 1977. But it would appear that Mpenzo was more concerned about killing men whom he regarded as having dishonoured him by sleeping with his wife. The women were not important enough to kill. He saw them as objects to satisfy his lust. Berkowitz, on the other hand, centred his attack on the women, for he had contracted a venereal disease from a prostitute. Both men avenged themselves on couples because they could not maintain normal relationships.

Other South African serial killers who attacked couples were Joseph Mahlangu, known as the Lovers' Lane Killer (1979) in Soweto (page 103), David Mmbengwa (1996-97) in Thohoyandou in the Northern Province (now Limpopo) (page 251), and Cedric Maake (1997) at the Wemmer Pan recreational area (page 281).

Couples in love enjoy sharing each other's company in secluded spots out of doors, little realising that they are easy prey for serial killers. Making love in the open leaves one in a vulnerable and precarious situation. Many men were literally caught with their pants down and were unable to defend themselves.

Inspector Matoti was an introvert. When he applied to attend the South African Police Service's course on the investigation of serial killers, he shyly informed the interviewer that he knew exactly what a serial killer was, for he was certain that he had arrested one. This proved to be true. Unfortunately serial killers were seldom recognised as such in the South African Police Service before 1994 and detectives in the rural areas had never even heard of this type of criminal. Many serial killers were probably caught, but the detectives who arrested them were not acknowledged as serial killer investigators. To have participated in a serial killer investigation is considered a highlight in the career of any murder and robbery detective.

Inspector Matoti died in a car accident a few years later when he was on his way to attend the First National South African Conference on Serial Killers in Paarl in the Western Cape in 1999. He had looked forward to the Conference, and to presenting his case to the other detectives. His family received a posthumous commendation and a cash award for Matoti's successful investigation.

BONGANI MFEKA

Kranskop, 1995

Bongani Mfeka differed from other serial killers in that he had relationships with his victims before he killed them. Although he called them his 'girlfriends', these women were more like a collection of dolls to him. He would play with them and then discard and destroy them so no one else could have them. He did not consider nor treat them as human beings with emotions. To him they existed solely as objects to fulfil his needs.

These women accompanied him as he travelled round the countryside, allegedly looking for work, but actually looking for an opportunity to commit crime.

Mfeka was a clever criminal and often posed as a traffic officer or a salesman before he started killing. He already had a record for assault, drug dealing, housebreaking, vehicle theft and taxi violence. On a particular day, as they walked in the veld, he would suddenly feel overpowered by an urge to kill. He would then rape his 'girlfriend' and strangle her.

The first of his victims was Babzile Nompumelo Mhlongo whom he strangled with a piece of string between 1 and 5 June 1995 at the Jammersdal Farm in the Kranskop area of KwaZulu-Natal.

Mfeka had met Babzile in the town of Stanger. He spent some time with her, flattering her and winning her confidence, and eventually he invited her to accompany him to his home at Silverstreams in the Kranskop district. On the way there he attacked and killed her and robbed her of two hundred rand.

She was discovered by farm workers. It could not be established whether or not she was raped.

Four months later, on 21 October 1995, Philile Happiness Masuku caught a taxi from Nkandla to Kranskop. At the taxi rank in Kranskop she met Mfeka and spent the following two days in his company at the Mathafeni location. Some time between 23 October and 3 November Mfeka took Philile to the Cubhu river on the Patience Farm in the Kranskop district, where he strangled her with a tracksuit top. Her body was discovered on 3 November. It could not be established whether or not she had been raped.

Mfeka met Tholakele Ntombinhlophe Khanyile on 31 October 1995 at a taxi rank in Kranskop. He promised her employment and asked her to accompany him to his house at Silverstreams. He took a short cut to the same Jammersdal Farm, where he began strangling her. She struggled and he eventually grabbed a piece of wood and began hitting her. She fell down and he raped her, but Tholakele managed to free herself and got away.

The day before Philile's body was discovered, on 2 November 1995, Mfeka met Nono Princess Shezi at the taxi rank. He used the same ruse that he had used with Tholakele to convince Nono to accompany him to his house at Silverstreams. He took the same short cut to Jammersdal Farm where he strangled her with his belt.

Some time between 31 October and 6 November 1995, Mfeka picked up Phumuzile Tholakele Phungula at the Kranskop taxi rank. He used exactly the same modus operandi as in the other cases and also strangled her at the Jammersdal Farm.

Tholakele Khanyile reported her rape and attempted murder to the Kranskop police.

On 6 November 1995 the Kranskop detectives arrested Mfeka, when Tholakele pointed him out. He refused to cooperate with the detectives. Since no detective in the Kranskop area was trained in the investigation of serial homicide, Inspector Tjaart Pretorius from the Newcastle Murder and Robbery Unit was asked to oversee the investigation. In the mean time, Captain Piet Byleveld of the Brixton Murder and Robbery Unit in Johannesburg was investigating the Nasrec serial killer case.* One of the victims in this case appeared to have come from Newcastle. Byleveld knew that Mfeka had been arrested and decided to bring him to Johannesburg for interrogation to establish whether he might have been involved in the Nasrec murders. At this stage, Mfeka had not yet confessed.

On the way from Kranskop to Johannesburg, Byleveld struck up a conversation with Mfeka. And when he stopped to have lunch alongside to the road, Mfeka was invited to participate in the meal.

On the journey, Mfeka told Byleveld that he regarded him as a father figure. Mfeka had been severely neglected by his own father and had always felt the lack of paternal love in his life. When they arrived at Brixton, Mfeka confessed to Byleveld. He also told Byleveld it was his dream to become a Methodist minister. (Nicolas Ncama also had a dream of becoming a Methodist minister; page 244.)

Mfeka was kept in custody at the Brixton cells close to Byleveld, whom he revered. Byleveld would sometimes book Mfeka out of the cells to clean his office. One day there was an uprising in the cells and an attempted escape. Mfeka grappled with the other inmates to prevent them from escaping. When asked why he had done this, he replied that he was afraid they would enter the building and harm Captain Byleveld.

Mfeka's trial was held in the Pietermaritzburg High Court. On 16 June 1996 at the age of thirty-two years, he was sentenced by Mr Justice Jan Hugo to four life terms for four murders and another fifteen years for the attempted murder and rape of

---

*A serial killer had been operative in Johannesburg since 1993. He was dubbed the 'Nasrec killer' since the bodies of his victims were found dispersed within a radius around the Nasrec sports complex in southern Johannesburg. In April 2002, 27-year-old Lazarus Tshidiso Mazingane, who had been identified as the 'Nasrec killer' was charged with seventeen murders. The case was sub judice at the time of going to press and cannot therefore be discussed.

Tholakele Khanyile and the theft of two hundred rand from Babzile Nompumelo Mhlongo. Byleveld attended the trial. Mfeka asked if he could be incarcerated in a prison close to Byleveld, but his request was refused for it would make it difficult for his family to visit him.

Notes

A photograph album with pictures of different women was found in Mfeka's house. He did not even know some of the women, but he collected their photographs. This album would be used as collateral evidence.

Collateral evidence refers to items, usually found in a suspect's home, which cannot necessarily be tied directly to his crimes, but point to his behavioural patterns and habits. For instance, paedophiles might make scrapbooks of photographs or pictures of children. These may not necessarily be pornographic, but depict children in what seem to normal people to be natural poses. Little girls on swings, doing ballet or gymnastics, or boys playing in the water in their swimming trunks hold an erotic attraction for paedophiles. They might also buy or steal children's clothing which they use as stimuli to enhance masturbation. A psychologist or a trained detective can usually testify on collateral evidence to provide the judge with a better picture of the personality of the offender.

Mhlengwa Zikode, the Donnybrook serial killer (page 219), had pin-ups of women in sexy underwear posing over chairs on the walls of his hut. Inspector Theo Goldstone, who had been trained to look out for and collect such items, confiscated these pin-ups. During Zikode's trial the victims testified that he liked to rape them while they were bent over a chair. Goldstone testified on the significance of the pin-ups which corroborated the victims' testimony.

Jeffrey Dahmer, the Milwaukee serial killer, had posters of naked men in his bedroom. After he had killed his male victims he would pose their bodies in the positions depicted in the posters and take pictures of them. Dahmer killed seventeen men between 1987 and 1991 and kept their dismembered corpses in his apartment. A serial killer who displays this behavioural pattern is termed a 'collector'. British serial killer Dennis Nilsen also kept the corpses of his victims in his apartment, under the floorboards. Like Dahmer, he would sometimes take one of them out, bath him and seat him on the couch or at the dining room table for company. Nilsen killed fifteen men between 1979 and 1983.

WILLEM GROBLER

Louis Trichardt, 1995

On the evening of 14 July 1995, 26-year-old Willem Grobler went to the Black Steer restaurant in Louis Trichardt. He was looking for company. He noticed 21-year-old Sonja Liebenberg and her boyfriend having an argument outside the restaurant. At first he tried to intervene, but then left the premises.

Grobler returned later and offered the distraught Sonja a lift home. They began arguing about Sonja's boyfriend and Grobler decided not to take Sonja home but drove to the bridge at the nearby dam. He parked the car, got out and opened the boot, taking out the jack and its handle. Sonja got out of the car and tried to run away, but Grobler hit her over the head several times with the jack handle. He dragged her body along the bridge, removed her pants, inserted the jack handle into her private parts and lifted her body up with the handle. The post mortem report indicated that it was impossible to establish whether she had been raped since her anus, vagina and bladder had all been torn. Grobler tossed Sonja's boots and pants into the boot of the car and threw her panties over the side of the bridge. He left her on the bridge and drove home where he threw her pants away and hid her boots under his bed.

Sonja was discovered by pedestrians the next morning and the police were called. She was still alive when she was found, but died shortly afterwards in hospital. Sonja had a twin sister, who had had a fight with Grobler some time before. Was he venting his anger on the innocent Sonja, without realising that she was not her sister? It seems more likely that he did not care and that his hatred extended to all women.

Initially, the case baffled Sergeant Japie Swanepoel of the Pietersburg (now Polokwane) Murder and Robbery Unit since the crime scene was located at a spot well known for satanic rituals. The case remained unsolved for almost a month.

Twenty-year-old Gertruida Elizabeth Breedt, nicknamed Lolla, was a friend of the Grobler family, but she allegedly caused trouble among the Grobler brothers who had fist fights over her. On the evening of 9 August 1995 Lolla and Willem Grobler visited several bars, as well as a friend of Willem's. When Grobler and Lolla left the friend's house he drove out on the Venda road. He and Lolla had an argument during which she apparently expressed the wish that his mother should die. Grobler parked the car and took a hammer from the boot. Lolla tried to escape but Grobler attacked her viciously. When Lolla lay unconscious on the ground, Grobler threw the hammer back into the boot and left the scene. He did not molest her sexually.

The following morning the police were called to the crime scene where they found Lolla barely alive. She was taken to the Ga-Rankuwa hospital where she died of her injuries later that day. Lolla was wearing a shirt with the name 'A Walchebach' written on the collar. In an attempt to identify the victim, Swanepoel contacted all the Walchebachs in Pietersburg and eventually traced Annelie Walchebach who told him that she had given the shirt to Susan Breedt who lived in Louis Trichardt. He traced Susan Breedt to her home, and she told him that she had given the shirt to her sister Lolla. Susan also told Swanepoel that her sister had left home with Willem Grobler the previous evening and had not returned home.

Swanepoel went to Grobler's home, which was in the same street. When he questioned him, Grobler told Swanepoel that he had taken Lolla to his friend Lucky Luke's home, but that she had left with three men in a red Citi Golf. Swanepoel spoke to Lucky Luke who maintained that he knew nothing about the three men in the red Citi Golf. In the mean time detectives had secured prints of the vehicle tyre tracks at the crime scene. Swanepoel went back to Grobler's house and found that his vehicle's tracks matched those left at the crime scene.

When confronted with the evidence, Grobler confessed to both murders and pointed out the crime scenes to Major Grobler. The detectives retrieved Sonja's boots, the hammer, the jack and jack handle.

Willem Grobler was sent to Weskoppies psychiatric hospital for observation. He was found to have border degree intellectual functioning and psychopathic tendencies, but was declared competent to stand trial.

Grobler's trial lasted from 1 September to 4 September 1997. He was sentenced to an effective thirty-eight years in prison.

Notes

Willem Grobler did not rape his victims. His basic instincts of sex and aggression were fused to such an extent that, in my professional opinion, he probably experienced an orgasm when violently hitting the girls and when he forced the jack handle into Sonja's private parts, thereby destroying her internal organs. Grobler provides an example of how a serial killer is dominated by the id. He acted out these fused instincts in anger. He had sufficient ego to know that what he did was wrong, but his superego was lacking for he did not give himself up to the police, showed no remorse, and tried to avoid responsibility by blaming his actions on his state of anger.

Grobler's case also illustrates how the system can fail the community. His career as a criminal had started in 1987 when he was found guilty of stealing a bicycle. He was sentenced to five strokes. That same year he was found guilty of negligent driving and was fined 250 rand. The following year, 1988, he was convicted for stealing tools and given a fine of 200 rand or forty days imprisonment, plus an additional fine of 800 rand or eighty days which was suspended for five years. Also in 1988, he was found guilty of attempted rape and given a two-year sentence, suspended for four years. In 1989 he was convicted for indecent assault, but served only six months in prison. Justice seems to have failed in the case of Willem Grobler, tragically for Sonja Liebenberg and Lolla Breedt and their families.

Although Grobler committed only two murders, the apparent lack of motive for his deeds identifies him as a serial killer. His early arrest, which can be attributed to good detective work, was extremely fortunate.

NICOLAS NCAMA

Eastern Cape, 1996-97

When Nicolas Ncama was a young child in the former Transkei in the Eastern Cape, he dreamed of becoming a Methodist minister, but after he had completed his matric, he qualified as an electrician. Ncama's parents died when he was a young child and he turned to his older brother for guidance. His brother was a Methodist minister and Ncama adored him. The brother was married and Ncama loved his sister-in-law as well. Their marriage provided him with the security and stability he had lost when his parents died.

Ncama's life changed irrevocably when his brother got another woman, Nomonde, pregnant and she forced him to divorce his wife and marry her. As a result, the brother was dismissed from the church. Ncama had to tell his beloved sister-in-law that his brother was going to divorce her. This infuriated him and when his brother later died in a car crash, his life was shattered. He hated Nomonde passionately, but she was the mother of his brother's children. His older sister also died around this time. Ncama subconsciously experienced the deaths of his parents, his brother and sister as rejection and developed an unusual sensitivity to rejection of any form.

Ncama married Madikobisho Euginia Mokeyana, a woman who had previously been married to a detective named Themba Zanto. She had a daughter named Sonia with Zanto and, although Sonia lived with her father, Ncama admitted that he was fond of her. Ncama's own marriage was unstable and he and Madikobisho separated. After the separation Ncama sometimes lodged with Nomonde, although he had no affection for her. As a self-employed electrician, he travelled around the Eastern Cape and had a number of girlfriends in different towns.

On 10 April 1996, Ncama gave Miss Zabo, the daughter of a family friend, a lift from Plettenberg Bay to Port Elizabeth. He found some excuse to stop the car close to a beach in Port Elizabeth, where he raped Miss Zabo. He also began throttling her, but did not kill her. When she recovered he took her to a house where he again tried to force her to have sex with him. When she refused, he assaulted her. She managed to get away and found refuge in another house, telling the woman who lived there what had happened to her. As happens so often with serial killers, Miss Zabo proved to have been Ncama's trial run.

Just over a year later, on 24 May 1997, Ncama, who was by now seriously intent on becoming a Methodist minister, borrowed Nomonde's car. He agreed to give 28-year-old school teacher, Miss Desi, a lift from King William's Town to Frankfort. On a stretch of road near Frankfort, Ncama stopped the car in the dark, grabbed Miss Desi and began to strangle her with one hand. With his other hand he tried to remove her clothing. She fought back, grabbing his private parts. Ncama was furious. He leaned over, opened the passenger door and kicked her out of the car before driving off. Miss Desi's luggage was still in the car. Miss Desi walked into Frankfort where she laid a charge with the police.

Four days after this incident, on 28 May, Ncama met an ex-girlfriend of his, 21-year-old Luyanda Gloria Nguzela, in Umtata. She was an inspector in the South African Police Service. Ncama asked her why she was avoiding him and she told him that she was not interested in his advances because he was unemployed. This rejection angered him, and he suspected that Nomonde had turned the woman against him. He lured Gloria into the car by promising her a lift. He parked the car at a secluded spot outside Umtata, reached for a piece of wire on the back seat and tied her hands behind her back. He then strangled her with the wire.

When she was dead, he untied her hands, and tied the wire around her neck to her belt. He drove on until he reached a bus station at Bityi, just outside Umtata. He dumped her body there after stealing her service pistol.

Nompumelelo Mpushe (26) also lodged with Nomonde in King William's Town. Both Nomonde and Nompumelelo worked as secretaries at the Bisho Parliament. On 12 September 1997, Ncama arrived at Nomonde's home to fetch his belongings as she had told him to leave. He once again felt rejected. Nomonde had already left for work and Nompumelelo was alone in the house. She told Ncama that he had to leave the premises immediately because she was late for work. This sparked Ncama's anger and he kicked her in the stomach. He then raped her and strangled her with her pantyhose. He wrapped her body in plastic sheeting and hid it under carpets stored in the garage. He stole her cellphone and new car kit. A few days later, on 17 September, Ncama returned when Nomonde was not at home, and loaded Nompumelelo's body into his car. He dumped her body, still wrapped in the plastic sheet, near a railway line at Fort Jackson station where it was discovered the next day.

On Sunday 5 October 1997, Ncama's 15-year-old step-daughter Sonia visited her mother Madikobisho at her home in Kwazakele outside Port Elizabeth. Ncama happened to be there too, but he had a fight with his wife who wanted him to move out permanently. An angry Ncama followed Sonia when she left to return to her father's house. He caught up with her at Njoli Square and managed to lure her to an empty apartment, to which he had the key, near a shop in Adonis Street. There he raped her brutally and strangled her with a nylon rope. He tied one end of the rope to a chair and left her bleeding body in the apartment.

Themba Zanto searched for his missing daughter. He suspected that Ncama was involved, but could not find him. Nine days later, on 14 October, he was horrified to discover the decomposed body of his daughter in the apartment.

Zanto, who was a detective at Kwa Dezi, reported the murder to his senior, Captain Deon Marais of the Kwazakele Murder and Robbery Unit. Marais traced and interviewed Nomonde, and she told him that Nompumelelo had been missing for weeks. Marais suspected that Ncama was involved in her disappearance as well. He contacted his superior, Superintendent Andrew Middleton, and told him of his suspicion that Ncama might be a serial killer.

It was on 19 November 1997, when Nomonde found Miss Desi's stolen luggage hidden in her garage, that this case was linked to the others. Nomonde informed Marais that she had discovered a firearm in her house. Marais traced the firearm and found it to be the service pistol of Constable Gloria Nguzela, whose body had since been discovered.

Nompumelelo's murder was being investigated by Inspector Tommy Jafta of the East London Murder and Robbery Unit. There were now three bodies to be accounted for. Middleton established a serial killer task team and centralised the investigations. In due course it was ascertained that Ncama had known all three victims.

Further investigation indicated that Ncama could have been involved in the rape and murder of Mrs Cynthia Nombeko Ndlaku. Ncama was friendly with both her and her husband, who was a Methodist minister. On 16 December 1996, he was repairing electrical faults at the Ndlaku home in Mase Street, Kwazakele. Mr Ndlaku was away, and Mrs Ndlaku was alone at home. A friend who used to sleep in the house when her husband was not there, was unable to stay over on the night Mrs Ndlaku was murdered. Ncama was aware of this. He left the house at about nine o'clock on the night of 16 December. He alleged that when he arrived for work the next day, he found Mrs Ndlaku's body. Her hands were tied behind her back and she had been raped and strangled.

The detectives managed to track Ncama down through Nompumelelo's cellphone, but he still evaded them. A reward of 50 000 rand was offered to anyone providing information as to Ncama's whereabouts. During October 1997 Ncama himself phoned Marais and told him he was not willing to hand himself over for he still had some business to attend to. At this stage Ncama was studying to become a Methodist minister, and he later told Marais that he was searching for a Methodist minister to whom he wanted to hand himself over. Eventually, in the early hours of the morning of Thursday 27 November 1997, the task team tracked Nicolas Ncama to a house in Debe Nek, just outside King William's Town.

He appeared in court for the first time on 1 December 1997 and the case was postponed to January 1998 pending further investigation. He was held in custody at the Louis le Grange police station in Port Elizabeth.

After his arrest, Miss Zabo and Miss Desi came forward and laid rape charges.

During April 1998, Inspector Jafta booked Ncama out of custody to accompany him to Cape Town for further investigation. On the way back, Ncama told Jafta that they should return to Debe Nek where other evidence was hidden. There Ncama managed to escape. He was on the run for a few days before he was rearrested.

Eventually, in November 1998, Nicolas Ncama, then thirty years old, appeared in the Grahamstown High Court on the following charges: four counts of murder – Mrs Ndlaku, Gloria Nguzela, Nompumelelo Mpushe and Sonia Zanto; three counts of rape – including Miss Zabo, Mrs Ndlaku, and Sonia Zanto; one count of attempted rape – Miss Desi; two counts of robbery – Gloria Nguzela's firearm and Nompumelelo Mpushe's cellphone; and one count of theft – Miss Desi's clothing.

Mr Justice Lex Mpati presided over the case. Advocate Terry Price acted for the defence and Advocate Johan Bezuidenhout for the State.

Nicolas Ncama was sentenced on 27 November 1998 to ten years for the rape of Miss Zabo, four years for the attempted rape of Miss Desi, one year for the theft of Miss Desi's clothing, twenty years for the murder of Luyanda Gloria Nguzela, eighteen months for stealing Gloria's firearm, twenty years for the murder of Nompumelelo Mpushe, six months for stealing her cellphone, and a life sentence for the rape and murder of Sonia Zanto. Themba Zanto sat quietly in court when Ncama was sentenced to life for killing his daughter. As an officer of the law he was satisfied that justice had been done, although it would never bring back his beloved daughter.

It could not be proved beyond a reasonable doubt that Ncama had raped and murdered Mrs Ndlaku. He had consistently denied this charge, claiming that he had the greatest respect for Mr Ndlaku because he was a Methodist minister. He said that he had committed the murders because of his hatred for Nomonde who, ironically, was also the wife of a Methodist minister. But he said he would never harm her because she was the mother of his brother's children.

Notes

Like Bongani Mfeka of Kranskop (page 235), Nicolas Ncama was one of the few serial killers who killed people he knew. The phenomenon of serial killers substituting others for the original aggressor or aggressors in their lives, is quite obvious in this case. Although the original trigger for Ncama's actions was his perception of his family members' deaths as rejection, Nomonde caused him psychological pain and was to him the personification of the evil, rejecting woman. Those he killed had known Nomonde and he believed she had turned them against him. Sonia was the daughter of his wife, who had also rejected him. Nomonde's marriage to Ncama's brother may have caused him to hate her, but it also saved her life. In his eyes, other women had to pay for Nomonde's mistake. Typically refusing to take responsibility for his deeds, Ncama blamed Nomonde for the deaths of his victims.

Nicolas Ncama described himself as a very proud, traditional Xhosa man. He did not tolerate rejection or resistance from a woman. The women whom he murdered were liberated and independent. They earned their own salaries and were not dependent on men to take care of them. Ncama was not very successful in his business as an electrician and resented these women because of their achievements. He described Sonia as a bright young student who would one day have been able to fend for herself.

It is interesting that Ncama, who professed to be a man of God and wanted to become a Methodist minister, should take God's power over life and death upon himself. Ncama resigned himself to prison life – after once attempting suicide while in custody – and endeavours to preach the word of God to other inmates. He expressed remorse only regarding Sonia's murder.

DAVID NDIVHALENI MMBENGWA

Limpopo Province, Brits & Kagiso, 1996-98

As a young boy, David Ndivhaleni Mmbengwa had bad luck with male role models. He grew up in the rural area of Thohoyandou in the Northern Province (now Limpopo). Thohoyandou means 'head of the elephant', bringing to mind the game, wild predators and elephants which used to roam there freely before they were slaughtered by hunters. The beautiful countryside, known as bushveld, is typically African, dotted with thorn trees and tall yellow grass.

All of this meant nothing to the young David Mmbengwa. He did not have a good relationship with his father, who died when he was a young boy. His mother remarried, but his step-father also treated him badly. Mmbengwa went to live with his grandfather, but his luck did not change. His grandfather also abused him and eventually he moved back to his mother's house. At school, he only managed to complete grade 8.

Some of Mmbengwa's most shocking childhood memories were watching his mother having intercourse with several of her boyfriends. Traditionally, the woman should be subject to her husband's authority and obedient in all matters. To David, a woman did not exist in her own right. She was the property of her husband. He had no quarrel with his mother's immoral behaviour; rather, his problem was with the men who stole another man's property. The code of honour between men had been transgressed. David never forgot this and it remained embedded in his heart where it festered to erupt in serial killing later in his life.

When he was about twenty, Mmbengwa was arrested for theft. He was sentenced to two months in prison, suspended for a year. At the age of twenty-eight, he had a fight with his uncle and stabbed him fatally. He was convicted of culpable homicide and sentenced to six years, two of which were suspended.

While in prison Mmbengwa was informed that his wife had been seen having intercourse with a taxi driver in the bush. This not only infuriated him, but also triggered memories of his mother's boyfriends committing adultery. When he was released from prison he rejoined his family in the Thohoyandou area. With his limited education and his prison record, he could not find employment and resorted to robbery.

On 16 February 1996 he accosted Zachariah Mudua on the Dwzerani road and stabbed him with a knife. He stole 3450 rand, a cellphone, a purse, some credit cards, a Z.88 pistol, a speaker and cassettes and Zachariah's vehicle.

Mmbengwa had tasted the addiction of power. To him, having power over another man was the ultimate feeling. At last the ill-treated child could stand up against adult men.

A month later, on 16 March 1996, he tried to rob a bread truck near Twinga and shot and wounded Simon Ndonyana. Scarcely a month after that, on 15 April 1996, he shot and wounded Norman Nthatheni who was visiting the Muhuru restaurant near Thohoyandou when Mmbengwa accosted him. Mmbengwa threatened him with a firearm and robbed him of 600 rand. On 28 May 1996, he ambushed another bread truck near Muledane and shot and killed Tshilidzi Thomas Gandula; and on 10 June 1996 he killed Lawrence Muofhe near Mashawana.

On 31 July 1996 Mmbengwa was roaming the bush near Dumasi when he came upon 34-year-old Hlekani Constance Khoza and her male friend. They had just made love and were on their way home in their vehicle, when Mmbengwa suddenly appeared in front of them with a firearm in his hand. He forced them to drive into the bush and told them to get out of the vehicle and lie on their stomachs. He indicated that he wanted to rape Hlekani but she struggled with him and he shot her, wounding her fatally. Her companion jumped up and ran and although Mmbengwa fired two more shots, the man managed to escape unharmed. He reported the incident to the police, but they were unable to trace Mmbengwa.

Perhaps Mmbengwa was aware that the police were looking for him and so he moved to the North West province. He was arrested in Brits on 14 November 1996 for robbery and the murder of Tshilidzi Thomas Gandula. On their way back to Thohoyandou the detectives stopped for the night in Pretoria and locked Mmbengwa up in the Silverton police station cells. He escaped.

He went to Tsisigi in the Thohoyandou district. During the night of 29 April 1997, Rendani Raphunga and his girlfriend were having intercourse in the bush near Dumasi. As they were leaving Mmbengwa suddenly appeared and without saying a word, shot Rendani. He completely ignored the woman and simply walked away. She reported the murder to the Thohoyandou police. Rendani died later in hospital.

On the morning of 24 October 1997, Azwieheli Lacter Mugwedi and his girlfriend were making love in the bush at Dovheni when Mmbengwa appeared. Without saying a word he fired at Azwieheli and killed him. Again, he ignored the woman and quietly left the scene. This time he was wearing a balaclava.

Mmbengwa had developed a pattern of roaming the bush, stalking couples making love. In his mind the men were committing the crime of adultery with his mother and his wife. He ignored the women because they were of no value to him.

On 15 November 1997 Bernard Nevhutalu and his colleague attended a funeral where they met two women, who accompanied them into the bush at Mutoti. Bernard and Rebecca Mulaudzi remained in the minibus while the other couple walked into the bush. Mmbengwa came upon the second couple and asked them if they were aware of the murderer who killed couples making love in the bush. He left them unharmed and walked to the minibus. He pulled out his firearm and fired several shots at

Bernard, killing him. He wounded Rebecca in the arm. Bernard's firearm was lying on the floor of the vehicle, but Mmbengwa did not take it.

During January 1998 the same fate befell Khorommbi Mukosi Ndou and his girlfriend at the Tshine Grazing Camp, and Richard Ramathikhithi and his girlfriend who were making love at Tshiulungoma. Both women escaped unharmed.

On 9 February 1998, Mmbengwa robbed Elvis Netshiavha of cash near the Makhuvha-Tshilivho residential area.

Mmbengwa and his family moved to Kagiso, near Johannesburg, where an uncle of his lived.

On 22 April 1998 Bushi Norman Fikilephi's vehicle broke down near the Kagiso cemetery. He was pleased to see a Golf pull over and approached the driver to explain his problem. But the driver pulled out a firearm and robbed Bushi of his firearm, cash and shoes. The Kagiso cemetery became Mmbengwa's last crime scene when, on 27 May 1998, Johannes Msakharum Mkhawane, a local murder and robbery detective, and his girlfriend Doris Kenyaditswe Rabothe were both shot and killed while making love in his car.

During June 1998, Captain Kwarra Nenswekhulu of the Thohoyandou Murder and Robbery Unit reported the possibility that a serial killer was active in his area to the Investigative Psychology Unit in Pretoria. Superintendent Tollie Vreugdenburg of the Bosveld Murder and Robbery Unit was alerted, for he was the most highly trained officer in that area. He established a task team and on Monday 7 June 1998 they left for Thohoyandou. They discussed the cases with the local detectives and the name David Mmbengwa was mentioned. Vreugdenburg drew Mmbengwa's record and found the culpable homicide sentence. On the Tuesday the team gathered information about Mmbengwa and on the Wednesday morning they visited the crime scenes. It was established that Mmbengwa had lived close to the scenes.

That afternoon Vreugdenburg and his team went to the house where Mmbengwa had lived. It was abandoned but inside they confiscated discarded pornography, documents on the traditional role of women, books on religion and legal aid, and a Venda Bible. One of the detectives, Inspector P Molele, who was a Venda prince, pointed out to Vreugdenburg that Mmbengwa had marked in the Bible certain passages relating to 'an eye for an eye' and the role of women, as well as passages relating to pure love. By now Vreugdenburg was certain he was on the trail of the right suspect. The collateral evidence corroborated the profile of the suspect drawn up by the Investigative Psychology Unit.

On the Thursday, Vreugdenburg and his team visited Mmbengwa's mother who told them about her son's childhood and her own infidelities. She said that he and his family had relocated to live with her relative in Kagiso and gave them his work address.

On the following Monday the team left for Kagiso. But the relative was not at work that day and the frustrated team spent the night in Johannesburg. The following morning, Tuesday 15 June 1998, at half past five, they met the relative at his place of work and explained the purpose of their visit. He took them to his son's house, but Mmbengwa was not there. One of the detectives spotted a police firearm next to the son's bed and confronted the son. He admitted that Mmbengwa had given him the firearm. It was Johannes Mkhawane's service pistol. Knowing that he was in serious trouble, the son led the detectives to a squatter camp near the Kagiso police station and pointed out a shack. At seven o'clock that morning, the detectives knocked on the door. It was opened by David Mmbengwa, who was living there with his wife and three young children. He was immediately arrested.

Initially, the squatter camp community was hostile towards the police, but when the situation was explained to them, they threatened to burn down Mmbengwa's shack. Vreugdenburg divided his team into two groups. One group was to accompany him and the suspect to Pretoria while the other was to assist the family in packing up their belongings and moving them to the safety of the relative's home in Kagiso. More pornography, another Bible and firearms were discovered in the shack.

Vreugdenburg and Inspector Molele interrogated Mmbengwa at the offices of the Investigative Psychology Unit in Pretoria. They were assisted by one of the unit's psychologists. Vreugdenburg began by asking Mmbengwa questions about his childhood and his religion. Mmbengwa was very aware of the fact that he was in the presence of a Venda prince and shyly asked Vreugdenburg's permission to ask a question. He wanted to know whether one was allowed to shoot back if one had a firearm pointed at one. Vreugdenburg knew immediately that Mmbengwa was referring to Johannes Mkhawane. He asked Mmbengwa what he did when the firearm was pointed at him and he replied that he had shot the man. Then he confessed. The process took an hour and a half.

When they got back to Thohoyandou Mmbengwa told Vreugdenburg that his uncle, Samson Nevhutanda, had provided him with firearms and initiated the robberies of the bread trucks.

The trial commenced in October 1999. Advocate Manyana acted for the state and Advocate Makafola for the defence. Mr Justice Makanya presided. During January 2000 the trial was disrupted by Cyclone Grace and was postponed. Samson Nevhutanda was a co-accused, but was eventually found not guilty.

On 26 July 2001 David Mmbengwa was sentenced to seven life sentences for the murders and another forty-six years for robbery, robbery with aggravating circumstances, attempted murder, escape from lawful custody, and illegal possession of firearms and ammunition. It was the court's firm view that he should remain in prison for the rest of his natural life. He was thirty-four years old.

Notes

The South African Police Service is proud of its international reputation for the speedy apprehension of serial killers. In this case it took Superintendent Vreugdenburg and his team eight days from forming a task team to the actual arrest of the right suspect. Vreugdenburg was following his intuition. The moment he entered Mmbengwa's abandoned house in Thohoyandou he had a feeling he was on the right track and he relentlessly followed his instincts. It paid off.

DANIEL MOEKETSI RAMAISA

Kroonstad area, 1997-98

The main agricultural produce of the Free State province is maize. Maize fields line the highways and stretch across the landscape. It is a pleasure to drive through this part of the country during the different seasons and to see the young maize, the full-grown maize higher than the height of a man, the crops being harvested and eventually the tractors ploughing the rich earth and preparing for the new season of planting.

During 1997 and 1998, the maize fields near Kroonstad – a medium-sized town in the Free State – the life source of thousands of people, became the killings fields of Daniel Ramaisa, a local taxi driver.

At about midday on 12 April 1997, a 13-year-old girl was walking along a dirt road on the Novacotia farm, when a man emerged from the maize fields and started chasing her. The young girl ran for her life, but the man caught up with her and dragged her into the fields. He forced her down among the stalks and tied her arms and legs. She screamed, but there was no one to hear. The man tied a ligature around her mouth to stop her from screaming. For hours he raped her repeatedly in the blistering sun. When she tried to scream again, he strangled her manually and left her for dead. But the girl recovered and ran home and reported the incident. She pointed out Daniel Ramaisa, who was at that time living on a neighbouring farm, as her assailant and he was charged with her rape, but acquitted on a technicality.

Four months later, on 11 August 1997, a woman was picking up ears of maize in the fields on the Gelukskraal farm when, to her horror, she came across the decomposed body of a young woman. The victim was dressed in a short-sleeved shirt, which was pulled up along with her bra. The body was face down but the hands had not been tied. As a result of decomposition and possible animal activity, the fingers and toes were missing and the head had come apart from the body. The victim was identified as 19-year-old Sophia Maria Ngatane. Although the body was badly decomposed, it was established that her death must have occurred some time during March or April that year.

On 8 May 1998 a herdboy discovered the body of seven-year-old Josephine Dibuseng Thuetsi in the maize field on the Mielieplaas farm. She was still wearing her school uniform and had been murdered about two weeks before, some time between 22 and 26 April. Her hands were tied behind her back with her school belt, and the belt was also tightly wound around her neck. It was later established that Josephine was last seen alive on 24 April at a local taxi rank in Kroonstad.

Two months later, on 25 July 1998, the body of a young girl was discovered in the grass fields of the Schoongezicht farm. The victim was wearing a dress with a floral pattern and she had her shoes on. Her stained panties were found a few metres from the body. The body was covered with vegetation. Tyre tracks were lifted from the scene. The victim was identified as 12-year-old Mittah Naong and she had last been seen alive on 24 May. She had left her grandmother's house and was on her way to her aunt's house, but she never arrived.

All the victims lived on the farms where they were killed. In July 1998, after the third body was found, a local teacher told the media that it seemed as though a serial killer might be active in the area. The press reported the four incidents and the killer appeared to quieten down for a while, as no more bodies were found.

Unfortunately no one linked these murders at the time but eventually, in January 1999, they came to the attention of the

South African Police Service's Investigative Psychology Unit, which specialises in serial homicide. Superintendent Gert Fourie, commander of the Bloemfontein Murder and Robbery Unit, was immediately contacted. Fourie drove to Kroonstad where he studied the dockets.

During the second week of January 1999, Fourie visited a shack in the local squatter camp, Koekoe Village, and arrested 40-year-old Daniel Moeketsi Ramaisa, a local taxi driver. He confessed to the crimes. Ramaisa was married and the father of two toddler daughters. He and his wife had previously lost two babies due to cranial deformity. Ramaisa told Fourie he had committed the murders because he became sexually aroused when the eyes of his victims dulled as they were dying.

Ramaisa's trial was held in Virginia in the Free State. The state prosecutor was Advocate Elize le Roux and Advocate Ilse Potgieter represented the accused. On 23 July 2001 Mr Justice van Kopenhagen found Ramaisa guilty of the three murders and the rapes of Josephine Thuetsi and Mittah Naong. In his confession he stated that Sophia Ngatana had consented to sex and the state was unable to prove otherwise. Mr Justice van Kopenhagen declared Ramaisa a dangerous criminal and sentenced him to thirty years imprisonment in terms of article 286 of the Criminal Procedure Act. This article specifies that the judge may sentence the offender to a minimum sentence without parole and after this term has been served another judge or magistrate may decide whether or not the offender has been rehabilitated. The Department of Correctional Services therefore has no discretion to release the prisoner on parole after twenty-five years.

Notes

There is no greater power than the power over life and death. Daniel Ramaisa was sexually stimulated by the sight of life fading from the eyes of his young victims and fixated on this sense of absolute power. It made him feel omnipotent.

It is tragic that the rape of the first victim and the murders of the other young girls did not initially receive full attention from the police. Although they are overburdened and work under extremely difficult circumstances, there is no excuse for their lack of interest. Fortunately, men like Superintendent Gert Fourie and his team are dedicated officers who are committed to their work.

The South African Police Service has since identified crimes against women and children as one of their highest priorities.

SIPHO TWALA

Phoenix, 1997

Sugar cane grows well in the tropical climate of KwaZulu-Natal. Cornubia Estate is a cane farm spanning 1200 square hectares in Phoenix, just outside Durban. Several suburbs surround this cane farm, one being KwaMashu. KwaMashu is what used to be called a 'township' and the Bester squatter camp is situated in KwaMashu, on a hill overlooking the cane fields. It was outside one of the three-roomed squatter huts that the Cane Killer, as he became known, would sit and stare out over his killing fields.

Some time in April 1996, Ms M was raped in Durban North. Her assailant attempted to murder her, but he was disturbed and she managed to escape. She identified the man as Sipho Twala and DNA samples were taken during the investigation. Unfortunately she did not turn up at the trial and the case was therefore not prosecuted.

On 17 February 1997 the body of an unidentified woman was discovered by cane cutters in field 301 of the plantation. She was wearing a dress, but her shoes were missing. Her hands were tied behind her back with a piece of green cloth. The body was badly decomposed so no smears could be taken to determine whether or not she had been raped.

Two months later, on 30 April 1997, another unidentified body was found in field 431. Her blouse had been pushed up to reveal a pink bra. The woman had been strangled with her panties, which had been torn into strips, but her hands had not been tied. Her skirt and shoes were missing. As in the previous case, the body was badly decomposed.

A month later, on 27 May 1997, the decomposed body of another woman was discovered in field 673. She lay on her back and her hands were tied in front with a piece of cloth. Her ankles were tied with the same cloth. She was wearing black panties and a blouse. Her handbag and shoes were lying next to her body. As there were only skeletal remains, no DNA smears for semen could be taken.

Just over a week later, on 4 June 1997, the charred remains of a woman were discovered in field 243. Cane cutters burn the cane fields before they harvest the cane to get rid of vermin. It seemed as if the woman was lying on her stomach and that her hands had been tied behind her back. Her white tackies did not burn in the fire.

Five days later, on 9 June 1997, another burnt body was discovered in field 673. The woman was lying on her stomach and her hands had probably been tied behind her back. There was a gag in her mouth and it was also wrapped around her neck. The torso of the woman had been pressed between cane stalks, seemingly to prevent her from squirming.

On 18 June 1997 the burnt body of yet another woman was discovered in field 671. Her hands were tied behind her back with plastic hessian and her feet were tied at the ankles with the same material. Again, a gag was found in her mouth and the material was wrapped around her neck. The gag was made from a piece of red T-shirt and a bra. Inside her mouth was a separate wad of material, which seemed to be made from her panties. The rest of the T-shirt was found on the scene.

Two days later, on 20 June 1997, the decomposed body of a woman was discovered in field 671. She was lying on her stomach and her hands were tied behind her back with a petticoat. Her ankles had been tied with strips of petticoat. Again, there was a gag in her mouth, also made from the petticoat, and it was wrapped around her neck. Her torso was wedged between two cane stalks.

All seven cases were reported to the detective unit at the Phoenix police station, but they were allocated to different investigating officers. The fact that the bodies were either badly decomposed or burnt complicated the investigations. Many pedestrians walk through the cane fields every day but no one came forward with any useful information. Fortunately one of the Phoenix detectives realised that something was terribly wrong. He asked that the cases be brought to the attention of detectives at the Durban Murder and Robbery Unit who had been trained in serial killer investigations. In July all the cases were transferred to Superintendent Philip Veldhuizen, who was second in command and had been trained in serial homicide investigations.

Veldhuizen immediately formed a task team consisting of Murder and Robbery detectives who had also been trained, including Superintendent Alan Alford, who had completed his training the previous week. Veldhuizen included two of the Phoenix detectives in the team. An operations room was set up and other support in the form of forensic experts and profilers were flown in from Pretoria.

On 12 July 1997 the detectives found the naked body of a woman in field 462. Her hands were tied behind her back and her feet were bound closely together. She had a wad made of her panties in her mouth and a gag, also made from the panties, was wrapped around her mouth and extended to her neck.

Veldhuizen asked that members of the Dog Unit and their dogs drive down from Pretoria to search for bodies in the cane fields. His foresight paid off.

On 23 July the decomposed body of a woman lying on her side was discovered in field 461 by the detectives and the Dog Unit. Her hands and feet were tied with hessian rope and she had been gagged with a piece of petticoat. Strips torn from a bra were found on the scene.

On the same day, in field 434, the body of another woman was found. Her hands were tied with strips of petticoat and the wad in her mouth had been carefully folded with the lace of a petticoat. She was gagged and strangled with a strip torn from the hem of a petticoat and her panties covered her head. Her feet were not tied.

The following day the detectives and the Dog Unit returned to the scene and discovered another badly decomposed body in field 461. She was still clothed and lying on her back. Her hands had been tied in front of her and there was a wad made of petticoat in her open mouth. Her feet had been tied with a strip of fabric from her polka dot dress.

Later that same day in the same field the dogs discovered another decomposed body. She was lying on her back. Her legs had been tied with petticoat but the ligature had come off. She had been gagged and strangled with a petticoat. Her panties were torn, but had been left around her ankles.

In the mean time the dogs had been sent into another field, 434, where they discovered another decomposing body. Her legs and hands were tied with strips of a bra and floral material. She had been gagged with the same floral material and a bra strap which had been tied in a knot on top of her head. In the same field on the same day yet another body was found. Her feet were tied with strips of her panties and a scarf. There was no gag and nor were her hands tied.

While these crime scenes were being processed by the detectives, the dogs discovered yet another body in field 434. She was wearing only a petticoat, but her hands had been tied with a black scarf and her feet were tied with strips of the same scarf. She had been strangled with a strip of a black bra and her panties had been thrown on top of her body.

Eight bodies were discovered in those two days. Most of the victims had head or face injuries, which indicated that the assailant probably knocked them unconscious before tying them up. This illustrated his need to act out his bondage fantasies because the unconscious women could not offer any resistance and he had no need to tie them up.

The last body was discovered on 5 August 1997. She was naked except for a blue jersey. She had been strangled with a pair of red panties and there was no gag in her mouth. Her hands and feet had not been tied. Pieces of petticoat were tied around cane stalks just one metre from her arm. Three condoms were picked up at this crime scene.

A total of sixteen bodies had been found.

Veldhuizen had requested that all dockets pertaining to rape and murder with a similar modus operandi for the previous year be transferred to him. In this pile of dockets he discovered the case of Ms M. As DNA had been identified in the last two cases he requested the Forensic Science Laboratory in Pretoria to compare the DNA identified in Ms M's case with the DNA in the series. A few days later it was confirmed that the DNA was that of the same person, Sipho Twala.

The task team were elated that they had identified their suspect, but they still had to find him. They were unable to trace Ms M. Informers were sent into KwaMashu to find Sipho Twala's dwelling and by eleven o'clock on the morning of Wednesday 13 August 1997, word came that Twala's hut had been located. By eleven o'clock that night, Veldhuizen had briefed the detectives, as well as members of the Internal Stability Unit who would provide protection, the profilers, the photographers and the forensic experts, and sent them all home for a few hours' sleep.

At three o'clock on the morning of Thursday 14 August 1997, a mere six weeks after the task team had been formed, Veldhuizen and a handful of detectives knocked on Twala's door. He opened it himself and was immediately arrested, shackled and seated on a small bench in his room. When the detectives shone their torches around the room they found that it was stacked with women's clothing. Clothing hung from the rafters in the roof and was piled on the floor. Women's watches lay next to Twala's mattress.

The rest of the team who had waited outside KwaMashu were alerted and silently moved into the sleeping squatter camp. Twala's mother and sister and her children were taken to the Durban Murder and Robbery Unit to be interviewed.

In the mean time the forensic experts collected and photographed the clothing. Outside Twala's hut the detectives discovered that he had practised making his knots with strips of underwear on the cane stalks growing there. He could do this while he looked out over his killing fields, fantasising about the murders, as serial killers like to do.

When first light dawned in the squatter camp, the community became aware of the commotion and gathered around the hut. This was why the heavily armed Internal Stability Unit had been called in. The detectives needed protection from the community, for KwaMashu was known to be a dangerous hot spot for violence. However when the community realised that the notorious serial killer had been arrested they broke into spontaneous cheers.

Twala was taken to the district surgeon for examination to prove that he had not been assaulted during the arrest and was then taken to the offices of the Murder and Robbery Unit in Durban. He arrived mid-morning, and one of the profilers was asked to interview him before the interrogation started. Within half an hour he had voluntarily confessed to the profiler and was thereafter interrogated by Veldhuizen.

During the interrogation, and using the interpreter as a 'model', Twala demonstrated to Veldhuizen how he had tied up the victims. He admitted that he had watched the detectives processing one of the crime scenes from a distance. He said that he left the bodies close to each other so that they could be easily found and given decent funerals.

Twala told the profiler that he had killed the women because they reminded him of his girlfriend who had aborted his baby and who had since rejected him. He said that she had broken his heart.

Twala did not know his exact age, but he was between thirty and forty years old. He had attended school only up to grade 2. He had been to prison for vehicle theft and claimed to have been trained as a cadre of the African National Congress's military wing, Umkhonto weSizwe. He was unemployed and made a living by stealing cane and selling it.

During the investigation and before Twala was identified, the profiler had predicted that the killer would be a Zulu male between the ages of thirty and forty years; he would be divorced or single and would be living in KwaMashu. He would be unemployed and would make his living by illegal means. He would not own a vehicle, preferring to walk. He would spend most of his days in the cane fields. He would have a previous criminal record, such as car theft, and would have faced a previous charge of rape. The killer would be aggressive, a loner with a short temper who bore grudges and was unforgiving. He detested women and had been wronged by an adult female shortly before the murders started. It could have been a girlfriend whom he wanted to marry who had jilted him.

The bondage evident at the crime scenes was symbolic of his fear of intimacy. He had tied his victims' hands and feet to prevent them from touching him. He gagged them and placed wads in their mouths so that they would not be able to talk to him, since he felt that a woman injured him emotionally when she spoke to him. He cut their underwear and used it mostly as ligatures, for underwear represents the mysticism of women, which he also feared. When he tore the underwear, bound and raped the victims, they were probably unconscious as a result of their head injuries and they could therefore offer no resistance.

The profiler made only one mistake, predicting that the killer would have had a secondary school education.

When Veldhuizen and his team inspected the ligatures, they found that one of the wads which had been folded from a strip of petticoat and inserted into one victim's mouth, belonged to the same petticoat with which another victim was tied up. Twala had taken some of the material home and had folded the wads there, probably while he fantasised about his next murder. When the time was right he would walk down to the crossroads, pick up a victim, promise her employment and accompany her through the cane fields, all the while playing with the wad in his pocket and knowing what he was going to do to her. He gave one or two garments to his mother and sister as presents, but mostly they were not allowed to touch any of the women's clothing which adorned his room.

Sipho Twala's trial began early in 1999. He was charged with the rape and attempted murder of Ms M who had been found just days before the trial commenced, and with sixteen rapes and murders. Advocate Gary Williams was the state prosecutor and Advocate Kenneth Samuels defended Twala. On 31 March 1999 Mrs Justice Niles Dunér sentenced Sipho Twala to an effective 506 years in prison. He was sentenced to twelve years for raping Ms M and to two years for attempting to murder her. He was found guilty of rape in the last two cases and sentenced to twelve years for each rape. In seven cases he was found guilty of indecent assault rather than rape, since although the victims' panties had been removed, no traces of semen were found. In seven cases he was acquitted of rape since the bodies were badly decomposed and the clothing had been burnt. He was sentenced to thirty years for each of the sixteen murders. Some of the sentences were to run concurrently.

Only a few of the victims were identified. During the trial Twala's mother was assaulted and her home was wrecked because the community believed that he was there. Twala showed no remorse throughout the trial and never apologised.

The community of KwaMashu's memory was short and it did not take long before they became hostile towards the South African Police Service again.

Notes

A day after Twala's arrest another murderer tried to copycat what he had read about the Cane Killer in the press. He dumped the bonded body of his female victim in the cane fields, but even if Twala had not already been under arrest the detectives would immediately have recognised this crime as a copycat attempt, since the killer did not know about Twala's modus operandi of tearing underwear, folding wads and securing gags. No one could copy an obsession symbolising the hatred and fear of intimacy which crystallised in Twala's particular modus operandi. Detectives have learned that in order to prevent copycat killings it is important not to divulge finer details of crimes to the press.

The movie 'Copycat' attempted to depict a person who copied various serial killers' modus operandi. It is highly unlikely that this would happen. True serial killers have their own idiosyncratic choice of victims and their modus operandi has a special personal meaning for them. Someone like the person depicted in the movie would not be a true serial killer, but rather a misguided and possibly disturbed individual looking for attention. Attention-seeking is a discernible motive and cannot be considered in the same light as the deep psychological motivation of a true serial killer.

VELAPHI NDLANGAMANDLA

Piet Retief, 1997-98

Piet Retief in Mpumalanga province is a picturesque town. It is situated in an area dubbed the Black Forest of South Africa because of the many plantations which are reminiscent of the celebrated area of the same name in Germany.

As with most other towns in South Africa, the so-called 'township', or predominantly black area, of Piet Retief is situated on the outskirts. The township is called eThandakukhanya, which means 'we want a clean place'. Behind the formal settlement lies the informal squatter camp of Phoswa Village. Dwellings in the squatter camp are built from numerous materials, including clay, mud, corrugated iron, hardboard and sometimes bricks. The roads are unmade, nameless and disorderly. Only a few houses have numbers painted on them. The village sprawls up the hill, covering a radius of some 10 kilometres. There are many shebeens or bars. Usually one room of a two or three-room dwelling serves as the bar. The woman of the house is known as the shebeen queen and her children usually sleep in an adjoining room while she serves her clients. Patrons also sit outside and drink.

On 4 April 1997, in the district of Blesbokspruit near Piet Retief, a .22 Anschutz rifle was stolen from the home of Mr Jacobus Christoffel van Schalkwyk. This .22 rifle is also called a Saloon and the serial killer who used it became known as the Saloon Killer. Apart from the rifle, another shotgun, ammunition, radios, jewellery, clothing, cash and food were also stolen from Mr van Schalkwyk.

On 24 April 1997, twenty days after the robbery in which the rifle was stolen, another burglary took place at the Corner Store in the Commondale district near Piet Retief. Nightwatchman Shaka Eliot Nkosi Dlamini was shot and killed during this incident. The burglar broke into the home of a second nightwatchman, Sandlankosi Simon Vilakazi. He fired a shot at him and ran off with his togbag.

The Saloon Killer had begun his murderous career which lasted a year and four months. Twenty people lost their lives and eleven others were wounded.

Khonzaphi Qwabi owned a shebeen. It was business as usual on the evening of Friday 13 June 1997. Khonzaphi was sitting in her kitchen with her friend Aaron Mtshali. Her daughter Thandazile had just informed her that she was tired of serving the guests and she retired to the other room in the house to go to bed. It was already past eleven o'clock.

Khonzaphi and her friends were discussing the shooting incident that had occurred earlier that evening. Two men and a woman had been shot on a road leading to Kempville, a suburb situated two kilometres from Phoswa Village. At about half past seven that night a woman, Nomsa Nelisliewell Ndlangamandla, had been walking along the footpath. A man had approached her and shot at her without warning, wounding her in the arm. As she fell to the ground she heard another shot. The same man had shot and killed Sitende Dhlamini who had been walking close behind her. Sitende was shot above the left eyebrow. Then the same man walked past Abson Avril Scheick and shot him in the back. He survived, but the man robbed him of his possessions.

News travels fast in a rural community. Mandla Zacharia Ngwenya joined in the conversation in Khonzaphi's kitchen. They were all shocked by the meaningless shooting of the three adults.

Suddenly two men entered the shebeen. One was wearing an army coat and a black balaclava covered his face. Without warning, he produced a .22 rifle and shot Mandla in the stomach. He pointed the rifle at Aaron, who had leapt to his feet, and

272

shot him two centimetres above his left eyebrow. Khonzaphi demanded to know why the man had shot her two friends. He swung the rifle in her direction and shot her two centimetres above her left eyebrow. Drunken clients rushed out of the shebeen and into the night.

The two men left the shebeen. Thandazile came out of her room and stumbled over the body of her dead mother. Aaron and Mandla had fled, only to die later in hospital. Twelve-year-old Thandazile could not comprehend the situation, nor did she know what to do about it. In a state of denial, she went back to bed.

A short while later she stared into the face of the man who had shot her mother. Both men had returned to the shebeen. The man in the army coat told the other that he had found another person he was going to kill. The second man took Thandazile by the hand and led her out of the shebeen. Then he went back inside. Thandazile crept back into the house and saw both men having sex with the corpse of her mother. After they left she hid under her bed, where neighbours found her the following morning.

These cases were reported to Captain Danie Hall of the Secunda Murder and Robbery Unit. Secunda is about 200 kilometres from Piet Retief, but Piet Retief fell within the jurisdiction of the Secunda Murder and Robbery Unit.

On 18 June a man stormed into the house of Amelia Dumakude Mbenyane in Phoswa Village and shot her in the head. She died instantly.

A little more than a month later, on 28 July 1997, Dingindawo Robert Twala was shot and killed on the Kempville road, but the local detectives did not alert Captain Hall. He only traced this docket in April 1998.

On 21 August 1997, the shop of Leonard Nhlabathi in Phoswa Village was broken into and a carton of cigarettes was stolen. Shots were fired at the scene, but no one was hurt.

On the night of 5 September 1997, Lucky Douglas Mbuli and his girlfriend were sleeping inside their hut in Phoswa Village.

They both woke when someone rattled the window. Lucky stormed outside and chased the would-be intruder towards the river, where he was shot in the chest. He managed to stumble back in the direction of his hut, but the perpetrator caught up with him and shot him again. This time the wound, slightly above the left eyebrow, was fatal.

Yvonne Nonhlanhla Nkambule lived in a mud hut in Phoswa Village. On the evening of Thursday 25 September Yvonne, her boyfriend, his friend and her sister had just finished dinner and were looking forward to discussing the events of the day. Yvonne had washed the dishes in a plastic wash tub. There was no running water or electricity in her hut and Yvonne opened her front door, picked up the wash basin and stepped outside to throw the water out. The next moment her sister and friends heard a loud noise.

'It sounds as if someone is playing cricket,' said Yvonne's boyfriend. The door burst open and Yvonne stumbled in, clutching her breast. 'I'm dying,' she said as she fell into her boyfriend's arms. A few moments later she was dead. Like Lucky, Yvonne had also been shot in the chest.

An hour and a half after Yvonne was killed, Paulo Jimba Manana and his friend Jacob Ngobeni alighted from a taxi and began walking along the road behind Phoswa Village. They became aware of a man walking behind them. He called to them and told them to hand over his possessions. Paulo and Jacob did not understand what he meant. The man then pulled out a .22 rifle and shot at them. Paulo and Jacob were petrified. They had no means of defending themselves so they picked up stones from the road and threw them at the man. More shots were fired and Paulo and Jacob ran for their lives. The man shouted that he had run out of ammunition and disappeared into the trees. A few moments later he reappeared and shot at them again. Paulo was hit in the left hand and Jacob was shot in the stomach, but both men managed to get away.

The following night, 26 October 1997, Bongani Mlipha and his friend Petrus Lala Maduma were walking on a dirt road next to the Welverdient plantation, close to Phoswa Village. They had been gambling at the Lunch Box, a tavern in Piet Retief. A man appeared from the trees and began shooting at them. He hit Bongani two centimetres above his right eyebrow, killing him. Petrus fled, but left his hat and shoes behind. Later that same night, the Piet Retief charge office got an anonymous call about a body lying next to the road at the abattoir, about a kilometre away from the place where Bongani was killed. Members of the uniform branch found the body of Amos Mjayi Nkosi. He had been shot in the left side of the chest and robbed of cash.

Within the space of two days it seemed as if the killer had gone mad. Fear spread like a veld fire through Phoswa Village.

Then, for three months, the killings stopped. They started again during January 1998, following the same pattern as the previous year. On 5 January 1998 Maria Khumalo was raped and strangled in the corn fields at Zaaihoek, close to Piet Retief.

On the night of 15 January, a shop in Phoswa Village was broken into and the nightwatchman, Ambriose Nthalintholi, was found dead. He had been shot in the right side of his chest. No one had seen anything. Absalom Nkosi, was shot and wounded in the neck on 26 January as he was riding his bicycle on the road to Kempville. His bicycle was stolen.

On 5 February 1998, at about 6.45 pm, Michael Dumi Shongwe was walking along a road in Phoswa Village when he encountered the killer. They had a short conversation after which the killer shot Michael in the face, but he survived the incident. At 7.50 pm that same night, the man broke into a hut in Phoswa Village. The occupants, Thokozile Mkhwananzi and Nellie Mdluli, were sitting inside when the door burst open. A man with a .22 rifle entered and shot Nellie two centimetres above her left eyebrow, killing her instantly. Nellie was eight months pregnant.

Two days later, on 7 February, Fanie Gilbert Malinga and a female companion were walking on a footpath in Phoswa Village. They were approached by the killer who shot and killed Fanie, but the woman managed to escape.

A month later, on 6 March 1998, the body of Rebecca Thandi Manana was found next to the road in Phoswa Village. She had been shot above the right eyebrow.

Three days later, the killer moved to the farms about 27 kilometres south east of Piet Retief. Some time during the night of 9 March 1998, he entered the homestead of Babili Esert Nduba. He kicked open the door of Babili's hut and shot him in the left side of the chest, killing him. Then the man took a bowl of porridge and a tin of fish and ate his meal outside the homestead wall.

He moved on, reaching the home of Johannes Nhleko at eight o'clock. Johannes heard someone moving about outside but was too frightened to investigate. No shots were fired, but the killer stole a chicken and two loaves of bread.

By half past ten he had reached the neighbouring farm and entered the homestead of Andries Mthimkhulu. He kicked open the door of Andries' hut and fired a shot, but no one was injured. He shot at Andries' dogs, killing one of them. Then he went to the neighbouring hut of Leonard Hadebe and kicked open the door. He felt underneath the pillow of the sleeping grandmother for money, but did not find any. He assaulted Leonard and pointed the rifle at him, but before he could shoot, the grandmother, Thema Hadebe, had woken and, in a drunken stupor, chased the perpetrator out of the hut. He fled into the night.

On Saturday 4 April 1998, several people made complaints about a man who had threatened them with a rifle on the farm at Goedertrouw, which is five kilometres east of Piet Retief. At 1.30 pm that day Zodwa Lucy Malinga was on her way to her house on the farm when she encountered the killer. He threatened her with the rifle and ordered her to remove her underwear. He assaulted her and attempted to rape her but could not get an erection. At about six o'clock that evening the killer met Phiri Johan Nqothani in the plantations at Goedertrouw and threatened him with the rifle. Phiri managed to flee. By seven o'clock that evening he had killed Elphas Mbuli, and by ten o'clock he had wounded Zweli Moses Nkosi in the chest. Zweli managed to get away, although several shots were fired after him.

During May 1998 a formal investigation team was assembled at the detective offices in Piet Retief. Superintendent Koos Fourie, Commander of the Secunda Murder and Robbery Unit, was in charge and the investigation was conducted alternately by Captain Hall and Captain Rudi Neethling. Detectives from Piet Retief, Vryheid, and Secunda were called in. Several suspects were interrogated, but the killer managed to evade the detectives.

The killer struck again on the night of Friday 2 July 1998 when he shot Mbuyise Zwane. Zwane's body was discovered on a footpath in Phoswa Village. And on the night of Sunday 4 July the body of Muzi John Mavuso was discovered at the dam at Phoswa Village. Both victims had been shot above the left eyebrow.

During the day on 21 August 1998, the killer broke into the home of Michael Kunene and stole security guard uniforms, bed sheets and primus stoves. At about five o'clock that afternoon he met Neliswe Mkhonza and her daughter Simangele Mkhwanazi in Phoswa Village. He began shooting at them, killing Neliswe. Simangele was wounded, but survived. A security guard uniform was discovered at the scene.

At about 6.30 pm on 28 August 15-year-old Mduduzi Vundla was riding his bicycle in Moolman in the Piet Retief area when he was shot at and fatally wounded in the back by a man who stole the bicycle.

At four o'clock in the morning of 6 September 1998 the killer shot and wounded Thembinkosi Simelane at the dam in Phoswa Village.

Four days later the detectives' hard work finally paid off. Alerted by an informer they managed to find Velaphi 'Soldier' Ndlangamandla, who confessed to Inspector Jan Sithole that he was the Saloon Killer. Ndlangamandla had been living with his wife in Phoswa Village.

His trial began in September 2000 before Mr Justice C J

Claassen. On 18 September 2000 he was found guilty on nineteen counts of murder, nine counts of attempted murder, three counts of housebreaking, one count of illegal possession of a firearm and one count of illegal possession of ammunition, six counts of robbery, one count of attempted robbery, two counts of housebreaking with aggravating circumstances, one count of indecent assault and one count of pointing a firearm.

On 19 September 2000 Ndlangamandla was sentenced to twenty life sentences plus 135 years. Due to lack of evidence, he was found not guilty of the murders of Ambriose Nthalintholi, Fanie Gilbert Malinga, and the attempted murder of Thembinkosi Simelane and Zweli Moses Nkosi.

Notes

Because he wore an army coat and was such a good marksman, Ndlangamandla was profiled as possibly having been a soldier at some time in his life. However, although he had applied to join the army he had been rejected. Since it had always been his dream to be a soldier, he was given the nickname 'Soldier'.

Ndlangamandla said he could not achieve an erection during normal intercourse and this emasculated him. It was only when he was holding a rifle in his hands that he could achieve an erection. He would ejaculate when he pulled the trigger. The rifle became his penis substitute. It made him feel powerful and manly. The fact that his victims were both males and females made no difference to him.

Ndlangamandla's case brings to mind that of David Berkowitz, alias 'Son of Sam', who between 1976 and 1977 killed three young women, one young man and wounded three young women with a .44 Bulldog revolver in New York, USA. The victims were young people who sat in cars late at night. He did not interfere sexually with his victims.

Berkowitz was adopted by a Jewish family, after his biological mother rejected him. His adoptive mother died when he was fourteen years old and this had a devastating effect on him. He disliked his stepmother and searched and found his natural mother. The happy reunion did not last very long. During his first sexual encounter with a prostitute Berkowitz was infected with a venereal disease and from that time his hatred for women blazed into a killing frenzy.

Both Berkowitz and Ndlangamandla released their sexual frustrations through the barrel of a gun.

Time frame and summary

4 April 1997	Robbery at home of J C van Schalkwyk .22 rifle stolen
24 April 1997	Corner Store robbed Shaka Eliot Nkosi Dlamini shot and killed Robbery at home of Sandlankosi Simon Vilakazi
13 June 1997	Nomsa Nelisliewell Ndlangamandla attacked Sitende Dhlamini shot and killed Abson Avril Scheick attacked
	Shebeen attack: Khonzaphi Qwabi shot and killed Aaron Mtshali shot and killed Mandla Zacharia Ngwenya shot and killed
18 June 1997	Amelia Dumakude Mbenyane shot and killed
28 July 1997	Dingindawo Robert Twala shot and killed
21 August 1997	Robbery at shop of Leonard Nhlabathi
5 September 1997	Lucky Douglas Mbuli shot and killed
25 September 1997	Yvonne Nonhlanhla Nkambule shot and killed
25 September 1997	Paulo Jimba Manana attacked Jacob Ngobeni attacked
26 October 1997	Bongani Mlipha shot and killed Amos Mjayi Nkosi shot and killed
5 January 1998	Maria Khumalo raped and strangled

15 January 1998	Shop in Phoswa Village broken into Ambriose Nthalintholi shot and killed
26 January 1998	Absalom Nkosi attacked
5 February 1998	Michael Dumi Shongwe attacked Nellie Mduli shot and killed
7 February 1998	Fanie Gilbert Malinga shot and killed
6 March 1998	Rebecca Thandi Manana shot and killed
9 March 1998	Babili Esert Nduba shot and killed Theft from home of Johannes Nhleko Break in at home of Andries Mthimkhulu Break in at home of Leonard Hadebe
4 April 1998	Complaints about man threatening people with rifle Zodwa Lucy Malinga – attempted rape Phiri Johan Nqothani – threatened with rifle Elphas Mbuli shot and killed Zweli Moses Nkosi attacked
2 July 1998	Mbuyise Zwane shot and killed
4 July 1998	Muzi John Mavuso shot and killed
21 August 1998	Robbery at home of Michael Kunene Neliswe Mkhonza shot and killed Simangele Mkhwanazi wounded
28 August 1998	Mduduzi Vundla shot and killed
6 September 1998	Thembinkosi Simelane attacked

CEDRIC MAAKE

Johannesburg, 1997

Cedric Maake can be considered one of the most cold-blooded serial killers in South Africa's criminal history. From a purely academic point of view, he is also one of the most interesting. Unlike most serial killers, Maake did not stick to one modus operandi, nor did he experiment with different modus operandi as some serial killers do. Rather, Maake had five different modus operandi which he applied to different sets of victims.

Little is known about Maake's personal history except for the fact that he was born on 10 September 1963 in the Giyani area in the far Northern Province (now Limpopo). He was the youngest of four children. Although Maake must have had a deprived childhood, the only early trauma he was willing to acknowledge was his initiation at the age of twelve or thirteen. Maake had no wish to elaborate on this experience, except to say that he had had to live in the veld for three months without clean water and food and that he considered this to be barbaric. Maake's father died when he was in grade 10 and he had to leave school. He went to Johannesburg to search for work. He became a plumber, working for himself. He had a wife at home in Giyani and a girlfriend in Johannesburg. He had fathered four children. At the age of thirty-three, when he was living in La Rochelle in Johannesburg, he began to commit his murders.

At about ten o'clock on the morning of Monday 6 January 1997, Magan Khanjee (78) was alone in his tailor shop on Madison

Street in Jeppe when a man entered, claiming to be a plumber. He said that he wanted to buy a pair of second-hand trousers. Magan handed the man a pair of trousers which he proceeded to try on. While Magan was placing the trousers into a bag the man suddenly lashed out at him with a shifting spanner, hitting him in the left eye. Magan fell down and the man struck him again. He could not remember anything after that. The man left the shop, but also stole five pair of trousers. Magan spent a week in hospital and although he survived the attack he did not make a complete recovery.

Magan was Maake's second victim. Eight days before, on 28 December 1996, the same fate befell Antonio Alfonso who was working at Hill Extension Gardens Café in High Street, Rosettenville, when Maake entered the shop and attacked him with a hammer. He stole 400 rand from Antonio. Antonio also survived the incident.

Two days after Magan was attacked, Maake struck at Terminus Butchery in Bezuidenhout Avenue, Troyeville. He bludgeoned Kenny Chan with a hammer and stole money from him before leaving the shop. Kenny survived.

On 17 January 1997, Maake entered Vellaph Brothers in Rockey Street, Doornfontein at about half past ten in the morning. He told the proprietor, Kantilal Lutchman (56), that he wanted alterations done on two pairs of trousers. He sat on a chair waiting for Kantilal to complete the work. He said that he also wanted to buy a pair of shoes for which he paid a deposit, signing his name as Patrick Makwena of Walmer Street, Bedfordview. Then he took out a hammer and told Kantilal that the head of the hammer was loose and that he needed to buy a new one. Kantilal directed him to a hardware store. A short while later he returned and told Kantilal that he wanted to buy underwear. As Kantilal turned around to take the underwear off the shelf, Maake attacked him with the hammer. He stole Kantilal's wallet and left the bloodied hammer behind in the shop. Kantilal suffered multiple skull fractures and a clot on the brain, but he survived.

Five days later, on 22 January, Abdool Samad Bulbulia was alone in his shop at Shamiana in Bree Street, Newtown serving Maake when Maake attacked him with a hammer. He stole Abdool's wallet containing 600 rand and left the shop. Abdool survived.

The next day, 23 January, Dhansuklal Thakor Patel was alone in his shop in Von Wielligh Street in downtown Johannesburg when he was bludgeoned with a hammer. His wallet was stolen. He was rushed to hospital but died later that same day.

Some time during February 1997 Hossen Amod, who worked at JB Cash & Carry in Main Street, Fordsburg, was attacked in a similar manner by a man wielding a hammer. Two hundred rand was stolen. Hossen survived.

On 26 February David Sadka was working at The Pawn Shop in Rockey Street, Yeoville, when he was attacked by a man using a hammer as a weapon. His wallet containing credit cards and cash was stolen. He survived the attack.

At eight o'clock the next morning, just after Amratlale Gopal (63) had opened the doors of City Shoe Repairs on Von Wielligh Street Johannesburg, two men entered his shop and attacked him with a hammer. Amratlale suffered brain damage and could not remember what had happened. His wallet was stolen.

A month later, on 26 March 1997, Lawpit Law, of the Modern Butchery in De la Rey Street, Vrededorp was also attacked by a man with a hammer and robbed of 900 rand.

Then, another month later, at about lunchtime on 22 April 1997, Yogi Dheda (34) was serving a customer at Jays Wholesalers in Commissioner Street. The customer wanted to know whether Yogi could mend shoes and he bent down and took them off. When Yogi turned his back, the man attacked him with a hammer. Yogi fought for his life and the man fled, leaving behind his shoes and a bag of clothing. Unfortunately Yogi sold the clothing and it could not be collected for evidence.

These eleven incidents account for the first cases in what was later dubbed the hammer series. At this stage, the crimes were being investigated by different detective branches in Johannesburg and the investigation was not coordinated.

On 27 April 1997, Maake changed his modus operandi and targeted couples relaxing in the Wemmer Pan area. The first couple he attacked was Muntu Elijah Hlatshwayo (58) and his companion Eunice Nkosapantsi, who were sitting in Muntu's Toyota Cressida in the veld next to the N17 highway on Rosettenville Road, Village Deep. Muntu was shot in the back and robbed of his wallet and a 9mm pistol. Maake dragged Eunice to the nearby mine dump where he shot her too. The state could not establish whether or not she was raped. On this same night, Maake met another woman in the Wemmer Pan area. He raped her and struck her repeatedly on the head with a rock until she died. The woman was never identified.

So Maake began what became known as the Wemmer Pan series by killing three people on one night. However he departed from this second modus operandi to his third modus operandi the following month when he targeted taxi drivers.

On 25 May 1997, Maake got a lift in Sipho Ndima's taxi. When they reached Compound Road in Springfield, close to Wemmer Pan, Maake took out a firearm and threatened Sipho. He robbed him of 300 rand and then shot him several times. Sipho survived.

During June 1997, Maake was travelling in Michael Mkhize's taxi and when they reached Colyn Road, Village Deep, close to Springfield and Wemmer Pan, he drew his firearm. He robbed Michael of a watch, a pair of shoes and 150 rand. Then he shot him twice. Michael survived.

These two attempted murders and robberies with aggravating circumstances concluded Maake's third modus operandi. That same month he reverted to the Wemmer Pan modus operandi.

On 14 June, Ralph Jeremia Ngwenya (49) and his companion Christina Mashigo (42) were enjoying each other's company at Wemmer Pan when they were accosted by Maake. When the ambulance and paramedics arrived, Ralph was still alive, although he had been shot twice in the back. He died while they were trying to resuscitate him. Christina's body was found a short distance away. Maake had raped her and shot her several times.

Two days later, on 16 June, Maake changed his modus operandi for the fourth time by randomly attacking people walking in the street. He attacked, raped and fatally shot Dorah Duduzile Dladla as she was jogging along the Soweto Highway at Crown Mines. On 21 June Sonti Simon Mohokoni was walking near the Highveld Technical College in Riverlea – which is close to Wemmer Pan – with two female companions, when Maake approached them. After a short conversation, Maake pulled out his firearm and shot Sonti, wounding him fatally. The women fled and Maake stole Sonti's shoes, 20 rand and his identity document.

During July 1997 a special investigation team was established at the Brixton Murder and Robbery Unit to coordinate the Wemmer Pan murders under the leadership of Captain Piet Byleveld.

On 11 July 1997 Maake reverted to the Wemmer Pan modus operandi when he attacked Jerry Khanya Naidoo (44) and his companion Charlotte Ndlovu (28) while they were sitting in Jerry's parked car at Wemmer Pan. Maake first asked Jerry to show him how a cellphone worked and whilst Jerry was distracted, he shot and fatally wounded him in the stomach and chest. Maake robbed Jerry of his wallet and then dragged Charlotte out of the car and pistol-whipped her. He made her walk with him for a short distance and then robbed her of her leather jacket, watch and spectacles. Maake also instructed Charlotte to entice a taxi driver to approach them, but she managed to get into the taxi and escape.

At about five o'clock the next evening, Maake encountered Moses Ramothlhwa (35) and Dorcas Makhatsane (26) at Wemmer Pan. He shot Moses twice in the back, killing him instantly. He stole his wallet and then turned his attention to Dorcas, forcing her to walk with him into the woods. Maake pointed to a vagrant walking in the woods and told her that this man worked with him. He instructed her to remove her clothing and raped her twice. He then gave her a few rands to take a taxi home and tried to make a date with her. He also asked her if she was going to attend Moses' funeral. Dorcas took a taxi home.

Four days later, on 16 July, Maake accosted Stanley Speelman Kolobe (26) and his companion Emily Madiba who were sitting in their parked car at Wemmer Pan. Maake forced the couple out of the car and into the woods at gunpoint. He told them to undress and to have sex with each other. In the mean time he stole Stanley's wallet from his trousers. He told them to get dressed again and to walk further into the woods. Stanley managed to get away, but Maake raped Emily and then shot her in the chest. He stole her leather jacket and watch. She survived.

Two days later, on 18 July, Maake reverted to attacking people randomly in the street. On this day he truly vented his fury for he killed five people and raped three women.

Late in the afternoon of 18 July, 25-year-old Samuel Moleme and his friend of the same age, Catherine Lekwene, were walking along Main Reef Road, Langlaagte, when they were approached by Maake. Maake tried to rob Samuel of his wallet but he put up a fight and so Maake pulled out his firearm and shot Samuel three times in the head. He shot Catherine in the knee, dragged her into the veld and raped her twice before running from the scene.

From Langlaagte, Maake proceeded to Claremont. In Princess Road he came upon David John du Plessis and his girlfriend Sarah Lenkpane in the veld. He shot and killed David, raped Sarah and then shot her too. He stole David's shoes. Close to midnight he encountered Martin Stander (19) and his girlfriend Lelanie van Wyk (15), sitting next to a wall in Plateau Drive, Claremont. The teenagers were on their way home and had stopped for a smoke. Maake shot Martin in the head, raped Lelanie and then shot and killed her too. He robbed them of their clothing and jewellery.

A week later, on 26 July, Heniel Mampuele Motioutsi and his companion Doris Phumla Mangaphela were walking along

Booysens Reserve Road when they were confronted by Maake and another man. The men demanded money from Heniel and when none was forthcoming they assaulted him. Doris was dragged into the veld, raped and battered to death with a stone. Maake stole her trousers and a pair of shoes.

In August 1997, Maake reverted to his initial modus operandi of the hammer series. One day during that month he asked Luvio Vittone (64) of Levios Shoe Repairs in Main Street, Jeppe, to repair his shoes. He returned the next day to collect them. Maake enquired about some belts hanging behind the counter and tried one on. Then he suddenly produced a hammer and attacked Luvio, hitting him in the face. Luvio discovered later that Maake had left behind a bag containing shoe polish, an empty wallet and the shoes. He sold these articles and they could not be processed as evidence. The hammer was also left behind in the shop.

Just after 8 am on 16 August, Natvarlal Gangaran (53) opened Eskay Tailors in Tramway Street, Turffontein. The last thing he remembered was switching on an iron to press some trousers. Maake attacked him from behind with a hammer and stole his wallet. Natvarlal survived the incident.

On 19 August, just before half past ten in the morning, Issop Hassen was tending to business at Korolia Stores in Bertrams Road, when he was attacked by a man with a hammer. The cleaner arrived at the shop a short while later and found the bloodied Issop on the floor. He spent a long time in hospital and although he recovered, he could not remember anything about the attack.

At about seven o'clock on the morning of 29 August, Kanoo Pharboo (56) opened KB Patel Tailors in Rockey Street, Yeoville. It is not clear what actually happened, but Kanoo was evidently the victim of a hammer attack and he was also robbed of his wallet. He was taken to hospital but never regained consciousness and died of his wounds on 20 September 1997.

On 14 September 1997, Abdool Hamed Cariem was attacked by a man with a hammer at SA Wholesalers, Pine Avenue,

Fordsburg. His wallet and cash were stolen. Abdool survived the attack.

Five days later, at about 10.15 am on 19 September, Harjivan Dhaya (75) who worked at Ndaya Tailors in Crown Road, Fordsburg, left his shop to go to the toilet. As he was entering the shop on his return he was attacked from behind with a hammer. His wallet and a bag of clothing were stolen. He survived.

On 4 October 1997 Mahomed Akojee Ebrahim was at work at Badats Stores in La Rochelle when he was attacked. His body was found with wounds to his neck and head. He died in hospital later that same day. Cash had been stolen from his shop.

Ten days later, on 14 October, Maake attacked Jacinto Mendes Serrano with a hammer in his shop, the Good Hope café in Hay Road, Turffontein. Cash was stolen. Jacinto died later that day in hospital.

The next day Maake implemented his fifth modus operandi by attacking someone in their own home. He entered the home of Jose Armando Vieira de Caires at 32 Bertha Street, Regents Park, and stabbed him to death. He stole a TV set, a video recorder, a wallet containing cash, a pair of shoes and keys.

On 18 October Maake reverted to attacking people with a hammer. Eduardo Augusto was relieving the owner of Soweto Wholesalers in Ophir Road, Booysens, when Maake entered and asked him for a plastic bag. When Eduardo bent down to get the bag, Maake attacked him with a hammer. He stole the cash register containing 500 rand, an identity document and a further 30 rand from Eduardo. Eduardo survived.

At about 11.10 am on 25 October, Mahesh Jairam Vallabh (36) was at work at Jays Tailors, Von Wielligh Street, when Maake entered the shop in the company of a woman. Maake said that wanted to buy underwear and then attacked Mahesh with a hammer. He also stole about 500 rand. Mahesh survived the incident.

At six o'clock in the morning of 4 November 1997, 55-year-old Anil Metha's son dropped him off at his shop at the Protea shopping centre in Brixton. At eight o'clock the saleswoman arrived and saw Anil's bloodied body through the window. The door to the shop was locked. She alerted the security guard who kicked the door open. A bag containing jeans and two invoices was found on the counter. Anil had been attacked with a hammer and his watch and wallet were stolen. He died on the scene.

Three days later, on 7 November, Maake committed the second last of the house series when he entered the home of Arthur William McIntyre at 51 South Rand Road, South Hills, and killed him with a hammer. He stole a video machine, a portable radio, jewellery, clothes and a .38 revolver.

Later on the same day Maake went to Victoria Fashions on Main Street, Rosettenville. This time the proprietor was not alone in the shop, but this did not deter Maake. He attacked Chaun Yang Cao and Qi Cao with a hammer and robbed them of cash. Chaun died the following day, but Qi survived.

On 14 November, Thakor Ranchod was at work at Boston Tailors in Commissioner Street in downtown Johannesburg when Maake entered and bludgeoned him with a hammer. He robbed him of cash. Thakor died five days later in hospital.

Because of public pressure all the incidents in the hammer series were now assigned to Captain Piet Byleveld at the Brixton Murder and Robbery Unit, who was also investigating the Wemmer Pan series. Captain Byleveld had planned to keep all tailor shops in central Johannesburg, which seemed to be the principal target of the attacks, under observation on the last weekend of November in an attempt to catch the suspect red-handed. This project had to be aborted, however, since the press reported the details of the hammer series investigation on their front pages.

Maake had obviously read the newspapers for he committed no more hammer murders. He did however resort back to three other modus operandi, namely the house series, the random pedestrian series and the Wemmer Pan series.

On 28 November, Gerhard Lavoo was riding his bicycle among the trees at Wemmer Pan, when Maake shot him fatally in the back. Maake stole the bicycle, which he later sold.

On 12 December 1997, Mini Jacob Nkabinde (40) and his friend Thandi Ndaba were relaxing at their shack at the Blue Dam in Homestead Park when Maake approached them. He claimed to be a policeman. Perhaps Maake was concerned about the press coverage and decided to move from Wemmer Pan to Blue Dam, although they are not far from each other. He searched Mini and Thandi's belongings, pretending to look for stolen goods. According to Thandi, he ordered them to follow him to his car. He then took out his firearm and raped Thandi in the bush, while holding Mini at gunpoint. Mini's bullet-riddled body was discovered not far from the rape scene.

On the same night Maake entered the home of Cyril Norman Slattery at 109 Donnelly Street, Turffontein, and killed him with a hammer. He stole a television set.

On 14 December, Enoch Mngoma (25) and his companion Deliwe Ngogela (24) were walking through the veld near South Klipriviersberg Road in Moffat View when Maake accosted them with a firearm. He directed them to a big rock where he ordered them to remove their clothing and have sex with each other. He fired a warning shot in the air to remind them that he had a weapon. Maake then attacked Enoch with a rock. He raped Deliwe, but promised to let her go when she said she would not identify him. He robbed Enoch of his clothing and a watch. Enoch and Deliwe both survived.

On 19 December Maake committed his last crimes, although he did not know it then. At about eight o'clock on that Friday evening, Bongani Gama and his friend Ntombifuthi Nxumalo were walking through Pioneer Park in La Rochelle when Maake approached them from behind. Without warning he shot Bongani in the back and robbed him of cash. He forced Ntombifuthi to accompany him to Wemmer Pan where he raped her. He then dragged her to the top of the nearby koppie, where he raped her again. He forced her to continue walking with him. They encountered two men, one of whom was Richmond Thembalabo Febana. Maake fired at the men, wounding Richmond. He robbed him of his tackies. Maake then forced Ntombifuthi to go with him to Faraday Station in Village Main where he raped her for the third time. He let her go, telling her that she was lucky that he had not killed her.

Four days later, on 23 December 1997, and an after intensive investigation, Captain Piet Byleveld and his team arrested Maake at a taxi rank in central Johannesburg and charged him with the Wemmer Pan series. In the course of the investigation Byleveld had traced the man to whom Maake sold Gerhard Lavoo's bicycle. This man showed Byleveld the receipt that Maake had given him. It was signed in the name of Patrick Makwena. Byleveld immediately realised this was the same man who had committed the hammer murders, for this was the name he had signed when he paid Kantilal Lutchman a deposit for a pair of shoes.

In April 1998 Maake was brought to trial. He faced 133 charges. The trial lasted 335 days. On 16 March 2000 Mrs Justice Geraldine Borchers found him guilty on 27 counts of murder, for each of which he received a life sentence; 26 counts of attempted murder; 41 counts of robbery with aggravating circumstances; one count of attempted robbery; 14 counts of rape; one count of assault with grievous bodily harm; three counts of illegal possession of a firearm, and one count of illegal possession of ammunition. Maake had one bullet in his possession when he was arrested. In total, his sentence amounted to 1835 years and three months. The three months was for the illegal possession of ammunition.

Notes

The press can either assist or hamper a police investigation. In the initial stages of the investigation into the hammer murders there was no coordination, as the cases were being investigated by different detective branches all over central Johannesburg. At that time the South African Police Service did not have the computer software that would enable them to establish links between similar crimes.

Because they seemed to be the target of the killer, the Asian community soon became aware of the similarities in the attacks and brought the issue to the attention of Mrs Jesse Duarte, who was minister of safety and security of the local provincial council at the time. After this, the cases were all transferred to Captain Byleveld, who had been trained as a serial killer investigator. Although initial investigations might have been uncoordinated, Captain Byleveld, to his credit, arrested Maake a mere six months after the Wemmer Pan investigation team was established.

The Asian community had also alerted the press to the possibility that the hammer murders were the work of a serial killer. It is understandable that the community was disappointed with the slowness of the police investigation and felt justified in taking the story to the press. Unfortunately this gave rise to certain problems.

Firstly, a surviving victim gave the whole story to a newspaper, with details of the other victims' names, including the surviving victims, the addresses where the attacks took place and the exact modus operandi, including the weapon used. The press gave this front page coverage, notwithstanding the fact that Captain Byleveld had requested them to hold the story until after the weekend of a surveillance operation. If the police had had the opportunity to keep the tailor shops under surveillance, Maake would more than likely have been arrested earlier.

Secondly, it is irresponsible of the press to print the exact details of a case, for once the suspect goes on trial, he may well maintain that he was tortured during interrogation and that he confessed to the facts because he had read them in the papers. The police then have to prove that he confessed and pointed out the crime scenes of his own free will and that he was not under duress. Had the details never been made public, the accused could only have confessed to them because he had prior knowledge of them.

Thirdly, it is dangerous to print the names and addresses of surviving victims for the killer might go back and kill them to avoid being identified. Maake never used any form of disguise.

It would be highly desirable for the press to take responsibility for their actions and cooperate with the South African Police Service in combating crime. The public needs to be aware that they may be hindering an investigation by giving details to the press. Once the suspect has been tried and sentenced, the public can sell their stories to the highest bidder if they choose to. Newspaper clippings often feature in the defence counsel's presentation of his case in an attempt to get his client acquitted. Everyone in South Africa, be it a detective, a member of the public, a member of the press, defence counsel or state prosecutor, has a role to play in combating crime, but not everyone is equally committed to taking on this responsibility.

Cedric Maake remains an enigma. He targeted very specific groups – Asian tailors, Portuguese café owners and courting couples – but other than saying that he 'hated people', Maake gave no clues that could elucidate his behaviour. He has refused to be interviewed.

Time frame and summary

Hammer series	28 Dec. '96	Antonio Alfonso, attempted murder
	6 Jan. '97	Magan Khanjee, attempted murder
	8 Jan. '97	Kenny Chan, attempted murder
	17 Jan. '97	Kantilal Lutchman, attempted murder
	22 Jan. '97	Abdool Samad Bulbulia, attempted murder
	23 Jan. '97	Dhansuklal Thakor Patel, murdered
	Feb. '97	Hossen Amod, attempted murder
	26 Feb. '97	David Sadka, attempted murder
	27 Feb. '97	Amratlale Gopal, attempted murder
	26 Mar. '97	Lawpit Law, attempted murder
	22 Apr. '97	Yogi Dheda, attempted murder

Wemmer Pan series	27 Apr. '97	Muntu Elijah Hlatswayo, murdered
	27 Apr. '97	Eunice Nkosapantsi, murdered
	27 Apr. '97	Unidentified woman, murdered
Taxi series	25 May '97	Sipho Ndima, attempted murder
	June '97	Michael Mkhize, attempted murder
Wemmer Pan series	14 June '97	Ralph Jeremia Ngwenya, murdered
	14 June '97	Christina Mashigo, raped, murdered
Random pedestrian series	16 June '97	Dorah Duduzile Dladla, raped, murdered
	21 June '97	Sonti Simon Mohokoni, murdered
Wemmer Pan series	11 July '97	Jerry Khanya Naidoo, murdered
	11 July '97	Charlotte Ndlovu, robbed
	12 July '97	*Moses Ramothlhwa, murdered
	12 July '97	Dorcas Makhatsane, raped
	16 July '97	Stanley Speelman Kolobe, robbed
	16 July '97	Emily Madiba, raped, attempted murder
Random pedestrian series	18 July '97	Samuel Moleme, murdered
	18 July '97	Catherine Lekwene, assaulted, raped
	18 July '97	David John du Plessis, murdered
	18 July '97	Sarah Lenkpane, raped, murdered
	18 July '97	Martin Stander, murdered
	18 July '97	Lelanie van Wyk, raped, murdered
	26 July '97	Heniel Mampuele Motioutsi, attempted murder
	26 July '97	Doris Phumla Mangaphela, raped, murdered
Hammer series	Aug. '97	Luvio Vittone, attempted murder
	16 Aug. '97	Natvarlal Gangaran, attempted murder
	19 Aug. '97	Issop Hassen, attempted murder
	29 Aug. '97	Kanoo Pharboo, murdered
	14 Sept. '97	Abdool Hamed Cariem, attempted murder
	19 Sept. '97	Harjivan Dhaya, attempted murder
	4 Oct. '97	Mahomed Akojee Ebrahim, murdered
	14 Oct. '97	Jacinto Mendes Serrano, murdered
House series	15 Oct. '97	Jose Armando Vieira de Caires, murdered

Hammer series	18 Oct.'97	Eduardo Augusto, attempted murder
	25 Oct. '97	Mahesh Jaraim Vallabh, attempted murder
	4 Nov. '97	Anil Metha, murdered
House series	7 Nov. '97	Arthur William McIntyre, murdered
Hammer series	7 Nov. '97	Chaun Yang Cao, murdered
	7 Nov. '97	Qi Cao, attempted murder
	14 Nov. '97	Thakor Ranchod, murdered
Wemmer Pan series	28 Nov. '97	Gerhard Lavoo, murdered
House series	12 Dec. '97	Mini Jacob Nkabinde, murdered
	12 Dec. '97	Thandi Ndaba, raped, attempted murder
	12 Dec. '97	Cyril Norman Slattery, murdered
Random pedestrian series	14 Dec. '97	Enoch Mngoma, attempted murder
	14 Dec. '97	Deliwe Ngogela, raped
	19 Dec. '97	Bongani Gama, attempted murder
	19 Dec. '97	Ntombifuthi Nxumalo, raped
	19 Dec. '97	Richmond Thembalabo Febana, attempted murder

SAMUEL SIDYNO

Pretoria, 1998-99

South Africa's capital city, Pretoria is characterised by wide streets bordered with jacaranda trees that turn the cityscape mauve in early summer when they flower. Many government offices are housed in graceful stone buildings erected in the first half of the twentieth century, giving the city a more graceful atmosphere than Johannesburg, the frenetic high-rise commercial heart of the country which lies just 50 kilometres to the south.

It was in this city, at about 5 pm on the afternoon on 18 January 1995 that 22-year-old Thembelihle Mtobi Gasa made her way to the Pretoria station to meet her friend Nicolas, a security guard, who had promised to help her find work. Instead, Thembelihle met Samuel Sidyno, also a security guard, who offered to help her in place of the absent Nicolas. After he had examined her matric certificate and security training certificate, he asked her to wait in the guardroom while he supposedly contacted his supervisor and discussed Thembelihle's qualifications. A few minutes later he told her that his supervisor had suggested that he accompany her to the security training school in downtown Pretoria.

Elated at the prospect of possible employment, and grateful for Samuel Sidyno's apparent helpfulness, Thembelihle readily agreed to go with him. He suggested that they take a short cut across the hill in Fountains Valley, a nature reserve and popular recreational area. Hesitant about accompanying a stranger through a secluded area, she complained that her stockings would be damaged if they followed the footpath. Sidyno assured her that she had nothing to worry about, but her instincts warned her. She stopped and refused to accompany him any further. Infuriated, he turned around and assaulted her, punching her in the face. In control now, he told her to remove her pantyhose and warned her that he had a firearm in his bag and would shoot her if she did not obey him.

Sidyno pushed Thembelihle to the ground, ripped off her panties and raped her. Afterwards he made her lie on her stomach and grab hold of a tree in front of her; he then proceeded to rape her again. When he had finished he threw her panties at her and told her to get dressed, threatening to kill her if she informed the police.

Just then Thembelihle saw two men approaching; both wore the distinctive metal star badge of the Zionist Christian Church. Ignoring Sidyno's warning, she managed to scream for help, telling the men that she had just been raped. The men overpowered Sidyno and handcuffed him with his security guard handcuffs. They went with Thembelihle to the Pretoria Central police station, where she laid a charge of rape.

On 12 May 1995, Sidyno was sentenced to four years' imprisonment for rape, but just over three years later, in July 1998, he was given parole. He was now thirty-five years old, unemployed and without a place to stay. Although he was married and his wife lived in Valhalla, a south-western suburb of Pretoria, one can only surmise that she did not want any contact with him, since he apparently did not get in touch with her. Instead, he found shelter in a small abandoned tower room on the crest of Capital Hill in Pretoria North. To the left of the hill lay the Pretoria Zoo and the Langenhoven Secondary School was situated at the foot of the hill. The suburb of Capital Park lay on the other side of the ridge. Sidyno earned a meagre living buying vegetables at the market and selling them for a small profit at train stations. He also worked as an 'informal' parking attendant, directing drivers to available parking bays at the zoo for small gratuities.

Five months after Sidyno's release from prison, on 14 December 1998, Patrick Mahlabanya, who worked at the Langenhoven Secondary School, was on duty at the school's golf course. He spotted children removing the flags that marked the holes on the course and started chasing them. The children ran up Capital Hill, with Patrick in hot pursuit. Stopping to pick up the flags which had been hastily discarded by the children, he detected a bad odour coming from a nearby bush. He investigated and made the gruesome discovery of the decomposing body of an adult woman. He ran to the nearest house to telephone the police.

The woman was wearing a black dress and a black and white jacket. A pair of orange slip-on shoes was found on the scene. She was lying on her stomach and was covered with branches. It appeared that she had been strangled with a cord of material.

Detectives from the Pretoria Murder and Robbery Unit used fingerprint analysis to establish the identity of the victim as Elizabeth Ramasela Senwamadi. Elizabeth was the daughter of Maggie Senwamadi who had worked as a domestic helper at a house at the foot of the hill. When Maggie became too old to work, she introduced her daughter to her employer. Elizabeth worked as her mother's replacement until the end of November 1998, when her service was terminated.

After losing her job Elizabeth moved in with 63-year-old Christinah Mabatle who lived close by. Christinah had last seen Elizabeth on 8 December. Maggie had last seen her daughter alive in October 1998, at which time Elizabeth had promised her mother that she would be home for Christmas. Paulina Menene Vuma, a close friend of the deceased, identified the pair of orange slip-ons as belonging to Elizabeth.

At about 10 am on 26 December 1998, Maureen Thoko Mavuka saw her 15-year-old grandson, Sipho Emanuel Mavuka, alive for the last time when he told her he was going to the Scheiden Station to attend swimming lessons. Sipho was wearing a red and blue striped shirt, grey trousers and black shoes. Later that day Sipho's 15-year-old friend, Johannes Rawane, spotted

Sipho talking to an adult man at the Hercules station. Johannes called to Sipho to accompany him home, but Sipho said that he was going with the man, who had promised him a bicycle. Johannes recognised the man as someone who 'used to sell chips at the station' and who was later identified as Sidyno. He never saw his friend alive again.

Being close to residential areas, Capital Hill is a popular place for walking and it is not uncommon to see groups of people climbing the ridge with a dog or two in tow. On Saturday 2 January 1999, Mr D Rautenbach, his son and his son's friend decided to climb the hill behind their house in Capital Park. On the summit of the hill there is a stone wall and Mr Rautenbach sat down on this wall to catch his breath. His German shepherd dog was sniffing around in the surrounding bush when he began to bark excitedly. Mr Rautenbach walked over to the dog and to his horror discovered a body beneath a tree. It had been covered with branches. He hurried home to call the police.

Captain Henning van Aswegen of the Pretoria Murder and Robbery Unit arrived at the scene soon afterwards and uncovered not one body, but two. Beneath the first was another more decomposed body. Both victims were male. The second body had no skull, but on exploring the area Van Aswegen found the skull a few metres away. He suspected that it had been dragged away by dogs or rodents. He also found a pair of black shoes about 20 metres from the bodies. With a sense of foreboding, he deployed his men to search the hill and an hour later was called to a spot about 600 metres from the first scene, where another body had been left. It was also male and he was barefoot. Like the others, the body was also covered with branches. A pair of shoes and an identity document belonging to an Andries Maoka were found near the body.

All three bodies were removed from the crime scenes.

The following day the detectives searched the hill for further clues. They came upon the tower room, which was situated between the crime scenes. A fence with a padlocked gate surrounded the room; however there was a hole in the fence large enough for a person to climb through. The door was also padlocked but it, too, had a large opening in it. Inside the room the detectives found a grey Coin Security coat with the name Sam and the number 14280 printed on it, together with several articles of clothing, two belts and a tin of snuff. These items were photographed by the police and taken possession of.

On 4 January 1999, the Murder and Robbery Unit was once again called out to the hill. Early that morning, Mr Rautenbach had gone for another walk and, unbelievable as it may seem, he had found another body at exactly the same spot where the previous bodies had been discovered. In fact, this body – a young woman – was covered with the same branches that the detectives had removed two days before from the previous two victims. It was clear by now that a serial killer was active on the hill.

Captain André Fabricius, who had been trained to investigate serial homicide, was put in charge of the investigation. The crime scene was duly processed and Fabricius asked members of the Special Task Force to keep the hill under surveillance. They stayed there that night and the next. During the early hours of 6 January 1999, they arrested Samuel Sidyno as he returned to the tower room. On 7 January 1999 Fabricius attempted to interrogate Sidyno who asserted his right to silence and refused to cooperate.

Meanwhile, two of the victims discovered on 2 January were identified. One was Sipho Mavuka. Since his disappearance, Sipho's uncle, Bangeni Raymond Mavuka, had been searching the hospitals and train stations for his nephew. On 26 January he went to the mortuary where he was shown the skull of a 15-year-old boy. Fearing that he had found the remains of his nephew, he contacted Sipho's mother, who went to the Murder and Robbery Unit where she was shown the clothing of the boy. Nomsa Gladys Mavuka identified her son's T-shirt; she even had a photograph of him wearing it. His grandmother confirmed this by identifying the T-shirt and the shoes he was wearing on the day he disappeared. DNA samples taken from Sipho's parents were the final pieces of evidence the police needed to confirm the identification of Sipho.

The second victim was identified as Tsholofela Ronald Maoka. Detectives had traced his mother, Jeanette Maoka, through the identity document found on the scene. The identity document belonged to another son, Andries, whose whereabouts were known. However, Mrs Maoka's son Tsholofela was missing. Andries Maoka was interviewed on 22 January and identified the pair of Lynx shoes found at the crime scene as belonging to his brother Tsholofela. Jeanette Maoka supplied the detectives with a photograph of Tsholofela and her third son, Lesego Frederick Maoka, was able to identify Tsholofela's clothing.

The third victim remained unidentified, but it was established he was an under age boy.

The young woman found on 4 January was identified as Paulinah Ledwaba from her fingerprints. Her boyfriend Daniel Baloyi and her sister Eunice Mashamaite identified a belt and the tin of snuff found among Sidyno's possessions as belonging to Paulinah.

On 14 January Sidyno was confronted with the evidence against him. He decided to cooperate and to point out the crime scenes. Senior Superintendent Poerie van Rooyen managed the pointing out procedure. As a member of the Special Investigation Unit and not the Pretoria Murder and Robbery Unit, Van Rooyen was not familiar with the particulars of the case. It is customary that an independent officer conducts a pointing out, so that no allegations of irregular influence can later be made by the suspect.

At each crime scene Sidyno told his story. He could not remember the names of his victims and gave them fictitious names to distinguish the bodies. He said he met a man named 'Petros' in November 1998 in Pretoria West. They were both looking for work and decided to direct cars in the parking area at the Pretoria Zoo. They earned a few rand doing this and decided to buy beer and cold drinks with the money. Sidyno led Petros up the hill close to his hideout. They had an argument about the money and Sidyno ended up strangling Petros. He hid his body under some branches on the hillside.

Sidyno said he met 'Timothy' during the second week of

November 1998 at the foot of the hill and suggested that they look for work in Hercules, a suburb on the other side of the hill. When they reached the top of the hill, Timothy apparently refused to go any further, which resulted in an argument. Timothy pulled out a knife and attacked Sidyno, but he managed to get the upper hand and strangled Timothy. He left his body under a tree, covered with branches.

The third scene Sidyno pointed out was that of 'Oupa' (the unidentified male) who he said he had met at Daspoort, a suburb to the west, during the third week of November. Oupa had told him that he was on his way to the zoo to sell ice creams. Sidyno went with him, but when they reached the school at the foot of the hill Sidyno suggested that they go to the market to buy vegetables instead and he led the way up the hill. Once again, there was an argument, during which Sidyno strangled Oupa. He stole 14 rand from the dead man before covering his body with branches, as he had done with his other victims.

He pointed out the crime scene of a woman he called 'Hilda'. He said that he had met her during the last week of December in the city centre. He escorted her up the hillside to have sex with her, but when she demanded to be paid he strangled her as he had no money. He said that he had noticed that the bodies of Timothy and Oupa had been removed, so he dumped her body in the same space where their bodies had been. He took off Hilda's jeans and wore them himself. (The bodies of Timothy and Oupa were removed by the detectives on 2 January – after Hilda's murder. It was characteristic of Sidyno's statement that he not only confused the names of his victims, but also the dates on which he murdered them.)

Sidyno led Van Rooyen to yet another crime scene where he said he had killed a boy. Van Rooyen noticed a skull here – this crime scene had not been found by the police. Sidyno said he met the boy 'Thabo' during the first week of 1999 at the Hercules station. Sidyno had bought some apples to sell and Thabo offered to help him. At about seven o'clock that night, Thabo met up with Sidyno and said he wanted to come and live with him in town. He led Thabo up the by now familiar path of death. When they arrived at his tower room he asked Thabo for the money from the sale of the apples. An argument ensued during which Thabo was strangled. Sidyno found about 24 rand in the boy's pockets, which he took. He then covered the body with branches.

Van Rooyen asked Inspector Eddie Olivier, a member of his unit, to remain at this scene and to inform Captain Fabricius of the discovery of the skull.

Sidyno moved on to the next crime scene where he said he had killed a woman called 'Rosina' during the last week of October. He met her at the Capital station and she said she was looking for work. As he had done with Thembelihle Gasa, he offered to help her and led her up the hill, which he told her was a short cut. En route Sidyno asked her for sex, calling it a favour. He said that she agreed, but asked him to hurry for she still had to look for work. This remark angered him and so he strangled her. Like the others before her, her body was covered with branches. Sidyno said that this was the last of his victims.

Captain Fabricius went immediately to the crime scene where Thabo had been killed and found the body as well as the skull. The body was in a state of advanced decomposition. A pair of black shoes, a piece of newspaper and a green pen were found at the scene. Thabo had been wearing grey nylon trousers and a shirt, but no underpants.

On 16 January 1999, Leslie Liebenberg and his friend Frikkie Mosterd decided to climb the Magaliesberg Mountain in Pretoria North. At about four o'clock that afternoon they smelled something rotten and on investigation found a body covered with branches. They called the police.

Van Aswegen was on duty and found the skeletal remains when he arrived. He tasked two policemen with guarding the crime scene overnight as it was already too dark to conduct a proper examination of the area. He returned the next morning to process the scene. Fabricius questioned Sidyno about this murder since there was a similar modus operandi. Sidyno confessed to it, identifying the victim as 'Mannetjie'.

On 21 January 1999, Fabricius requested Senior Superintendent Vinol Viljoen,* of the Serious and Violent Crimes Component of the SAPS to officiate at the pointing out of the place where Mannetjie's body had been found. Sidyno directed Viljoen to the Pretoria North mountain and not to Capital Hill.

Sidyno told Viljoen that he had met a certain 'Samson' (the name he was now using to refer to Mannetjie) in Pretoria North while he was looking for work. He had suggested to Samson that they look for work in Daspoort and that they take a short cut across the hill. At the top of the hill, the inevitable argument broke out during which Samson was strangled and his body covered with branches.

On 9 February 1999 Sidyno stated that he wanted to make a confession in front of a magistrate. Fabricius arranged for him to see Magistrate Johannes Kruger.

On 31 May 1999, the managing director of Coin Security identified the coat found in the tower room as belonging to Samuel Sidyno who had been a member of the Coin Security staff from March 1991 to August 1993.

After thirty days' observation at Weskoppies Psychiatric Hospital in June 1999 a panel of psychiatrists found Sidyno competent and fit to stand trial.

Samuel Sidyno's trial commenced in August 2000. He appeared before Mr Justice Johann van der Westhuizen and was charged with seven counts of murder, two counts of rape and one count of robbery. He was found guilty on seven counts of murder and one count of theft. The state could not prove the rape charges. On 5 September 2000 Samuel Sidyno was sentenced to seven life sentences for the murders and one year for theft. The sentences were to run concurrently which means that effectively he will be in prison for forty years.

Three days after his conviction, Sidyno's parents gave an interview to the *Sowetan* newspaper. His mother, Mamalebano

---

*Viljoen was the detective in charge of the Moses Sithole/Atteridgeville serial killer investigation in 1996.

Sidiyo, said Samuel's real name was Malebanye Samuel Sidiyo and she had no idea why he had changed his surname. The family lived in Klipspruit, a suburb of Soweto to the south of Johannesburg, and was very religious. They regarded what had happened to their son as God's will and could provide no other explanation for it. Sidyno's father, Bra Mannenberg Sidiyo, said his son's story was a long and sad one and he was too emotionally exhausted to elaborate. He said Sidyno grew up in Klipspruit and completed grade 11, although prison records gave his educational level as grade 7.

The family had been following the case in the media. Sidyno had contacted them when he was awaiting trial, but when his sister arrived at prison he refused to see her. She tried to visit him five times, but to no avail.

Notes

Samuel Sidyno lived a few hundred metres from his crime scenes. He had the audacity to leave bodies in exactly the same places where previous bodies had been removed by the police. One might think that he did this deliberately to provoke the detectives, or that he was perhaps stupid. But neither assumption would be correct. He was just a creature of habit, like most other people. This principle of habit is a fundamental aspect of criminal profiling.

When Robert Ressler, John Douglas and their colleagues from the Federal Bureau of Investigation in the United States began interviewing serial killers in prison, they found many indications of habit. One of the most important was that serial killers tend to return to their crime scenes. Everyone likes to return to a place that holds a special meaning for them. People return years later to their honeymoon hotels, the towns they grew up in. Serial killers do the same, but the difference is that most serial killers return to their crime scenes to relive their fantasies and to masturbate.

Possessiveness is another human trait that serial killers are prone to. Many of them, like Samuel Sidyno, Moses Sithole, Sipho Twala and the Station Strangler left the bodies of their victims in clusters. They commit the murders and leave the bodies in places where they feel safe. This becomes their 'graveyard' and they resent other people passing through it. They dislike the police 'scratching around' in their graveyards, in the same way a child resents his parents snooping around in his room or cupboards. Some of them also dislike 'releasing' the bodies to the police. They often watch when the police remove the bodies and sometimes visit the mortuaries where the bodies are held, or they attend the funerals of their victims. Some of them even visit the graves of their victims. This behaviour is not a manifestation of compassion; it is possessiveness.

Sidyno raped his first victim in 1995 in the Fountains Valley in Pretoria. The Fountains Valley is flanked by a few hills, one of which is called Klapperkop. An old fort was built on this hill by the Boers to protect them against the British forces during the Anglo-Boer War at the turn of the twentieth century.

Klapperkop has a notorious connection with the Panga Man, who terrorised Pretoria citizens during the late 1950s. The place has always been popular with lovers, for they have a beautiful view of the city and they can make out undisturbed in their parked cars.

In 1946 a gang of five robbers began operating in the Pretoria areas of Skanskop, Swartkoppies, Klapperkop, the Fountains, the Union Buildings, Meintjieskop, Tom Jenkins Lane, Queenswood and Koedoespoort, their principal modus operandi being attacking people in cars and robbing them. They also broke into people's homes.

In 1952 one of the gang members, Alfred Malazi, was shot dead by Sergeant Jan Roux in Queenswood and the following year two more were arrested in the Fountains Valley and sentenced to death. A fourth member, Jack Dibakwane, was arrested in 1957 and sentenced to twelve years in prison. The last member, Phineas Tshetandizi became the dreaded Panga Man.

When his friends were arrested, Tshetandizi decided to go solo. He made himself a panga and targeted couples making out at the Klapperkop Fort. He would silently approach the cars and then viciously attack the couple and rape the women. Some victims lost limbs and others were severely wounded but, miraculously, none of them died.

A task force under the leadership of Captain Fred van Niekerk investigated the cases with tenacity, but the Panga Man evaded arrest. Then on 30 September 1959 an army recruit made a complaint to the military police that a man had assaulted him. He gave a good description of his attacker. One of the military policemen recognised the description as that of Phineas Tshetandizi who worked as a nightwatchman at the South African Police Headquarters in Schoeman Street, Pretoria. But before they could arrest him, Tshetandizi launched his last attack on 9 October 1959. On being interrogated after his arrest, Phineas Tshetandizi confessed to being the Panga Man. He was a 40-year-old Venda and the panga, jewellery and clothing of his victims were discovered in his house at Vlakfontein.

Ironically, while working as a watchman at the police headquarters, he often eavesdropped on the generals while they discussed the Panga Man investigation.

Initially there were thirty-two charges against him, but when he eventually appeared before Mr Justice Roper in May 1960, the the state prosecutor, Advocate Rein, had reduced the number to nineteen.

On 6 May 1960, Phineas Tshetandizi was sentenced to six years each for three charges of assault with the intention to murder, four years each for two charges with the intent to rape, two years for assault, one year for robbery and one year for theft. He was also sentenced to death for two rapes and three charges of assault with the intention to murder and to rob.

On 14 November 1960, as Tshetandizi approached the gallows, his last statement was that God should ensure that every policeman and prison warder should die and that South Africa should be returned to the black people. He was hanged a few minutes later.

Had his victims died, Tshetandizi would have been a particularly vicious serial killer. A lifelike scenario depicting the Panga Man attacking a couple in a car is exhibited at the South African Police Service Museum in Pretoria. The panga used by Tshetandizi is an exhibit.

FRANK NDEBE

Mpumalanga, 1999

Frank Ndebe was born on 17 August 1968. His mother was a live-in domestic worker and his father worked on the mines, so Frank was brought up by his grandmother on Louw's Creek farm, between Barberton and Malelane in Mpumalanga Province.

Frank did not have an easy life as a child. He was lonely and his grandmother was poor. She also had some strange notions about child rearing. She told Frank he was not allowed to masturbate for it would spoil her tobacco. Every morning when he woke up, she would smell his penis to make sure he had not ejaculated during the night and then she would smoke her tobacco. When Frank came home late from school, his grandmother would wake him up at three o'clock the next morning and chase him into a river with a knobkierie. She made him stand shivering in the water until it was time for him to leave for school.

Frank looked forward to the times when his mother came to visit him. He adored her although he saw very little of her. As a child, whenever his mother was angry with him, Frank would cut the skin over his heart with a knife. He had nightmares about being lowered into a grave in a coffin.

Frank attended school up to grade 9. He dreamed about becoming a film producer and loved to read books and watch movies about film stars. When he left school, he worked as a gardener at Sheba mines. His parents had divorced by then and both had remarried. Frank did not get on with his step-parents.

In 1990, at the age of twenty-two, Frank Ndebe was sentenced to ten years in prison for committing two rapes. A serial rapist had been active in the Donga area near Komatipoort. Ndebe was identified as the suspect by two victims and was convicted. His involvement in the other cases could not be proved. Both his parents distanced themselves from their son at this time. Ndebe was sodomised in Barberton prison and he got hold of pornography. He was finally released on 20 December 1998 and returned to the town of Barberton.

On 16 January 1999, prison warder Mabuza was jogging along a road outside Barberton when he noticed a woman, Beauty Madsane, walking along the road and a man following her a short distance behind. Mabuza recognised the man as Frank Ndebe who had been released from prison just one month before. He stopped and chatted briefly to Ndebe before continuing with his run. Ndebe caught up with the woman and dragged her into the veld. He tied up her hands and raped her for about an hour until two women walking past heard her screams. Ndebe fled. He realised that Mabuza would guess he was the culprit and that he would once more be sent to prison. He blamed all three of the women as well as Mabuza for his predicament and hastily left Barberton. Eventually he arrived at Elekwatini, a township outside the town of Badplaas, where he met 23-year-old Emma Skosana. She was the mother of a one-year-old boy.

Four months later, on 11 April 1999, Frank asked Emma to accompany him to Nelspruit. Emma took her child and a relative, 22-year-old Cynthia Ngwenya, with her on the trip. After walking in the hot sun for a while, the child began crying and this irritated Ndebe. They stopped, and while Emma was trying to comfort her child, Ndebe took Cynthia into the bush and raped her. When he returned, Emma was visibly upset, so he assaulted her. He tied her hands behind her back and strangled her and then strangled the child. He covered the bodies with grass and the branches of trees. He forced Cynthia to remain with him.

That night they slept in the veld. Cynthia was too terrified to try to run away. The following day they continued walking past

Nelspruit and arrived at Pienaar where they stayed with Ndebe's sister. On 15 April Ndebe decided to return to Badplaas. He and Cynthia left his sister's house at about six o'clock that evening and once more slept in the veld. They continued on foot, but on 17 April they were offered a lift to the town of Carolina. On the way to a farm outside Carolina they saw an adult woman walking along the road. Ndebe waylaid her and dragged her into the veld. He tied her up, raped and strangled her and then robbed her of her clothing.

The pair continued their journey towards Delton, sleeping in the veld every night. On the morning of 18 April Ndebe ordered Cynthia to dress herself in the murdered woman's clothing, which she did reluctantly. At about three o'clock that afternoon they took a taxi to Middelburg and walked from there to Nkodwana.

At about six o'clock on the morning of Sunday 19 April they arrived at the Badplaas-Barberton intersection. Ndebe spotted a woman, 45-year-old Zodwa Shonge, walking to a café. He waylaid her and dragged her to the tree where Cynthia was waiting. He told the woman he was going to murder her. She pleaded with him and begged Cynthia to help her, but Cynthia was too scared of Ndebe to do anything. Even the woman's plea that she had children dependent on her did not help. Ndebe subdued her and ripped her headscarf into pieces which he tied together and then bound her hands and feet. He wrapped the scarf around her throat and strangled her. When she was dead he turned her on her stomach, removed the ligatures and threw them on to the ground next to her. He stole the contents of her bag, including cash.

Cynthia pleaded with Ndebe to take her home. They got a lift to Badplaas and were walking towards Elekwatini when a police van drew up alongside them. The police searched their bags and then asked Cynthia if her parents knew where she was. She told them she wanted to go home. Both Cynthia and Ndebe were loaded into the back of the police van. When they reached Cynthia's parents' home she told the police her story. Ndebe was taken into custody. Late that night, Cynthia took the police to the body of the victim in Carolina.

On the morning of Monday 20 April the case was referred to Captain Thinus Rossouw of the Nelspruit Murder and Robbery Unit. He had been trained in serial homicide investigation and had worked on the Atteridgeville serial killer case (page 198). Rossouw asked Superintendent Koos Fourie, commander of the Secunda Murder and Robbery Unit, to officiate at the pointing out of the crime scenes. Superintendent Fourie had been involved in the Saloon Killer investigation (page 271). Ndebe pointed out the crime scenes but denied killing Emma's child.

Ndebe was quite forthcoming when he was interrogated by Rossouw. When Rossouw asked if he had ever hit a woman, Ndebe replied that a woman was beautiful and there was no place on her body that he would hit. Rossouw was aware of the fact that Ndebe had whipped Cynthia during her captivity. He asked Ndebe if there was anything that he feared and he replied that when he was a young boy he had feared the *tokoloshe*.* But once one has had sex, Ndebe said, one no longer fears the *tokoloshe*.

On 20 November 2000 Frank Ndebe was charged in Nelspruit with the rape of Beauty Madsane, the abduction of Cynthia Ngwenya, two charges of raping Cynthia, two charges of assaulting Cynthia with grievous bodily harm, the murders of Emma Skosana and her son, the robbery and murder of the unidentified woman in Carolina and the murder of Zodwa Shongwe. He was also charged with possession of a firearm, but this turned out to be a toy pistol. Mr Justice M K de Klerk presided.

Much to everyone's surprise, Ndebe pleaded guilty to all the charges. The judge called for a short recess and then sentenced Frank Ndebe to seven life sentences for the rapes and murders, ten years for the abduction, six years for the assaults and thirty years for the robberies. The trial lasted just forty-five minutes.

Ndebe returned to the Barberton prison, where he had

---

*The tokoloshe is a mythical small man who has great power and commits dreadful deeds against people.

previously served his sentence for two rapes. He had been a principal member of one of the notorious prison gangs and resumed his status there.

Notes

Ndebe's case brings to mind that of Elias Msomi who also had a female companion who accompanied him on his travels. Although neither of these women participated in the murders and were held against their will, there have been cases where a man and a woman have joined forces as a serial killer pair. The most notorious of these were Ian Brady and Myra Hindley (1963-1965, UK) and Fred and Rosemary West (1974-1994, UK).

Hindley and her boyfriend Brady killed 12-year-old John Kilbride and ten-year-old Lesley Ann Downey in 1963. Photographs of the distressed Lesley Ann and a tape of her pleading for her life were found in their house. On 6 October 1965, they teamed up with Hindley's brother-in-law David Smith and killed 17-year-old Edward Evans. David was horrified and notified the police, who investigated and found Edward's body in Hindley and Brady's house.

Brady had grown up in the slums of Glasgow, but Hindley had a normal middle-class upbringing in Manchester. The two met in January 1961 when they were working for the same company. Hindley dumped her fiancé for Brady and lost her virginity to him. Brady, who was into Nazism and sadism, soon seduced Hindley to his ways, which eventually escalated to torture and murder. The bodies of the children were left on the remote Saddleworth Moors outside Manchester.

Rosemary West played a much more active part in the murders she committed with her husband Fred. Fred, who had 'divorced' his first wife, met 15-year-old Rosemary, twelve years his junior, in 1969. Despite her young age, Rosemary was as interested in sadistic sex as Fred. Fred had already killed his first wife Rena and a young girl named Anne McFall. Fred and Rosemary were married and Fred's daughters Anne Marie and Charmaine lived with them. Both Charmaine and Fred's daughter Heather were murdered. By 1994, Fred and Rosemary West had killed twelve young girls between them. Some of them were buried beneath their house in Cromwell Street, Gloucester, and the remains of the other bodies were found at Letterbox Field and Fingerpost Field in Kempley, 25 kilometres from Gloucester. Fred and Rosemary's children told police how she would hold them down while their father raped them.

Fred West committed suicide in custody. This posed a predicament for the police as they had no evidence that Rosemary was involved in all the murders. They charged her with the murder of Charmaine, who had been killed during a short period when Fred was in prison for petty theft. When she was found guilty of this murder, the jury was convinced that she had collaborated with her husband in the other murders. She was sentenced to life in prison.

The four youngest West children were given new identities to protect them.

RESOURCES

Bennett, B & Timmins, H (1954). *The Noose Tightens.* Cape Town Archives.

Bennett, B & Timmins, H (1956). *Freedom or the Gallows.* Cape Town Archives.

Cameron, D & Frazer, E (1987). *The Lust to Kill.* Cambridge: Polity Press.

Criminal Procedures Act (Act 51 of 1977) South Africa.

Freud, S *The Complete Works of Sigmund Freud.* London: The Hogarth Press.

Harrison, S (1998). *The Diary of Jack the Ripper: The chilling confessions of James Maybrick.* England: Blake Publishing Ltd.

Hollin, C R (1989). *Psychology and Crime.* London: Routledge.

Holmes, R M & De Burger, J (1988). *Serial Murder.* Newbury Park: Sage Publications.

Ivey, G (1993). Psychodynamic aspects of demon possession and Satanic worship. *Suid-Afrikaanse Tydskrif vir Sielkunde* 23 (4): 186-194.

Jeffers, H P (1993). *Profiles in Evil.* London: Warner Books.

Kaplan, H H & Sadock,B J (1991). *Synopsis of Psychiatry.* Baltimore: Williams & Wilkens.

Lane, B & Gregg, W (1992). *Encyclopedia of Serial Killers.* London: Headline Book Publishing.

Leibman, F H (1989). Serial Murderers: Four Case Histories. *Federal Probation* 53 (4): 41-45.

Levin, J & Fox, A J, (1991). *America's Growing Menace – Mass Murder*. New York: Berkley Books.

Leyton, E (1986). *Compulsive Killers: The Story of Modern Multiple Murder*. New York: Washington Mews Books.

MacCulloch, M J, Snowden, P R, Wood, P J W & Mills, H E (1983). Sadistic fantasy, sadistic behaviour and offending. *British Journal of Psychiatry* 143: 20-29.

Money, J (1990). Forensic Sexology: Paraphiliac Serial Rape (Biastophilia) and Lust Murder (Erotophonophilia). American Journal of Psychotherapy. XLIV (1): 26-36.

Nordby, J J (1989). Bootstrapping while barefoot (Crime models vs theoretical models in the hunt for serial killers). *Synthese*. 81 (3): 373-389.

Prentky, R A, Wolbert-Burgess, A, Rokous, F, Lee, A, Hartman, C, Ressler, R K & Douglas, J (1989). The Resumptive Role of Fantasy in Serial Sexual Homicide. *American Journal of Psychiatry* 147 (7): 887-891.

Ressler, R K, Burgess, A W & Douglas, J E (1988). *Sexual Homicide, Patterns and Motives*. Lexington: Heath & Company.

Ressler, R K & Shachtman, T (1993). *Whoever Fights Monsters*. London: Simon & Schuster.

Schwartz, A E (1992). *The Man who could not kill enough – The Secret Murders of Milwaukee's Jeffrey Dahmer*. New York: Carol Publishing.

South African Police Service.

The Star Newspaper, Johannesburg.

Van der Merwe, K. Vroue sterf wreed in skemerwereld. *Die Huisgenoot* 29 Augustus 1975.

Catch me a Killer   Micki Pistorius

'Serial killers experience the power over life and death as omnipotence. Since they have little control over their own lives and feelings, they become addicted to the omnipotence that control over someone else's life gives them. Therefore, they will kill repetitively. It restores the mental imbalance they experience whenever their self-worth is challenged . . . when I interrogate a serial killer I dive into the blackness of his soul. I am familiar with his feelings of emptiness, loneliness, depression, death, omnipotence and fear. I dive deeply and get a grip on his torment . . .'

A profiler who wants to understand the mind of the serial killer must have been prepared by life experiences before he or she can dare to venture into the abyss. A person who has led a protected life will not survive . . .

Micki Pistorius, who has a doctorate in psychology, spent six years as a profiler with the South African Police Service. As head of their investigative psychology unit, she has been involved in more than thirty serial killer cases and has participated in the training of more than a hundred detectives in the investigation of serial homicides.